THE CHURCH OF THE FUTURE

Other works by Walbert Bühlmann
published by St Paul Publications (U.K. edition)
and Orbis Books (U.S. edition)

The Coming of the Third Church

Forward, Church! (U.K. edition)
Courage, Church (U.S. edition)

The Missions on Trial

All Have the Same God (U.K. edition)
The Search for God (U.S. edition)

The Chosen Peoples (U.K. edition)
God's Chosen Peoples (U.S. edition)

Walbert Bühlmann O.F.M. Cap.

THE CHURCH
OF THE FUTURE

A model for the year 2001

Epilogue by
Karl Rahner S.J.

ORBIS BOOKS
Maryknoll, New York

DOVE COMMUNICATIONS
Melbourne, Australia

ST PAUL PUBLICATIONS
Slough, England

Chap. 1 first appeared in *Theologisch-praktische Quartalschrift*, Linz, 1981, and chap. 6 first appeared in *Ordenskorrespondenz*, Cologne, 1982; both articles were revised by their author for inclusion in the German original of this book. The Epilogue (with some reworkings by its author, Karl Rahner) first appeared in *Diakonia*, Vienna, 1981.

Translated from the German
Welt Kirche: Neue Dimensionen – Modell für das Jahr 2001
by Dame Mary Groves OSB, Oulton Abbey, England

Manuscript editor: William E. Jerman

282
B931ch
1986

Orbis Books
Maryknoll, New York 10545, U.S.A.
ISBN 0-88344-253-1

Dove Communications
Box 316 Blackburn, Victoria 3130, Australia
ISBN 0-85924-600-0

St Paul Publications
Middlegreen, Slough SL3 6BT, England
ISBN 0-85439-242-4

Copyright © Walbert Bühlmann
English translation copyright © Orbis Books, Maryknoll, New York and St Paul Publications, Slough 1986
Typeset by Grove Graphics, Tring, Great Britain
Printed by Billings & Sons, Worcester, Great Britain

Contents

Chapter 4

Chapter 5

Chapter 6

Chapter 7

Chapter 8

Chapter 9

Chapter 10

Chapter 11

Chapter 12

Epilogue by Karl Rahner

Preface

Recent decades, notwithstanding all the dubious changes they have brought with them, have immensely broadened our horizons and so added to what it means to be human. Newspapers and television allow us to take part daily, from our homes, in what is going on everywhere in the world. Jumbo jets fly inquisitive tourists to all parts of our world and shuttles will soon be doing the same in space. Science and technology are moving so fast they are almost out of sight and hearing.

In such a world too the lives of Christian men and women will no longer revolve around their parish church and be concerned merely with their own salvation. The church where they were baptized and received the other sacraments can only now be rightly seen as part of a world church. A broadening of ecclesiastical horizons is needed in our time, and to this end the present work seeks to make a contribution. It does not attempt to develop a complete ecclesiography or ecclesiology but only calls attention to some outstanding features of the new ecclesial situation.

We shall have to concern ourselves especially with questions of the church in the Third World, for this is where the biggest changes originated in the period from 1960 to 1980, and where leadership can be expected in the next 20-year period. That Third World already has more than two-thirds of the votes at the UNO and will in the foreseeable future account for two-thirds of Christendom and four-fifths of humanity. We can no longer pass it off as a sizable minority. The new dimensions of the world church bring pressing demands for the integration of the Third World into the First World picture of world and church, whether for its understanding of the church or for evangelization.

After the stormy upheaval in the church during the conciliar and postconciliar period, a certain quiet has settled in. Many churchgoers obviously rejoice at this and think we have gone through enough 'experimentation', had enough 'upset', enough 'adaptation' in line with the real or seeming requirements of the time. Now, the promulgation of the new Canon Law, the impetus of Vatican II, is interrupted and brought to an end. A period of consolidation surely must follow. Order and discipline within, decisiveness and uniformity without — in the direction of 'enemies' — are to be the important passwords now to be passed on and carried through.

But many others, myself included, are deeply convinced that the council has not yet had its last word, not spent its ultimate strength, not yet achieved its final aims. For quite apart from new orientations within the church, which will continue to influence the future, Vatican II was the first council of a church now become worldwide in fact. It did not merely attend to passing needs, but signalled the start of a truly new era, a 'third age'. In the wake of the church of the first millennium — the Eastern church — and the church of the second millennium — the Western church — now follows, with the irruption of the Southern church, the church of the coming millennium, the age of the world church in short.

Of course it is not for us to sit down at a drawing board and plot the future. The future is the secret of the Lord of history. But yet we can conceive something of it and ask ourselves what we can do to serve and further God's plans, and how the church of the future must to a certain extent appear when it starts out on the third millennium of its history — no longer as a North Atlantic church with a missionary outreach in other parts of the world, but a church in and of all peoples.

It is striking how often Pope John Paul II speaks of the church on the way to the year 2000: four times in *Redemptor Hominis*, then in various addresses, and again at the promulgation of the new Canon Law on January 25, 1983. There may and must be therefore, in spite of the unavoidable obscurity of the whole future and so also of the church, an enquiry made into the church of the future.

Much that can be foreseen and said and desired of the future of the church remains of course a matter of interpretation. I do not imagine that everyone in the church will subscribe to every opinion set out in this book. Many may hold much of it to be utopian or indeed undesirable. But even a cursory look at the history of the church in recent years will show that much has become a reality that not so long ago went for utopian or undesirable. If our horizons are never widened by utopian notions, we go along in a rut and vegetate in everyday dullness — and so it is with the church.

In order to avoid as many misunderstandings as possible, let me emphasize what should in any case be taken for granted — that I base my stand unequivocally on the teaching of the church. My ecclesiology is that of the church, that of Vatican I was well as that of Vatican II. But within this general teaching of the church on the church there must be allowed room for shifts of emphasis, as the whole history of the church shows. In this way both extremes always remain valid but sometimes one, sometimes the other comes to the fore. To turn away from a static legalism, therefore, is not to deny that there are and must be laws. To advocate greater pluralism in the church is not to deny that there must be a fixed foundation of doctrine and a teaching authority in the church. To call for more community among the Christian churches is far from holding all churches to be simply equivalent expressions of the one Christian church. To recognize the Spirit of God at work even in the non-Christian religions in no way sets Christianity on a level with other religions. To criticize the Roman Curia because one can give examples of how, together with the church itself, the curia always stands in need of reform, does not overlook the fact that the whole church, in spite of the need for reform, remains the mystery of the presence and love of God.

In order to give greater support to my main theme, I asked permission of my friend Karl Rahner to include one of his essays, written independently of this book. I thank him for his kind cooperation.

This book, as the table of contents shows, comprises two parts. Part 1 gives an assessment and analysis of the present state of the world church. The first four chapters consider its new geopolitical framework; the next four set new kerygmatic accents on the themes of justice, peace, hope, and worldwide fellowship. Part 2 sketches a utopian response to this situation, a model for the church in the near future, which, I hope, my present contribution may help get off the ground.

In 1978 I published a book, *Wo der Glaube lebt: Einblicke in die Lage der Weltkirche* ['where the faith lives: glimpses into the situation of the world church']. Karl Rahner said of it that it was 'the best Catholic book of the year'. Certain themes from it are taken up again here, brought into line with how things stand today, enlarged, and built up into a model for the church for the year 2000 — for the close of the second millennium and the opening of the third millennium, for which we should even now be setting a course.

Part One

New Dimensions

Chapter One

From Western Church to World Church

At the close of the 1974 Synod of Bishops in Rome on evangelization in the modern world, Pope Paul VI handed a copy of the
Acts of the Apostles to each of the participants as they left. His
meaning was that this account of the church still retains its importance today and the same Holy Spirit still guides the church.
I would go still further and maintain that a kind of Acts could
be written for every century but that the 'Acts of the Twentieth
Century' would be the one most like that of the first century, both
for the rapid spread of Christianity and in reference to tensions in
the church: then, the transition from a Jewish to a gentile church;
today, the transition from a church of the West to a world church.

Reflecting upon the present state of church and mission, we can
make two new and important assertions: the church today is found
in six continents, but so also is mission — in North and Latin
America, Europe, Africa, Asia, and Australia. It will be worth-
while to reflect on these two statements a little, not entering into a
description of church and mission in six continents, but simply
dwelling on the fact that church and mission are in six continents
and some consequences of that fact.[1]

Church in Six Continents

The Church of the West

Today, standing at the close of a period of history, we are
for the first time conscious of how long the church has been
concentrated in the West. From the moment when Paul wanted
to turn back from Troas and head toward Asia, the church has
been in fact throughout its whole history a church of the West:
even the so-called Eastern churches are to be found largely in

3

European countries. Paul would perhaps have gone as far as India and the history of the church would have unfolded in Asia, but 'the spirit prevented [him] ... would not allow it' (Acts 16), and he went instead to the West, to Macedonia, Corinth, Rome.

As a result we find that in modern church histories a good 95 percent of the material is on the church of the Western world. Furthermore, all theology, the whole of liturgy, the whole of church discipline, are the fruit of the 2,000-year-old Western church. Statistically the picture was that at the start of this century 85 percent of all Christians lived in the West.

That was the time of the European hegemony in world and in church. All lines of world politics, world economics, world church met in Europe. It was the wealthy, donating, teaching church; the others were the poor, receiving, learning missions, entirely dependent on it. Missionaries, children of their age, went out to those lands of 'savages' and 'heathen', and laid there, certainly at enormous sacrifice, the foundations for what was later to be the new Africa and the church of Africa, but they did it in a way that today would be called paternalistic.

This age of European hegemony reached its peak and at the same time its close during the Second World War. Asians and Africans were still under the thumb of Europe but very quickly after that the empire of colonialism, from Jamaica to the Cape of Good Hope to Singapore, collapsed like a house of cards. At the end of the war there were 57 nation-states worldwide, 51 of which were the founding members of UNO. There are now 159 members (1985).

Only now can we speak of a world history in the proper sense. What until now was called 'world history' was divided into the three stages of European history: antiquity, the Middle Ages, the modern period. But now the first stage of real *world* history has begun.

World Church

Recent decades brought about a quite new situation for the church also. What is effectively the centre of gravity of Christianity in the West has shifted more and more, and 1970 reached a critical point: by then 51 percent of all Catholics were living in the southern continents: Latin America, Africa, Asia-Oceania. Until

4

1980 the proportion went on rising to 57.76 percent. By the year 2000 a good 70 percent of all Catholics will be living in the southern hemisphere.

The church is making an approach to culturally very ancient peoples: we know today that civilization developed in the valley of the Indus and the Ganges, in the Yellow River valley, in Indonesia, Africa, America, and finally also in the eastern Mediterranean. By the same token, Third World peoples have very youthful populations. The West is becoming more and more an aging community and church. But in the Third World as a whole, 42 percent of the population is under 15 years of age. The church there is a church of youth, hope, the future. These peoples are also still very poor. The church there has the opportunity of becoming the church of the poor and for the poor, not merely on paper but in deed and in truth.

With hindsight it is plain that the pontificate of Paul VI was marked by the genesis of this new state of affairs. For me Paul VI will go down in history as the pope in whose pontificate the church of the West became the church of the world. In those fifteen years the shift of the statistical centre of gravity took place: indigenous bishops came into their own, so that today in Asia around 95 percent, in Africa around 75 percent of the bishops are local in origin. Another significant fact: since Peter went to Rome, no pope had ever left Europe. But Paul visited all six continents as a sign that now the church has really become a church of the six continents. Pope John Paul II has continued this practice of world pilgrimage.

The religious and sociological fact of the church in six continents was undergirded by Vatican II. We know now that the one universal church with its strong centralized power (Vatican I) exists concretely in countless local churches all of which have the right and duty not to be any longer 'only' missions, carbon copies of the European church, but to stand on their own feet and be allowed to contribute their full say within the framework of the whole church.

In view of this phenomenon I have maintained that the Third Church is approaching, church of the Third World but also church of the third millennium. Roughly speaking we can say that the first Christian millennium, with the first eight councils all held in the East, stood mainly under the leadership of the First Church,

5

the Eastern church; the second millennium stood under the leadership of the Second Church, the Western church, which shaped the Middle Ages and, from the time of the 'discovery' of the New World, undertook all missionary initiatives. Now the coming third millennium will evidently stand under the leadership of the Third Church, the Southern church. I am convinced that the most important drives and inspirations for the whole church in the future will come from the Third Church.

This theory has already been confirmed by experience — at the 1974 Synod of Bishops on evangelization in the modern world. Just as Vatican II and the first three Synods of Bishops were conducted by the Second Church, bishops and theologians of the Third World took over the leadership in the 1974 Synod. It was they who raised the burning issues that finally went into *Evangelii Nuntiandi*. Not for nothing did Paul VI note twice in *Evangelii Nuntiandi* the special contribution of the Third World bishops (30, 31). It is good to let this new state of things sink into our consciousness. Americans speak of 'cultural lag', when someone does not keep up with new ideas, new currents of theology, philosophy, ideology, and so lives twenty years behind the times, lives in the past. That can happen in church circles too. One of the most important new duties of Second Church leaders is to bring to the knowledge of their people the fact that they are no longer *the* church but have become part of a greater church.

The Church Incarnated in a Variety of Cultures

The spread of the church in numbers and in importance in the Third World has consequences for the whole church. Up to Vatican II, complete uniformity reigned in the Catholic Church: the same catechism everywhere, the same Latin liturgy everywhere, everywhere the same centrally monitored church discipline. There was indeed talk of adaptation but it referred only to purely external details like dress, church music, and so on.

As long as the church lived in a European cultural setting, that was more or less acceptable. But today when the church lives in six continents, each having its own political, cultural, and ecclesial consciousness, the church there must not merely be accommodated in exterior things, but radically 'incarnated' into those cultures. That is why in Vatican II, still very cautiously because for the first

6

time, but then in *Evangelii Nuntiandi* more naturally and boldly, the incarnation of the church in diverse cultures was spoken of, and with it legitimate pluriformity, not as a threat to unity but as an enrichment, as a God-given expression of unity in diversity.[2] Geographically quantified Catholicism must be an offshoot of qualitative Catholicism. This alone mirrors the divine plan of creation, to which all cultural priorities must defer.

All this is plain in theory and has been set out and deepened in conciliar texts and since then in books and articles. But as soon as it is to be translated into practice, problems begin. As soon as a local church wants to take concrete steps to become really a local church, not merely a carbon copy of the Roman church, it is told by authority: in the name and in the interests of unity, that will not do. This tension between documents and deeds constitutes the testing and trial for the church in the present time. Just as the transition from the Jewish to the gentile Christian church took place under tensions and with victims — Paul was sacrificed for it — so also the transition from the Western church to a world church, from uniformity to pluriformity, will take place only under tension. One pole in the church, central power, concentrates on unity. This is its right and duty. All the more, however, must the other pole, the bishops and episcopal conferences, enter into dialogue defending their interests and their complementary viewpoints so that genuine parity and balance can come between the two poles. Unity certainly, but within pluriformity.

Mission in Six Continents

Teminology

Missions have been phased out because they have developed into independent local churches, even though still in need of help for some time. And yet we continue to speak of *mission* — in six continents. The apparent contradiction is resolved by its very terms: mission and missions.

Missions were juridical territories under the administration of Propaganda Fide (*Ad Gentes*, 6). They were therefore, according to the *jus communionis*, entrusted to missionary institutes. These missionary institutes bore the full responsibility for 'their missions'. Meanwhile, however, the *jus communionis* was abrogated for mis-

7

sion churches by an instruction of Propaganda Fide in 1969 and they became local churches with their own responsibility for evangelization in their area. Whereas missionary activity had been carried on by foreign missionaries and missions were the objects, recipients, of missionary activity, Vatican II declared them to be subjects and bearers of missionary activity (*Ad Gentes*, 20). And so it is anachronistic to continue speaking of 'our missions'. For churches to continue to call for 'prayers for the missions', 'alms-giving for the missions', is offensive. Such talk perpetuates the thinking of historical colonialism: here the metropolitan centre, there the overseas adjunct; here the church, there the mission. Nowadays it is no longer a question of 'missionary aid' to beggars but of mutual interchurch service in which all churches have some-thing to offer.

It is striking that both Paul VI in *Evangelii Nuntiandi* and John Paul II in his many addresses in Africa not only speak of the missions very much in passing, as though from habit, but continue speaking of the age of evangelization, of the missionary task, the missionary church. The expressions 'mission' and 'missionary' still have validity. They refer to the preliminary evangelization of those who are still far from Christ. This preevangelization must in future have priority among the tasks the church sets for itself, as is plain from *Evangelii Nuntiandi* (51 and passim). This document, how-ever, had not only pre-Christians but also post-Christians in mind, not only the 'not-yet' Christian but also the 'no-longer' Christian, those no longer practising, no longer believers, who stand again in need of preevangelization. This missionary situation, the area of 'not-yet Christians' and 'no-longer Christians', is found today in all six continents. That is why we speak today of mission in six continents. Missions were coming to an end, but mission goes on.

Preevangelization in the Third Church

When we know that in 1965 there were a good two milliard non-Christians (2,272 million) and that in the year 2000 there will be a good four milliard, no one can say the missionary age is at an end. Certainly today we have no need any longer of anxious zeal for saving souls, as though without our zeal, without baptism, millions of human beings will go off to hell. We can accept today that God has both the firm fatherly will and the necessary means to save all humankind. Missionary concern no longer arises today out of fear of hell but out of love of God, whose goodness and love we want to make known to the whole of humanity. Whether individuals then enter the church is not in our power but in the hand of God. The first can be termed evangelizing, the second christianizing.

In the sense of evangelizing all humankind through personal witness and through the mass media, there is certainly much more call for missionary activity today than ever before. Talk of 'missionary crisis' must therefore be taken very relatively. Until now only one continent was missionary. But because now all local churches in all six continents have become actively missionary, mission activity has developed sixfold. The 'missionary crisis' is a Western phenomenon: the radical decline in missionary vocations. But perhaps it was necessary, providential, so that Second Church personnel might draw back from their almost monopolistic leadership role and give all the churches room and scope to become missionary. So it is not mission as such that is in crisis but only the missions run almost exclusively by foreign missionaries.

Missionary activity is also ordered differently today. In the past it was an organized, hierarchical apostolate: bishop/priest/catechist. The catechist was the 'long arm' of the priest, on the payroll of the local church. But now everywhere in Africa, Asia, and Latin America communities have developed with an elected council of lay persons who perform the various ministries: reading and explaining the gospel in a divine service without the priest, leading the singing, instructing candidates for baptism, visiting the sick or families in need. They are spreading Christianity now quite on their own, as communities, as in the early days of the church.

What, then, should be the task of missionary institutes regarding these self-reliant local churches with leaders chosen from among themselves? The answer could well be that the missionary institutes have fulfilled the task for which they were founded. When today they are denied a visa to some countries, they do not leave behind a vacuum but a more or less developed and viable local church.

Where possible, they should continue to work together with local churches for as long as their assistance is necessary and possible. In not a few places there are still real shortfalls; missionaries are needed to bridge the gap to an indigenous clergy.

9

The classic type of missionary who like Abraham left home and country behind has the function of animator and will indeed to a certain degree always be useful in a young church for it not to become 'parochial', falling into the danger of thinking only of those already in the church.

Missionaries will not be merely stop-gaps but messengers between older and younger churches, conveying theological insights to both of them and mutually enriching them. True *koinonia*, a community of churches, will come into existence not in dependence but in mutual giving and receiving, teaching and learning.

Missionaries will also widen horizons for older churches. Until now they have been sending missionaries to other continents and have not noticed that missionary situations were at the same time building up at home with no one to attend to them. That should no longer be the case.

Preevangelization in the Second Church

In the West, 'missionary situations' have again been developing — that is, groups of persons (isolated individuals do not constitute an ecclesial situation in the church) standing outside the church, living apart from Christ. They can be called post-Christian. They are in need of preevangelization. Their situation calls for 'missionaries', for persons who in systematic fashion pass across the boundaries of the Christian community and announce Christ again to those far from him, with new methods and in a new language (*Evangelii Nuntiandi*, 55–56).

An analysis of this new situation was made for the first time in 1943 in a book by Henri Godin and Yves Daniel, *La France pays de mission?* [Is France a mission land?]. The book caused a considerable stir at the time, and, outside France, much opposition. No one wanted it to be true. Twenty years later the World Council of Churches, meeting in Mexico City, coined the expression 'mission in six continents'. Catholic circles did not go along with the idea.

But more and more it was necessary to come to terms with the fact that, for example, in Germany, church attendance among young Catholics, from 1963 to 1973, fell from 52 percent to 19 percent; in 'Catholic' Vienna church attendance was down to 10 percent; in the suburbs of French cities 3 percent to 5 percent;

10

in the U.S.A. there were 80 million 'unchurched'. This state of affairs has been described in books and articles.[3] John Paul II confirmed this analysis when he said to the European Bishops' Conference: 'Europe is at the point of again becoming a missionary continent; that should not be a reason for pessimism, but be understood as a great challenge' (*Osservatore Romano*, Dec. 21, 1978).

Foreign missions are, in a certain sense, coming to an end, but home missions are starting up as a new task calling for new initiatives.[4] The human values upheld by post-Christians must be recognized and acknowledged. There must be contact made with them on the common ground of humanity. Their secret longings for fulfillment must be detected, interpreted, and so answered that the church, sacrament of salvation for all, says to them not a word of damnation but of salvation and hope.

It can indeed be said without exaggeration that the 'Christian West' has become the most difficult mission area. Evangelization of persons alienated from the church cannot be expected of priests, who are already too few. They can at most be animators, encouraging and prompting the laity. What once applied to all disciples of Christ ought again to become self-evident: 'every Christian a missionary'. Those who take this seriously and want to act accordingly need new courage, a new language, new inspirations, which will doubtless be given to those who are open to the Holy Spirit.

Chapter Two

A Continental Church in Latin America

On the politico-economic level we have witnessed the formation, however laborious, of regional blocs — for example, the NATO countries, the Warsaw Pact countries, the Arab bloc, the Latin American countries, and so on. This has been called macro-regionalization.

On the ecclesiastical plane something similar is occurring. The Catholic Church is not merely a conglomeration of 2,452 dioceses or similar ecclesiastical districts (1983). There are also unifying bodies: the national episcopal conferences and the symposia of continental episcopal conferences, which are slowly but surely promoting integration. I turn now to the three southern continental churches, beginning with Latin America.

In 1980, Latin America counted 323 million Catholics (Europe, 271 million). But I am not concerned here with statistics and power shifts. I shall consider each of the three southern continents from a distinct viewpoint. For Latin America the theme of poverty is the most obvious.

To speak of the Third World is at once to think of the stigma that overhangs it like a menacing black cloud: poverty. The Third World, the tropical zone encircling the globe, is in fact the empire where poverty holds unlimited sway; where still today 800 million human beings, twice the population of Europe, live below a minimum subsistence level; where racial wars and natural catastrophes repeatedly carry off whole sections of the population; where the ruling class enslaves the poor by corruption and exploitation; where unfavourable conditions of trade widen still more the gulf between rich and poor; where there are mostly only two extremes in effect: communism without freedom or capitalism without justice.

All this characterizes, alas, the entire Third World. But it is in

Diagram 1 — World Catholic Population, 1980

First World
42%

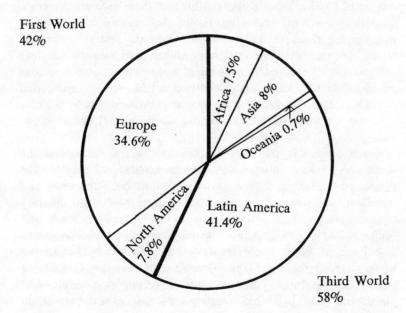

Africa 7.5%

Asia 8%

Europe
34.6%

Oceania 0.7%

North America
7.8%

Latin America
41.4%

Third World
58%

Latin America more than elsewhere that crimes against the poor cry out to heaven for vengeance — crimes that are cemented into de facto power structures and therefore seemingly legitimized. Here more than elsewhere churches and peoples have become aware of the true state of things and are seeking liberation and justice.

A Continent Rich in Resources

Latin America was in no way consigned by fate to go down in history as a poor continent. If today it stands as a symbol of poverty and extortion, once it was a rich, a blessed continent, one might almost say a Garden of Eden. So far as we know, the inhabitants of the two Americas, originally a branch of the Mongol race, migrated in several waves between 50,000 and 30,000 B.C. across the Bering Strait, frozen in winter.[5] Here they came upon ideal country, land in abundance, with forests for hunting and rivers for fishing. In the course of centuries they tended to move southward, toward a warmer, more congenial, climate. At the time of Christopher Columbus the entire population may have amounted to 35 or 40 million, two-thirds of them in South America.

In time many of these nomadic peoples became sedentary and developed agriculture. Later on they gave the rest of the world maize, the potato, tobacco, cocoa, rubber, and manioc. In their religion they honoured a paramount God supreme over various other spirits and knew many creation myths, with a primordial paradise, original sin, and a deluge. Amerindians today, whether Christian or not, are still remarkable for a very strong religious sense.

Three peoples in particular — the Mayas, the Incas, and the Aztecs — attained an astonishingly high standard of culture. The Aztecs of Mexico practised agriculture with both terracing and irrigation, and maintained an urban culture with tight military administration. Their achievements in the sphere of road- and bridge-building surpassed in some respects those of the Romans. The Incas of Peru, whose territory was larger than that of the Roman empire, built a 5,000-kilometre road over the Andes from present-day Quito to Talca in Chile. In ceramics, weaving, and metalwork they produced masterpieces. Museum treasures in Bogotá and Lima convey some idea of it.

The Aztecs knew a kind of sacrificial communion, a kind of confession that remitted temporal punishment, and a kind of baptism by which a newborn child was washed free of original sin. A well-organized hierarchical priesthood conducted the various rites to the accompaniment of psalmlike chants. Murder, adultery, sacrilege were punished with death. There was also a belief in eternal life, with heaven and hell. They believed they had conquered and held the land at God's command. A symbol of God's presence was kept in a depository and no decision was taken without consulting God. Finally, they awaited the return one day of the god Quetzalcoatl to restore the Golden Age. When the Spanish under Cortes arrived, the Aztecs thought to see in them sons and brothers of Quetzalcoatl. Therefore the Spanish were received with great friendliness.

A wonderful opportunity was offered to the Spaniards to form friendly relations with these peoples and enter into exchanges of trade, culture, and religion. A glorious chapter of history could have been opened. But the Spanish way of thinking, with its un-questioning sense of superiority, would not allow such a vision to be contemplated. The Amerindians were seen only as heathen and idolaters, savages who were to be absorbed by subjection and conversion to Western Christianity and become its servants. Instead of proclaiming the good news of the gospel, the Spanish instigated a reign of terror. Thus began a subjection, in successive stages, that has continued, in part, to the present day.

An Oppressed Continent

The Conquest

The Spanish and Portuguese explorers and conquerors are described as 'good Christian men'. They wanted to conquer the world for Christ and the church.[6] Fernando Cortes, the scourge of Mexico, the most outstanding of all the conquistadors, was very pious, always carried an image of the Mother of God about him, attended daily Mass. For the rest, however, he gave free reign to his passions and knew no political scruple. The same could be said of Francisco Pizarro, the conqueror of the Incan empire, in present-day Peru. He had an official proclamation read before King Atahualpa demanding that he and his people submit to the pope and the emperor, Charles V, or else be subjugated by force and enslaved — men, women, and children. Atahualpa declared himself ready to call Charles V his brother but not as a tributary subject. He insisted that he would hold to his own beliefs, for his God was alive and not, like Jesus, killed by his own people. Thereupon Pizarro sent his troops to confession and communion, himself preached a sermon, gave the signal for the attack, and had two thousand unarmed Amerindians massacred. The whole country was soon overrun.

After taking forced possession, it was a short step to 'peace-keeping', that is, systematic exploitation of the country, now that its riches had been discovered. In contrast to North America, where the climate was more agreeable to Europeans and which therefore was developed as a colonial settlement with almost total extermination of the indigenes, South American colonization was export-oriented. The Amerindians were ruthlessly enslaved and transported to sugar and coffee plantations and then to copper, silver, and gold mines.

A concrete example: between 1528 and 1540 most of the

15

two hundred thousand Amerindians of Nicaragua were taken prisoner and brought to Panama and Peru. In 1535 Spain was told the 'good news' that a third of the indigenous population of Nicaragua had been enslaved and carried off.[7] But the slaves died off like flies from contagious diseases and harsh treatment. In the whole of the southern continent their numbers were in a hundred years reduced by a third. Then the Dominican Bartolomê de Las Casas took up his crusade for the Amerindians. He achieved the abolition of their slavery by 1542. Slaves were imported from Africa to take their place, and a new chapter of horrors began. Estimates of the number of slaves deported from Africa vary from 7 to 15 million. Quite as many lost their lives hunted in Africa and in the ocean crossing with its callous disregard for hygiene. Little time was wasted on Christian scruples.

The motivation behind the whole undertaking was simply greed. It has been calculated that 185,000 kilos of gold and 16 million kilos of silver were carried off to Spain from 1503 to 1660. And gold was made lavish use of in Latin America itself, as various gilded churches — for example, the church of St. Francis in Salvador (Bahia) — bear witness.

All this evil was pursued with an easy conscience because it was widely believed that the Amerindians were not fully human and were bereft of reason. Even missionaries bore this out, after the fashion of Fr. Tomás Ortiz, O.P., who wrote of the Indians in Colombia in 1529: "They have no sense of justice, go around naked, feel neither love nor shame, they are asses, stupid, mad, insane; to kill or be killed is all the same with them; they are bestial in their vices, cowardly as rabbits, filthy as swine...." Petrus Martyr included this passage in his book *De orbe novo*, widely read at the time, and added: 'They are really wild animals. Never has God created a people so full of vices and beastliness, without a glimmer of goodness and culture'.[8]

Traces of this prejudiced attitude persist to the present day. In December 1967 seven Colombian ranchers invited sixteen Amerindian men, women, and children to a meal and then hacked them to pieces in cold blood with machetes because they allegedly had stolen some cattle. The murderers were at first set free by the court because they maintained they 'had not known it was a crime to kill Amerindians'.

It must in fairness be pointed out that the Spanish crown did

16

much to further missionary work in the interest of the Ameri-indians and, for example, strictly required that there be a school near every church for Amerindian children. But on the whole it remains true that the conquest of Latin America is the most un-worthy chapter in the history of Christendom.

Did the church keep silence on all this? Contrary to the general opinion that the Amerindians were, on account of their savage state, at best fit for baptism but not for the Holy Eucharist, Pope Paul III emphasized in the bull *Veritas ipsa* in 1537 that Amer-indians were 'truly human beings' and therefore certainly fitted for faith and the sacraments. Their traditional religion, on the other hand, was mostly considered to be idolatry and 'impersonation of the devil'. The missionaries certainly were faithful representatives of the land of the Inquisition! No false compromises were to be admitted and it was thought to be pleasing to God when idols were destroyed and a church built out of the stone of demolished temples of 'the religion of the devil'.

Besides the occasional prophetic figure who intervened in behalf of human rights, episcopal bodies sometimes took action. Worthy of mention in this connection is the Third Mexican Synod of 1585, at which the bishops, basing themselves on information from missionaries, spoke in terms that could not be plainer or more powerfully put even today:

> We are informed that of a hundred Amerindians going down the mines in one week, the greater part die, and those who stay alive may not return home to their children because they live in a kind of slavery. They are badly nourished, treated like savages, shut in like animals in foetid holes, victims of a fearful inhumanity never found even among barbarians and unbelievers.

Such injustice could not be condoned; it cried to heaven for vengeance and had to be stopped. The bishops issued a decree on the subject demanding just treatment for the Amerindians.

But the same synod also urged that idolatry be dealt with more rigorously. The punishment of death should be meted out to those who furthered it.[10] A typical expression of the thinking of the time, a thinking much less defensible than was the so-called idolatry! Unfortunately, the church fell more and more into absolutism and in the stage of feudalism became part of the system.

Feudalism

After the gruesome conquest there developed a patriarchalism in a feudal system not based on the inheritance laws of a nobility, as in the Europe of the Middle Ages, but on the power of the powerful. Basically, all conquered land was a possession of the crown. In practice, however, it was very quickly appropriated by individuals and the whole procedure was silently tolerated by the authorities. Thus, until the end of the seventeenth century, there was a firmly established landed aristocracy reigning over the land from the giant *haciendas* (Spanish) or *fazendas* (Portuguese). Sad to say, both religious orders and dioceses concurred with this system of vast landed estates or latifundia.

The latifundia, and the mining communities, were peopled by a central core of white families, augmented by Amerindian and black serfs. In time there came to be more and more workers of mixed genetic parentage: *mestizos* (of white and Amerindian parentage) and mulattos (of white and black parentage). Especially in the first hundred years, when there were few Spanish women in the Latin American colonies, the white conquerors practised unbridled promiscuity. Amerindian girls and women had no recourse but to submit to their will. This was especially the case in Brazil, particularly with respect to female slaves. It is still at work today, to the extent that Latin American countries are the first nineteen in the world in the number of children born out of wedlock.

Even later, when more Spanish and Portuguese women were brought to Latin America, extramarital relations continued apace. Girls and women of colour were handed over to the will of plantation owners and their adolescent sons, for work and for pleasure. Sexual rapine was part of the system. To father children by slave women was the cheapest way to increase, and maintain control over, the slave population.

The pattern of autocratic white families and dependent workers set the social structure in Latin American countries, and continues to do so today wherever a revolution has not put an end to it. The patriarchal extended family was accepted and confirmed ecclesiastically in that the *patrón* was automatically godfather to all the children born on his ranch. Even after the abolition of slavery, he retained, as their guardian, almost as much control as before. Workers had enough to live on, but no more. Landowner-

18

ship, personal development, and free choice of occupation were out of the question.

Today the overall population of Latin America is estimated to be 48 percent white, 32 percent *mestizo*, 11 percent Amerindian, and 9 percent black, the proportion varying a good deal from one country to another. In Argentina there are few nonwhites, whereas in Peru and Guatemala there are still very many Amerindians. Generally speaking the 'final solution' to the Amerindian question appears just around the corner whether in the form of ethnocide — socio-cultural extinction as they are integrated into the modern work world — or in the form of genocide. That is becoming especially clear in the current opening-up of the Amazon basin. Road construction and agri-business are bringing 'progress' to primeval forests, until now practically untouched, and so making widespread inroads on the last territorial regions of the local Amerindians.[11]

Who will there be to honestly rejoice when in 1992 the 500th celebration of the discovery of America is observed? Should we not speak rather of *invasion* than discovery? Already in 1762 Abbé Raynald was writing that it would have been best had America not been discovered. He calls the discovery a catastrophic event, which is no exaggeration if we think not of the white immigrants but of the then proud and happy inhabitants of the Americas who through the incursion of white Christians were robbed of their lands and their lives.[12] Will there be proclaimed in 1992, as a sign of international reconciliation, a great confession of guilt? or will this sinister tale merely be 'filed away' with so many others?

'National Security'

In not a few countries of Latin America there has been established by the three ruling classes — the monied elites, the military, and the government — the so-called National Security system, an ideology to the effect that basic personal rights must be entirely subordinated to the 'highest good', the 'requirements of the nation', or — more accurately — the interests of the privileged. The system stands in close relationship with international capitalism. These states apply in time of peace the tactics of war in order to 'uphold law and order' — that is, in practice to nip in the bud any attempt at insurrection against injustices. Often the ruling classes call

19

themselves Christian. They also control religion, to prevent it from falling under the influence of 'dangerous, subversive, communist ideas'.[13]

A series of works appearing in East Berlin, *Lateinamerikanische Analysen und Berichte* ['Latin American analyses and reports'], gives in the first volume a striking analysis of the overall situation:

> The general development in Latin America in recent years is taking a significant direction. Almost everywhere a capital accumulation model is being set up, indications of it being the systematic exclusion of the ordinary people from the collective wealth and from political decision-making, as also the centralization of economic and political power. On this model, economic growth has for long been possible only as a result of large capital investment, both foreign and internal. To attract these investments it is necessary to create conditions allowing high profits. Among these conditions are especially a planned reinsertion of the national economy into the international labour market, a reduction of the function of the state economic sector to that of a servant of private capital, and a drastic lowering of bank rates. These conditions are attainable only on the basis of a combination of economic liberalism and political repression.

This has fostered the growth of military dictatorships, the setting aside of democratic rights, the repression of 'unaligned' trade unions and political parties, as also the mushrooming of detention centres, the countenancing of death squads and murder commandos, and the systematic disregard for human rights in these countries.[14]

It was not by chance that this analysis was followed by a long article on Marxism in Latin America. Unfortunately, only Marxism appears to have the strength to break the fetters of the system in place. It is a tragedy of history that only communist states are in solidarity with the poor unprotected masses, whereas the U.S.A. is undergirding capitalist regimes and giving military support. Communism in Latin America needs to be confronted by quite other means!

It is not only communist circles that are calling for change. Bishops and episcopal conferences raise prophetic voices in various countries, especially Brazil. Repeatedly, and yet again in a declaration of August 27, 1982, on the autumn elections, the Brazilian bishops have championed a pragmatic economic policy aimed at greater social justice. The agricultural policy of the government is

20

a mistake because it is chiefly based on exports. The bishops call for a just distribution of land to be made to the dispossessed landworkers. And they want them to be organized fully so as to stem the catastrophic flight from the land and the overcrowding in the cities. What the bishops seek is the satisfaction of the basic needs of the masses blocked by the affluence of the wealthy few.[15]

A Continent Liberating Itself

Such an unequivocal stand by the hierarchy, such a complete reversal of the positions taken by the majority of the bishops to the side of the poor, argues that in the church in Latin America a powerful process for change is under way. The 'God of history' seems again to hear the cry of an oppressed people, seems again to be summoning a Moses to free the people from servitude and poverty.[16] It remains a mystery how this God is made to seem silent and unconcerned for decades, centuries even — five centuries — in Latin America.

What I shall next describe is a fabulous example of how something great can arise from small beginnings. It belongs among the finest and most moving episodes of modern church history.

It began with a few theologians and lay persons who made a *révision de vie* and came to realize that the firmly entrenched situation in Latin America could not be willed by God: a privileged minority upholding social injustice with all the means of repression and exploitation within the power of the state; a church concerning itself only with the supernatural truths of faith and the sacraments, and teaching the poor to wait in patience for God and their eternal salvation; the masses so long emasculated and dehumanized by slavery that they no longer questioned its inevitability; a mockery of the gospel teaching that all are called to fellowship and that in the Eucharist they form one communion with Christ and each other. Only the wealthy oppressors in their fine clothes were to be seen at divine services; the poor were ashamed to come to church in their rags.

These theologians came to a new understanding of economic dependency: the poverty of the masses was not simply a fact of life to be alleviated by almsgiving, but a by-product of the economic system in place. Even as theologians, then, they must concern themselves with problems of national and international economics

21

and after that help the people to a religious and economic con-scientization so that they might see the interrelationships and themselves gradually change their situation and the system.

These concepts were at first developed only in lectures and small groups. Then some influential bishops backed them, and boldly joined it. They tried then, in line with the 'church of the poor' of the Second Vatican Council — pioneered by Cardinals Suenens, Lercaro, and Montini, and Archbishop Helder Câmara — to under-take a radical review. What they achieved was that the Latin American bishops' conference at Medellín in 1968 adhered to this line and boldly declared:

> God has sent his son and he became man to free all people from every servitude in which sin, ignorance, hunger, misery and oppres-sion, in a word injustice and hate, hold them prisoner, which in their turn take their rise in human selfishness [Document 1.3].

The chief point of their pastoral programme was now the 'option for the poor'.

Medellín also gave the green light to the basic Christian com-munities, which then began to proliferate in country after country and have since then widely renewed the face of the Latin American church. Henceforth there was no longer a care of souls from above, the hierarchical church, with priests appearing at an outpost twice a year like meteors, dispensing the sacraments and disappearing again, leaving outstations for another six months with no church-related activities. Now a care of souls was developing from below. The church as the people of God now gathers, prays, sings, reads and interprets the gospel, and on this basis changes day-to-day living step by step.

This option of Latin America for justice, for integral salvation, for basic communities, has already exerted a great influence on the church as a whole. At the Synod of Bishops of 1971 the classic statement was formulated that to work for justice, development, integral salvation, is not preevangelization, not a means to an end, but 'an essential part of evangelization itself'. In *Evangelii Nuntiandi*, following the Synod of Bishops of 1974 on evangeliza-tion in the world today, Pope Paul VI twice expressly brought out the important contribution of the bishops of the Third World. The Puebla bishops' conference in 1979 confirmed the way taken until then, so there can be no going back.

22

It was in 1971 that Gustavo Gutiérrez published his now classic work *Teología de la liberación* (English translation, *A Theology of Liberation*, 1973). It fully expressed the aim of this theology, which was not to set up theories but to start out from praxis and serve it. This theology does not think of itself as an explanation of dogmas, still less as a defence of dogmatic orthodoxy, but as a faith-reflection on popular praxis.

Liberation theology does not begin by making an enquiry into the religious practices of a people, but by an analysis of the concrete everyday situation, the hopes and joys, cares and sorrows, of a people. The second step is an attempt to assess this situation prophetically and to ask how the God of history and life will want to free this people from this state of things, from personal sins and difficulties as well as from socio-political injustices. The third step concerns pastoral consequences — what is wanted is to give others courage and strength from the gospel message to be able to change their situation and in so doing to experience the exodus, liberation from slavery, salvation history today, as a foretaste of eschatological liberation. The five-volume work by J. L. Segundo, *A Theology for Artisans of a New Humanity*, which grew entirely out of praxis, shows how teaching the faith today can be close to life and therefore also full of meaning.

It cannot be denied that some liberation theologians make use of Marxist socio-political analysis in their study of the concrete state of affairs. This does not make them Marxists, as is said of them all too quickly. They simply make a choice among the different models of development that three political parties incorporate in their platforms. On the extreme right, landowners do indeed also talk about development but they understand it in the sense of a process continually renewing itself and so remaining the same, therefore supporting their capitalist thinking and their hierarchical, authoritarian structures. The liberals to the centre are aware of the need for radical change, a more just sharing of national wealth, a stronger participation of the people in responsible government. But basically they remain the managerial class, guiding everything and keeping everything in their hands. The left, on the contrary, sees only one way out of this stagnating situation: a change of economic structures, a creative transformation, a total involvement of the people in government.[17] This is explained in Marxist terms, which are convincing and attractive even though their concrete exemplification in communist states is in no way a recommendation. Liberation theologians incorporate Marxist concepts more or less expressly in their work. They propose a variety of models in their approach to the problem of violence as a defence or counterforce against the brutal violence of right-wing governments. There is a variety of 'liberation theologies'.

Liberation theology differs in many respects from the scholastic theory usual until now. The latter started out from eternal truths, was deductive, universal, everywhere applicable — and by that very fact abstract, divorced from life. Liberation theology on the other hand begins with an analysis of the concrete state of affairs, is inductive, contextual, and aims at changing life at close quarters. Further, scholastic theology was professorial, written by theologians in their studies and presented in lecture halls, uncontaminated by the world. Liberation theology on the other hand is out in the forefront of life. In the first instance it is produced by the people in grass-roots communities as a spontaneous response to the gospel, and only then perhaps written down. Again, scholastic theology remains uniform, the same throughout the world, and to that extent drained of colour. Liberation theology is shot through with as many diverse colours as life itself or as creation, and gives an idea of the boundless impulses of the Spirit of God.

What first came to expression in Latin America has been taken up and broadened in EATWOT (Ecumenical Association of Third World Theologians). In 1976 a group of theologians of the three southern continents met together in Dar es Salaam with the aim of sounding out their common positions and interests, and formulating them, and to that extent freeing themselves in a certain sense from Western theology. Then continental meetings were held: in 1977 in Accra, Ghana; in 1979 in Wennappuwa, Sri Lanka; in 1980 in São Paolo. In 1981 a general conference was held in New Delhi to evaluate progress up to that point. At that meeting there were lively speeches on the Third World as a growing challenge to theology. If theology was not to remain a luxury monopolized by ivory-tower professors, the causes relating to the grim world of poverty must be discovered and by all legitimate means removed in the strength of the word of God. Faith in God and in Christ's resurrection meant believing in love, justice, peace, the possibility of changing the world.[18] Finally in January 1983 there took place

24

in Geneva the first EATWOT meeting of Third World theologians and Western theologians.[19]

When the various reports of these conferences are read they give the impression that there was more economic analysis and politics going on than theology. But that is just the way to pursue exodus theology and paschal theology today. So it seems that Latin American liberation theology can become, via EATWOT, a world theology. The findings of such a theological venture can certainly not yet be assessed. Some shake their heads over it and call it a profanation of theology; others see in it the return of prophecy bringing freshness to a stale theology. In fact these theologians, who often voluntarily live in slum areas, do not want merely to do something 'for' the poor but to live 'with' the poor and 'as' the poor, and struggle together against poverty and misery, in order to eliminate it as being not the will of God but a blemish disfiguring God's plan for humanity.

This process will not soon reach its conclusion. It is only at the beginning of a new and arduous road. Perhaps the goal will never be reached. The structures of injustice and international capitalism stand like an almost impregnable fortress. Decision-making boards of multinational corporations and National Security regimes see the growing danger. They label 'communist' those theologians and bishops who identify with the poor, and think to harm them in this way, whereas the church, for that very reason, has again become credible to the people. The apathetic people is winning back, if not yet its rightful living standards, at least its self-respect, with a more fully human life and an eschatological hope, so that it no longer lets itself be discouraged even when some innocent individuals are made a sacrifice to violence. It is striking that at the funerals of such 'martyrs for justice' dejection does not reign but much rather a mood of exhilaration expressed in Easter hymns. Christians are orienting their lives more and more to the scriptural utopia of justice and peace, even though its implementation will be long in coming and meanwhile prophets die for its cause.

What has thus grown up from the grass roots and then been set down in scattered theological works is scheduled to appear in Latin America as a collection of forty volumes, under the collaboration of one hundred and fifty theologians, probably with the title *Mysterium Liberationis*. When the five volumes of *Mysterium*

Salutis appeared between 1965 and 1976, it was felt to have captured and expressed postconciliar theology once and for all. Certainly these volumes remain indispensable. But *Mysterium Liberationis* could, as the first great southern theology, with its new emphases and new methods of expression, represent a great expansion and enrichment. Slowly the church is becoming not only geographically and demographically, but also theologically, a church of six continents.

What does all this mean for European Christians? Latin America today stands as a great sign of hope. If such a hierarchical, sacramentalized, statistical church could renew itself to such a degree in so short a time, the European church too, with its history of clericalism, should not lose heart in its expectation of salvation from the grass roots and not react in fear as though the conciliar definition of the church as the people of God was a mistake.

Further, Europeans may not, like uncommitted onlookers, merely observe what is going on in Latin America. They must think in terms of *inter-esse,* 'standing by' it, as their church and part of the one human race. They should do all they can to eradicate the great guilt that the Western world bears toward Latin America. There is a papal commission Justitia et Pax. Members of religious orders and institutes are inspired by this concept. In capitalist America, organizations and movements for responsible investment and options for justice in the Third World are multiplying. Do Europeans not live in a rather bourgeois atmosphere and leave the challenge of radical change to so-called leftist groups? In saying this I am not forgetting what has been achieved by private initiatives, political parties, and church bodies. I only want to encourage and strengthen it.

The Latin American writer J. P. Miranda has written a book entitled *Marx against the Marxists.*[20] He demonstrates in it how Marx meant well by humanity and believed in a future of justice and peace. He would be horrified to see how today his ideas have become an ideology and a system of unfreedom and repression. I have a mind to write a book some time: 'Christ against the Christians'. Latin America would occupy a hefty chapter in it. To look at Latin America through the lens of 'justice and poverty' would yield a wealth of material, from the conquest to the present day, that would make Christians deeply ashamed. We can only murmur: 'God, be merciful to us poor Christians', and then confidently pray: 'God, help the Latin American peoples in their struggle for justice and peace, so that those seeking liberation may one day be liberated'.

Chapter Three

A Continental Church in Africa

A person would have to be blind not to see in Africa, as well as in Latin America, the ominous shadow of poverty stalking the land. Poverty in Africa means unfavourable climatic conditions with now too much, now too little, rain; the chronic state of under-nourishment in the Sahel; the lamentable situation in Tanzania, where, in 1978, a year of normal rainfall, 439,000 tonnes of maize could be exported, whereas in 1980, a year of drought, 258,000 tonnes had to be imported.

Poverty in Africa means unjust world trade conditions. Tanzania, in 1981, in spite of strict controls, had to spend 55 percent of its budget on crude oil. The equivalent of 5 tonnes of sisal paid for a tractor in 1960, which then cost 10 tonnes in 1970, and in 1980 as much as 20 tonnes.[21]

Poverty in Africa means being the football of international politics. The Soviets and Americans carry on their gruesome proxy battles in Ethiopia, Angola, and Mozambique, contending for spheres of influence.[22]

Poverty in Africa means shortages of food, medicine, and spare parts of all kinds; it means bureaucratic government; black markets; corruption and exploitation of the poor by the rich; a way of life that Julius Nyerere has termed 'spiritual slumming'. In the 1960s African nations, with much flag-waving and hand-clapping, entered upon independence. Not a few have taken names nostalgically reminiscent of their history, recalling the greatness of their peoples in precolonial days: Ghana, Mali, Benin, Zimbabwe.

It has to be admitted that, despite relatively favourable condi-tions, African nations have not succeeded in building solid and lasting superstructures, with the result that conditions are much harsher at present, with massive national debts, interior divisions, and inefficient administration. They appear to be headed toward a

28

rather bleak future. An indication of this sad state of affairs and a counsel of despair came in January 1983 when the richest country, Nigeria, decided to expel its 2 to 3 million immigrant workers almost overnight — something that went against all African tradition.

The Symposium of the Episcopal Conferences of Africa and Madagascar (SECAM) in the 1960s had concerned itself mainly with African cultural problems. In the 1980s it is more and more preoccupied with problems of justice and poverty. In 1981 it decided to launch a six-year study of justice and peace problems. A general concluding conference is scheduled for 1987.

The bishops, doubtless, do well not to spend all their time in the clouds of African cultural problems, and to turn instead to injustices in everyday life. But they cannot dismiss the problem of African culture. It remains a groundswell that ever and again breaks out in literature and pan-African congresses. Africa complains bitterly of having been robbed in colonial times not only of what it possessed but also of what it was, its cultural identity destroyed, its pride in its own culture soured. There is therefore a very strongly felt need to upgrade the culture of African peoples. The African EATWOT group rightly emphasized at the 1981 conference in New Delhi that poverty should not be thought a unidimensional concept: it should not be considered only in the perspective of economics, as Marxists are wont, but should also include anthropological and cultural aspects.

Here I should like to illustrate the subject of the church in Africa in its cultural dimensions, taking African names as an instance. In Africa a name, as in the Bible, expresses a person's being. A name is given to an infant in a special rite of naming, and it is changed at the initiation ceremony to indicate that now the child is grown up and a full member of the tribe. Woe betide anyone still calling that person by the childhood name! The same goes for the baptismal name. Woe betide anyone using the old name! In many tribes very meaningful religious names were known: 'God is great', 'God knows', 'God willed', 'Gift of God'.... With the aid of three historical collective names applied to Africans we can now pursue our theme and follow Africa's wearisome way out of the past into the present and on into the future.

Implications of Three Names

'Negroes'

This name symbolized the continent of Africa, nearest to Europe geographically but culturally the longest unknown. 'Negro' meant 'heathen, savage, barbarian, uncivilized', good only to serve the white man and gradually be civilized. Until recently, whole tribes bore names that meant nothing more than 'nigger': Galla in Ethiopia, Kaffir in South Africa, Kirdi in Cameroon — names no one dare use nowadays. Europeans have to recognize with shame that they did not take Africans seriously in colonial and missionary times. At best they were charitable to them. But they did not respect them. And so they remained blind to their cultural and religious values.

When at the turn of the fifteenth century the world stage broadened amazingly, and suddenly new continents came into view, there already was a fixed preconception, derived from traditional theology, about all persons of colour. The correlation between prejudice and its confirmation was automatic. The world proved to be divided into two: here Christendom, there the rest; here salvation and heaven, there damnation and hell; here truth, there falsehoods; here civilized persons, there barbarians and savages. And one hears what one wants to hear. For four centuries travellers and missionaries confirmed in their reports that things were just as they had always been known to be. That knowledge only grew somewhat more concrete and definite by the new information. I shall give proof of this regarding Africa, limiting myself to the religious sphere.

Duarte Lopez, a mariner who travelled through Africa from 1578 to 1587, shared his many experiences and impressions with Pigafetta, who published them in 1591 in a book that by the standards of the day became a best-seller. It came out in several editions in Latin, Dutch, English, French, and German, and helped to form the image of black Africa in Western minds. We read inter alia:

> Each one there honours and takes for his god whatsoever is pleasing to him, without measure, rule, or order. . . . [Lopez saw]: a great quantity of carved devil's images of every fearsome form: many prayed to winged dragons, which they kept in their houses and gave them all the best and costliest of food. Others held snakes

of strange shape and form to be gods, others toads, others tigers, or other horried and fearsome beasts. The uglier, more unshapely, more hateful they are, the higher they are held by them and respected.

Barely a hundred years later the Dutch geographer O. Dapper, with his thick volumes on the three 'new' continents, did much to spread knowledge of the new world. In his book on Africa he passes abrupt judgment: 'The Kaffirs attend no service for divine or idol worship: they know nothing whatever of God and live like cattle'. Of the Beninese he could report: 'As touching their worship of God or rather of idols, it consists in honouring and praying to the devil, to whom they offer human and animal sacrifice'. Of the Senegalese he says, 'They are all lascivious, thievish, unreliable, deceiving, and excessively gluttonous, so that they do not eat but feed like cattle'. The inhabitants of Upper Niger come out better: 'They earlier had a god, Guighime, the Lord of Heaven. Later they became Christian and then Muslim'.

From the same seventeenth century another traveller expresses his African experience thus: 'No one, however carefully informed, can ever be in a position to discover among all the Kaffirs, Hottentots, or coastal dwellers a single trace of religion, or the least sign of honouring God or the devil'.

In the year 1645 began the well-known missions of the Italian Capuchins to the Congo. These poor, ascetic missionaries sent an astonishing amount of information back to Europe, but still in the manner of their day. Recently an African scholar, Professor Mudimbe, has undertaken a study of these reports. He points out how Africans are spoken of 'with their outlandish customs, their devilish ways, their limited understanding, which make them like animals'. To this world, 'disordered, crazy, with its devilish illusions, must be brought order, truth, the eternal norms' and these peoples be 'led from animal to human behaviour, from barbarism to civilization, from the deceits of witchcraft and idol worship to the light of reason and faith'.

From the eighteenth century on, there spread the notion, which had indeed already been set forth by Luther in his *Commentary on Genesis*, that black Africans were descendants of Ham and were under Ham's curse. This was the explanation for their proneness to vice and also for their position of subservience to the white man. With Christian compassion the missionaries gave themselves to

31

these 'accursed children of Ham'. Bishop Augouard of Brazzaville (1921) repeatedly asked in his letters for prayers 'for the black tribes so that the curse of Ham may soon be lifted from them'. He opines outright: 'The black race is the race of Ham. You feel it: the blacks are lazy, gluttonous, given to all vice'. At the First Vatican Council, seventy bishops signed a petition for priests to be sent to Central Africa, for 'still today the oldest of all curses afflicts those wretched Hamites. . . . In spite of the efforts of Mother Church, the unfortunate Negro race is still under the fearful empire of Satan'.

This understanding of the whole of non-Christianity as devilish also entered into religious instruction in Africa. A typical example is the 1912 adult catechism of Fr. Willibald Wanger. The author had indeed gone to great pains to study Zulu customs well and to integrate Christian teaching with this background. In lieu of a 'short catechism', he wrote a handbook of 534 pages. But even he did not succeed in breaking away from the prejudice common to virtually all missionaries. He writes of heathenism:

> What an error! How can one so lose oneself, leave the true God, and honour something that is not God? . . . This fearful error called heathenism comes from the devil who wants to be as God, and from the stupidity of those who, deceived by the devil, hand on these lies from generation to generation.

Certainly there were also other voices. The founders of the Holy Ghost Fathers and the White Fathers, Fr. François Libermann and Cardinal Lavigerie, frequently advised their missionaries to study and cherish African culture and religion. That did not prevent the ideas just mentioned from going on working in the minds of most missionaries and in missionary literature until well into the twentieth century. The lower, more piteous, more unfortunate the blacks were painted, the more the good benefactors of the missions were touched and gave money to 'ransom black babies'.

Africans were therefore, by the mere presence of the 'superior' whites, so humiliated and alienated that they suffered at being black and had only one wish — to be like the whites. When I was in Tanzania in the 1950s, black youngsters would stroke my hand and say: 'We would like to be white like you'. More than material poverty, which they accepted, was the hurt of psychological under-development into which we had driven Africans. They felt them-

32

selves strangers in their own skin, outlaws in their own land, robbed
of their own culture and worth.[23] 'Father, forgive those whites,
for they knew not what they did'.

'Africans'

The name 'Negro' should no longer be heard. By using the
name 'African' racial difference is no longer degradingly under-
lined. Africans (like Europeans) live in their own continent and
have their own culture.

Very cautiously, but eagerly too, Africa began in the 1950s to
regain its cultural consciousness. The strength and persistence of
the reversal are in fact astonishing, and so too that it should have
survived slavery and colonialism and kept its joie de vivre. When
after the Second World War the nationalist movement started up,
above all in French-speaking Africa in the circle around the newspaper *Présence Africaine*, the political issue was always coupled
with the cultural: colonials were minors with no responsibility,
cripples who could do nothing for themselves; colonization was
essentially death to an indigenous culture; political freedom must
be fought for as a basis and starting point for cultural development. . . .

In 1956 there appeared the book *Des prêtres noirs s'interrogent*
['black priests raise questions']. *Présence Africaine* organized the
first international congress of black writers and artists in Paris.
This congress was considered the most important event since
unification for black Africans, a rendezvous for giving and receiving, speaking and listening. Until then the world had been divided
into two, the loud-speaker side and the muzzled side. For centuries
the European solo filled the world with its commanding tones. But
now the black world had made its entry onto the international
stage.

At that time there began, again in French-speaking Africa particularly, the poetry of *négritude*: blacks now stand up for being
black. They would no longer suffer it. Its acceptance gave psychological healing. It was idealized and shouted to the world: 'Black
is beautiful! Black is innocence! White is the devil!' Today this
stage is partly over, for there is no longer any need to fight for
rehabilitation. There is more talk today of *africanité*. With all the
differences within Africa itself, Africans point to common cultural

33

values, faith in the visible and invisible world with their hierarchical structuring, faith in a Supreme Being, Creator, Father of all that is, faith in community, to be developed in a sharing of energy and joy.[24]

Work has also been done on retrieving and writing down the past history of Africa, and collecting and publishing alongside modern African work the traditional oral literature as well.[25] Africa has good reason to be reconciled with the past: otherwise it would not have a future of its own and it would always remain a by-product of European culture. Meanwhile Europeans have had their eyes opened and gladly recognize today the comprehensiveness of the African worldview. So much so that Pope John Paul II, during his 1980 journey to Africa, not only emphasized African cultural values but went further and declared that 'Africa has much more to offer the world community than its raw materials'; that 'Africa is called to mediate fresh ideals and insights to a world showing signs of weariness and narrow self-seeking'. So now the tables are turned.

It must be understood, however, that many Africans have not yet overcome the trauma of colonialism and still continue to overreact with expressions such as 'alienation, depersonalization, carbon copies of the West, cultural and political dictatorships, colonial annihilation, the imperialistic metropolis'. Especially in South Africa, activists take up counterattack and now see in whiteness a symbol of racism, barbarism, sin. In South Africa there reigns, along with apartheid, a whole system that sits ill with the modern world and with a state calling itself Christian. The black majority there enjoys only very restricted political rights, but no longer allows itself to be badgered as previously. It is not by chance that South Africa, in cultural reaction, is producing more black writers than are the other African countries. Let us look by way of illustration at some passages from speeches by Steve Biko, the founder of the Black Consciousness Movement:

The unnecessary harassment of blacks by the police, the ruthless application of the pass laws, the continual humiliations of all kinds, are a permanent reminder that the white man stands on top and the black is only tolerated. The one is fully a human being: coloureds, Indians, and Bantu are lumped together by the concept 'nonwhite' into a group of underprivileged who have it written on their skin that their human worth is not recognized. We must react against the oppression and insult. That will be a proof that we are

34

not quite dead yet, that we are quite capable of reacting. . . . Meanwhile hatred has turned in us into a consciousness of victory. Black consciousness is awake. That is the most positive call ever to come out of the black world. It is the realization that now we blacks can take a hand in power politics. We are no longer afraid. For one who is afraid can be mastered. One who is not afraid can never be conquered. We are ready to die on our feet rather than live on our knees. Now we know that a real person is beginning to shine out of the black. . . . We have come to the point now where we no longer excuse ourselves to God for being black but thank God for it. We are at the point now where we no longer hate the whites but laugh at them. For we know that it is not us they are ruining with their cynical attitude but themselves, that their policy is nothing but the attempt of frightened people to convince one another that they could master the blacks for evermore. But now their paper palaces are falling in and we all sing to that: Amen! Alleluia!

It is not to be wondered at that white South Africans sought to silence such a voice with death and that such a man had to suffer a prophet's fate. Biko was several times in detention and on September 24, 1977, beaten to death in prison.[26]

Outside South Africa too there are now voices calling for reaction, advocating a return to the ancient African cultures and pitying black Christians for having made a poor exchange in turning away from the traditional African outlook with its closeness to nature, its cosmic mysteries, its sense of community. Prof. V. Mudimbe of Zaire believes that during the whole of the colonial period and up to the present day, to become a Christian meant to take on Christ along with the Western package. He opines: 'A genuine African theology would be what Africans have to say about God, which has nothing to do with the church, the apostolic tradition of Rome. The missionary has really nothing to say to the heathen'.[27] With this, however, we have already gone beyond the subject of Christianity in Africa.

'African Christians'

In the secular field too, Africa has been given the green light with independence. It can be as African as it likes. Europeans have no longer a say in the matter. The cultural problem resides now in the church, where universalism and africanization are somewhat at odds. In not a few countries of Africa Christians already make up half the population. In 1980 Africa counted 59 million Catholics, 7.5 percent of the Catholic Church. By the year 2000 black Africa will have a Christian majority, 57 percent. Africa is on the way to being christianized. Has the time also come for Christianity in this continent to be africanized?

Historically speaking we are faced with the fact that individual missionaries have indeed for some time already researched and published books about African custom and usages, languages and religion but that in spite of this there was simply the European model of Christianity available, with a European catechism, European hymnbook, European theological textbooks, European Latin liturgy. The majority of missionaries knew nothing of African culture and judged it lock, stock, and barrel according to the old prejudice. In the strongly developed centralization before Vatican II, unity meant uniformity. Woe to those who dared to go their own way!

Not until Vatican II was there talk, still very cautious, of 'legitimate pluriformity' (*Lumen Gentium*, 13, 24; *Sacrosanctum Concilium*, 37–40). Christ's incarnation was even referred to as a model of inculturation (*Ad Gentes*, 10). Ten years later Paul VI spoke much more forcefully of this in *Evangelii Nuntiandi*: the gospel must be translated not only into different languages but into different cultures, so that the young, who today have a great feeling for their own culture, should also really understand; this 'must' appear in theology, in liturgy, in secondary church structures (*Evangelii Nuntiandi*, 63).

The 1974 Synod of Bishops used this document as a starting point, the bishops of Africa speaking as vigorously for the concept of inculturation as the bishops of Latin America for integral salvation. After this synod the African bishops in Rome held a further meeting and in a joint declaration said:

> In the new mission context the bishops of Africa and Madagascar consider accommodation theology to be completely outdated, and they would replace it with a *theology of incarnation*. The young churches cannot ignore this basic challenge. Although the bishops recognize theological pluralism in the unity of the faith, they nevertheless encourage by all means research studies for an African theology. Such a theology, open to the fundamental aspirations of the African peoples, will bring Christianity to be truly incarnated in the life of the peoples of the black continent.

The same assurance, that Africans can now be fully Christian and at the same time fully African, was given by Pope Paul VI in his communication *Africae terrarum* of 1967 and during his first visit to Africa, in Uganda (1969). It has also been repeated by Pope John Paul II in his many addresses in Africa.

So the discussion stage is theoretically over. There should be no further recourse to 'accommodation' in externals — for example, dress and song; to take something of the prefabricated package of Western Christianity and 'adapt' it to African ways. Following the much more radical precedent of God Incarnate, the point is to bring the essential kernel of the gospel as a leaven to Africa and there give it the opportunity to become enfleshed in African culture and so begin a new history in Africa.

In practice this dream still comes up against great difficulties among the bishops themselves, because they lack courage and creative ideas. On the other hand in Roman circles also there can be opposition where there has not yet been a clean break from the old ecclesiastical model of Western Christianity in terms of absolute unity and uniformity. Now that the earlier symbol of unity, Latin, has been sacrificed, there is a desire to uphold uniformity in other matters. This, too, results from an almost panic fear that otherwise there will be a falling away, as in the different sects that are sprouting up everywhere, especially in the Third World. According to Barrett's *World Christian Encyclopedia* (Oxford, 1982), there are some 20,800 denominations, churches, and free churches — far more than was thought hitherto. The only problem is finding and adhering to a sound middle way between extremes. It could also be that in the Catholic Church, too, something of a schism could be caused in the future, with the Roman Curia stubbornly insisting on uniformity rather than magnanimously acceding to non-Western peoples and leaving final decisions more and more to local bishops and episcopal conferences.

Tension between broad-minded documents and narrow-minded practice is what marks the present stage of the church, and the present criticism of the church. It can reach a favourable solution only through active dialogue. Rome has indeed the right and the duty to guard unity. But local bishops have as much the right and the duty to act in behalf of their group interests and to take responsibility for legitimate pluriformity. Otherwise the church will miss its hour, now that it is no longer a Western church but a church in six continents, with the majority of its members in the southern hemisphere. Otherwise Africa, which has won a place for itself in literature, art, and cinema, will continue to show in the area of church activity so little originality except in the independent churches.

There is therefore in Africa more than elsewhere a very intense reaction against continuation of dominant European attitudes in the church. A few samples from theologians and pan-African congresses:

> We are still a by-product of the Christian West. We young churches are born with the signs of premature aging, with all the marks of the ancient churches of Europe. . . . We must put through a Copernican revolution and be able at last to perform on our own. . . . In spite of the introduction of African languages and African musical instruments into the church, liturgical reform misfired because it is bound up with the Roman rite. What use to us are translated prayers that were composed elsewhere and by non-Africans? Should not an African form of Christian prayer be found? . . . It is a question of stripping Christ's message of the Western garb that it has worn for two thousand years, so that the true religion of Christ can shine out in its original beauty. . . . The question of colonialism and neocolonialism in the religious field, still dependent on the churches of the West, will never be resolved so long as the churches of Africa look only to London or Rome instead of looking for heaven by way of Africa. . . . We are tired of receiving the gospel through the prism of European culture alone. Just leave us on our own for once with our gospel and our God. Leave us free at last of our state of pupillage and let us enter on our inheritance.[28]

It would be only too easy to ignore or condemn such voices. Basically inculturation implies nothing else than appreciation for cultures, which are a work of creation, a work of God. A person can be understandable and understood only from within the framework of a particular culture. For this reason God made use of a particular culture for the divine self-revelation in Jesus. There is no such thing as 'culture-free' religion, abstract religion. Religion can exist only as inculturated in a concrete human history. Just as the church took on a Western form of culture in accordance with its previous history, so also it should now become possible for it to assume an African dress in Africa, Asian in Asia, and in this way become 'catholic' not merely geographically and demographically but also culturally. What might that not effectively mean for Africa?

Christian Inculturation in Africa

Theology

Here African theologians are called on not merely to elaborate African themes, but produce an African theology. There have been scattered attempts at this but as yet they fall short of what has been done in Latin America and Asia.[29] Africans are perhaps rather less inclined to speculation and research; they are more intuitive life-artists. They will, once the wind of freedom blows, give form to their African Christianity in no time at all and create an African theology.

I should like to put forward the suggestion that, following on *Mysterium Salutis* for Europe and *Mysterium Liberationis* for Latin America, Africa might construct its theology around the subject of Christ's incarnation and publish it under the title *Mysterium Incarnationis*. This pivotal mystery of our faith would in fact offer both the material and the opportunity for a specialized theology from which could be drawn the radical conclusions for an incarnated African church.

In the course of history this mystery has been misconstrued in many ways. It has been thought, for example, that because Jesus used bread and wine to set before us a sign of his presence that was easily intelligible, bread and wine should always and everywhere be used, even where they are generally unknown, have no symbolic meaning, and must be imported at a high price. The correct incarnational response would be just as Jesus in his cultural context used bread and wine, so the equivalent could and should be used in Africa — for example, palm wine and manioc.

Liturgy

Liturgy is not merely the repetition of rites, or the fulfillment of a duty (Sunday obligation, Easter Communion). In the early church it opened the way by which the Christian could be led into the message of Jesus and the catechumen experience the communion of discipleship. As Jesus did not then come to destroy the law, the religion of the Old Testament, but to fulfill it and uplift it (Matt. 5:17), so the church ought not today destroy traditional African religion but fulfill it and bring all times and all religions to experience the unity of the saving act of God. That will not

39

happen if European rites are transplanted to Africa and simply translated into African languages, but only when pre-Christian African rites are utilized as a groundwork for understanding the Christian sacraments. The African, too, knew of sacramental birth rites (a sort of confirmation), sacrifice and sacrificial meal (a sort of Eucharist), a moral code with confession of sin (a sort of penitential rite), a marriage rite, and a rite of introduction to the priestly office. Such rites ought not to be merely interesting anthropological museum pieces, but studied as theologically significant symbols for conveying Christian grace.[30] This is still only the beginning of the task for the future.

As a foretaste of liturgical africanization we can take the Zairian liturgy in which the Roman Eucharistic prayer is not merely translated but enriched with an infusion from the African world of nature, tradition, and symbol, and carries the whole people along with it in a two-hour drama with singing and dancing. Here the Eucharist really is a 'feast' giving meaning and strength to the whole week. Rome has hesitated to give recognition to this liturgy but it is performed by permission of the bishops. This is another example of how, throughout history and still today, the real life of the church is not decreed from above but springs from the grass roots, grows, and expresses creative diversity in the church.

Discipline

Here I can only make suggestions. As regards the eucharistic elements, ministering to districts with no priest, the African approach to marriage, and so forth, there are still many issues remaining on the waiting list. The church has received far more powers from Christ than it has thought hitherto. It has to understand its 'tradition' not merely retrospectively and statically but also prospectively and vitally. It should have the courage in historically new situations to produce creative new traditions. But that is only done by persons close to life at ground level.

In this connection there has been discussion of the possibility and pressing need of an African council — not to repeat what has been said in Rome but to take up properly African problems and solve them by reference to de facto situations in accordance with the signs of the times. Anyone knowing only a little of conciliar history is aware that there frequently were synods and councils that came to decisions for a regional situation of doctrinal and disciplinary importance, and which often were later an inspiration for the whole church.[31] Why should that not happen today as well, when a churchwide council of 3,500 bishops — at Vatican II there were at most 2,500 — is perhaps unfeasible? The church must be more and more concerned, not with questions that are universal and therefore remote from life, but with the concrete problems of the different continents in which it should now be at home.

That may seem futuristic. Currently we see rather a tendency toward centralization and consolidation. But the pendulum will swing the other way in time. If, then, my considerations are not yet realizable for today and tomorrow, they can for all that awaken church members to the third millennium, soon to begin. During it the history of the church will not stand still, but draw out conclusions from the new situation of a church in six continents.

It could be objected that the time for diverse cultures is past and that on the contrary a global 'world culture' is spreading over the earth. If this is to be understood along the lines of a steam-roller flattening out all local contours, then I can only say: 'poor humanity'. A new world culture of this kind would be like an ice age in which everything would freeze up. I admit that the laws of science and technology are global in character. I also hope that particular achievements — the Charter of Human Rights, regulations for hygiene and medicine — should extend to all of humanity. But I wish very much, even so, with all Africans, that Africa may find its cultural identity again and bring it to full bloom, for Africa will be able to feel fully at home only in Africa, not in a monocultural world. That is, not in isolation and stunted growth, but in assimilation and development. Just as formerly the culture that arose in the Christian West was based on the Greco-Roman and Germanic cultures under the inspiration of the Christian faith, so Africa could take over the best of Western culture, cross it with African traditions and art, and so develop a Euro-Afran culture, and in this way make its due contribution to a world culture.

It lies with others to give sympathetic encouragement to this process and follow it with interest. It is a humanitarian exercise to explore the origins of one's own culture and cherish its values. But humanism in the context of the present-day world means following not only the current of one's own culture but eventually

41

going out onto the ocean of all cultures. In the North Atlantic schools, therefore, some attention should be paid to the literatures of Africa, Asia, and Latin America. In theological studies some time should be spent on what has been called 'comparative theology' (Anton Exeler).

So it will come about that with all our differences we shall live a true *koinonia*, which will mean above all symbiosis, a mutual exchange in theology, pastoral experiences, credible exemplars of Christian living, so that in liberty and union, in justice and peace, we may increasingly become one church and one humanity. So in African culture, which Europeans had nearly exterminated by their superiority', we may celebrate, to their and everyone's surprise and joy, an African renaissance, a Christian resurrection.

Chapter Four

A Continental Church in Asia

The thought of rendering an account of the whole of Asia is overwhelming. There is a fear of drowning in the mass of humanity in Asiatic cities, of feeling lost in the endless stretches of territory. You have to overcome barriers to talk about Asia. The Near East, the Middle East, and the Far East, the roof of the world (Tibet) and the many islands, are very different from one another in their geography, history, politics, culture, and religion. Donald Barrett, in his *World Christian Encyclopedia*, speaks of eight continents, three of them constituting Asia. To describe this giant, therefore, is possible only in limited and general terms.

Asia, to be sure, has the same experience of poverty as Latin America, the same problems of culture as Africa. But the theme that particularizes Asia is religion. If we consider the world from the point of view of major religions, there are five more or less Christian continents: Europe, the two Americas, Australia, and Africa, which, south of the Sahara, will in the foreseeable future have a Christian majority. Only Asia is left, the largest by far. It counts 57 percent of the world population. But after five hundred years of a Christian missionary presence, it is only minimally christianized. The 63 million Christians make up 2.42 percent of the overall population. But if the 40 million Catholics of the Philippines are not taken into account that leaves only 1 million Catholics, 17 million Protestants, and 5 million Orthodox — 1.73 percent. Missionary work here is still in its early stages; and it is high time, after a long history of unsuccess, to start thinking again. The reason for the opposition to Christianity is not to be found in want of religious feeling but in the very opposite.

The Most Religious Continent

Non-Christian Asia may well claim to be the most religious continent in the world. It has been the cradle of all the great religions: the three monotheistic religions — Judaism, Christianity, and Islam — in western Asia; the more ethical religions with their cyclic return and reincarnation, Hinduism, Buddhism and Confucianism — in eastern Asia. To travel from one end of Asia to the other is to be taken by surprise at the intensely religious atmosphere encountered at every step, whether shown in the number of mosques, temples, and pagodas, or in the masses of pilgrims expressing their faith with flowers and lights, lifting up their hands or kneeling in prayer. In a train, on an airplane, on the street, it is very easy to get into a conversation about religion.

When I left the plane at Benares in 1962 — I was wearing my Capuchin habit — and was waiting for the bus, an airport technician came up to me and surprised me with the request: 'Can you give me peace of soul?' Astonished, I wondered aloud why he should ask me, a stranger, such a question. He replied: 'People dressed as you are have peace of soul'. In Calcutta, on the same journey, a man stopped me in the street with the query: 'Can you show me the truth? I have been years looking for the truth'. I gave him the address of The Open Door in Poona, where small publications are sent out to enquirers. His reaction: 'I have read so many books already. I don't want to read any more books, I want to find a person who lives in the truth'. The like would hardly occur in the West.

Asia is the continent for the 'religious of the book'. The other continents had not developed writing; their religious traditions were handed down orally. Greece and Rome did indeed have a script but produced no religious writings to be compared with the Vedas and Vedantas of Hinduism, the Dhamapada of Buddhism, the Qur'an of Islam. These holy books are held and read with intense reverence.

Between the 6th and 5th centuries B.C. there was an especially rich outpouring of the Holy Spirit. Alive at that period were Zoroaster (ca. 570–500), Buddha (ca. 560–480), Confucius (ca. 551–479), Lao-Tzu, and the Deuteronomist (exact dates not known). They were all founding religious movements and conveying to humankind a sharpened consciousness of ultimate reality and eschatological hope.

Important for Asia is religious tolerance, stemming from the conviction that no historical religion can exhaust the fulness of eternal truth, that all religions contain fragments of truth that can be shared and mutually recognized, and so be enriching. In India there is intolerance for only one thing: religious intolerance. The violence between Hindus and Muslims since independence cannot be adduced to the contrary. It has not been a war of religion but a settling of political scores. The way in which Christians in Asia in the course of history behaved intolerantly, however, could never be accepted there — and rightly so — and was part of the reason why Asia has not become Christian.[32]

The Role of European Arrogance

Europeans must once again admit that, as for Latin America and Africa, so also for Asia their presence has spread anything but 'peace and light'. Through arrogance and sheer ignorance they have simply passed condemnation on Asian religions and cultures, and given great offence to India, Indonesia, and China, where great civilizations existed long before Greece and Rome.

St. Francis Xavier was only speaking according to the fashion of his day when he wrote from India: 'The Indians have no culture at all. It is hard to live among a people not knowing God and not obedient to reason because so sunk in sin'. It is astonishing that so holy a man could not recognize that he was living in the most religious country in the world. On his many journeys he had a faithful companion, a non-Christian. One day he suddenly died and Francis Xavier wrote: 'I can no longer repay him for all the good he has done for me. I can no longer pray for him for he is now in hell'. Further pronouncements of his: 'The true God cannot dwell among the heathen or hear their prayers. . . . The idols of the heathen are of the devil and they must be destroyed at the first opportunity'. Before setting off for China, he informed the king of Portugal: 'I have received a great mission from God. I am going to China to declare war on the devil and those who pray to him. The Chinese shall no longer serve idols and demons'.

Three centuries later it all sounded the same. Bishop Anastasius Hartmann (d. 1868) wrote in India: 'The Indians are on the lowest rung of civilization, in the crudest idol worship. They lack the simplest basic attributes for sociable living — namely, faithfulness, truthfulness, industry'. Yet he was a great pioneer; he founded a

Catholic newspaper in Bombay, built the major seminary there, laid the foundations of what is today the famed St. Xavier College, translated the New Testament into Hindustani. But in his judgement of the Indians he sadly remained a child of his time and spoke as did nearly all others.

A missionary to China in 1870 wrote: 'The religions of China are hideous, preposterous, the most ridiculous in the world. No idea of art, no aesthetic sense, devilish music, no conception of beauty. Their literature is senseless, childish, without thought or sentiment... complicated sentences enough to make one sick'. Such talk was repeated in the comprehensive work by L. Kervyn on the apostolate in modern China written in 1911. A scholar such as J. Beckmann remarked on it: 'Works such as this are typical neither of this Belgian missionary nor the missionary society to which he belonged, and certainly not of the Catholic Church, but of the average European'.

It raises a smile today to find that the Chinese and Japanese for their part cracked jokes at the expense of Europeans. They called them 'barbarians from the south' (because they came by a southerly route). They pitied them for not being born in their country. The artists of the day expressively caricatured the foreigners with their white faces and long noses.

The only Catholic missioners who seriously tried to enter into these religions and give Christianity an indigenous dress — Matteo Ricci (1552–1610) in China, and Roberto de Nobili (1577–1656) in India — were, after much uncertainty, finally condemned for their ventures. Catholic missionaries since then had to take the Missions Oath not to attempt similar ventures. This dispute over rites was not declared at an end until 1936 for Japan, 1939 for China, 1940 for India. Catholics were not allowed to take part in national festivals if they involved ancestor worship. This unfortunate dismissive attitude, lasting for centuries, was a further reason why Hindus, Buddhists, and Shintoists could not become Christian. They could not bring themselves — rightly, we would have to say today — to forget their forebears and deny their past. Thus Christianity was and is taken to be the religion of Europeans, not of Asiatics.

It is about time we stopped throwing stones into our neighbours' gardens and opened our eyes to the variety and beauty of the flowers growing there.

Interreligious Dialogue

Asian Religions 'Revisited'

To 'discover', occupy, and pillage Asia was one thing; to discover the peoples of Asia and make friends with them is another. So long as the weather and sports, economics and politics, are the only topics of conversation, persons remain strangers. Not until they are discovered to be religious beings is it possible to be fully united with them and carry on a religious exchange. 'Rediscovering' other religions belongs to the finest and most exciting part of contemporary church history.

The religious patrimony of Asia was brought home to the West in several stages. First, students of religion — M. Mueller, R. C. Zaehner, H. von Glasenapp, W. Fuchs, W. Gundert — opened the breach, translating Asian holy books and publicizing them in the West. Westerners became acquainted with Asian thinkers who truly earned their esteem: Ramakrishna, Sri Aurobinda, Vivekananda, Rabindranath Tagore. Then missionaries came to realize that they could not merely concern themselves theoretically with these religions but should live the life of a monk in the Indian context, about which they then wrote inspiring books — Jacques Monchanin, Henri le Saux, Bede Griffiths, F. Acharaia. Today we have a fine number of Asian Christian theologians: Raimund Panikkar, Lynn da Silva, D. S. Amalorpavadass, M. Dhavamony, M. M. Thomas, S. J. Samartha, J. Russell Chandran.

These scholars took a sympathetic approach to these religions and came to a feeling for much that to outsiders remains strange or strikes them as ridiculous. Love alone opens the way to the truth. Panikkar confirms this in the introduction to an almost thousand-page anthology of Veda texts: some will see in them only the manifestation of a primitive spirit, but anyone studying them prayerfully, in depth, discovers in them one of the loftiest expressions of the Spirit. Panikkar hopes that such texts will not only be read but sung and celebrated in paraliturgical Christian festivals.[33]

A theological congress held in Bangalore in 1947 pursued the same line of thought when thirty-two distinguished Indian theologians reflected on the significance of the Hindu holy books and came to the conclusion that in them also the voice of the Holy

47

Spirit could be heard. Consequently, the finest passages could be included in the liturgy — after fitting preparation of the faithful — not as a substitute for the Old Testament but to complement it, so as to make Indian Christians aware that the Spirit of God had loved and led their peoples from ancient times.[34] Roman authorities reacted coldly in the negative. Such new ideas take time and are at first best tried out and appreciated in small groups only.

In the meanwhile the basic assertion that the Holy Spirit is present and at work in Asian religions was to meet with no further difficulties. Pope John Paul II twice emphasized in *Redemptor Hominis* that these religions show the working of the Holy Spirit (6 and 12). The same pope on his journey to Japan in 1981 declared before representatives of Japanese religions:

> I find in the virtues of friendliness and kindness, courtesy and bravery, so commended by your religious traditions, the fruit of that divine Spirit who in our faith is 'friend of humankind', who 'fills the earth', 'holds all together' (Wisd. 1: 6–7). Above all, this same Spirit effects in all persons and in all religions the opening to transcendence, the tireless seeking after God, that can only be the reverse side of God's seeking after humanity.

Two members of the Roman Secretariat for Non-Christians have written important articles on the presence and the working of the Holy Spirit in all faiths.[35]

From these theological premises it is only a short step to drawing conclusions in concrete cases and naming praiseworthy non-Christians 'saints'. That is why I suggested via the international press on April 13, 1983, that Mahatma Gandhi, who has come to life again in the West through Richard Attenborough's magnificent film, should be officially proclaimed a saint by the church. He was such a deeply religious figure, had such a great respect for every religion, was so affected by Jesus and his gospel, and on the other hand struggled so dauntlessly, always in accord with the principle of passive resistance, for human values, human rights, the equality of all human beings, that the pope could declare by canonizing him that he too had been inspired and guided in his lifetime by the same Holy Spirit who inspired and guided Christian saints. Mahatma Gandhi could be pointed to as a shining example to be emulated not only in Hinduism, where he already enjoys public veneration, but also in the Christian world. Such an unprecedented course of action would at first spark a healthy shock but then indeed arouse great joy throughout the world, and could be taken as a silent reparation for Christian guilt in the past.

The Path of Dialogue

The Second Vatican Council made a great leap forward with the Declaration on the Relation of the Church to Non-Christian Religions (*Nostra Aetate*). Such a declaration was not on the agenda. Pope John XXIII intended to promulgate a declaration on the Jewish problem so as to put an end to the evil of anti-Semitism. When such a proposal came up for discussion, some Asian bishops remarked: 'All very good. But if the council says something on the Jews, it must also speak to the other non-Christian religions, which make up two-thirds of humanity'. This opening was made and with it, at long last, a bridge to the majority of humankind.

Until John XXIII such expressions as 'heathens', 'infidels', and 'devil worshippers' could be heard in papal utterances. The younger Roncalli likewise used such terminology, but no longer when he was pope. To whom do we owe it that he was enlightened and made the change? His private secretary at the time, Monsignor Capovilla, told me the answer: 'From the time he was apostolic delegate in Turkey and observed Muslims at prayer and talked with them, he could no longer speak of "heathen" but only of "brothers and sisters in the one God and Father in heaven" '.

Nostra Aetate speaks well of the religious values in the non-Christian faiths but does not say the last word. It affirms, along with *Lumen Gentium*, the possibility of individual salvation outside the church for those who live according to their conscience. But it did not raise the question of the salvation potential in those religions themselves — in other words, whether non-Christians could be saved in and through their religion or in spite of it. This question was left to postconciliar theologians for further clarification. Here, as in other areas, the council was not the end but the beginning of a new road.

Nevertheless it gave the starting signal and conferences on the non-Christian religions suddenly sprang up East and West like mushrooms in the night. The contemporary development in Christian ecumenism made possible a whole series of such conferences jointly organized and carried through by Rome and Geneva, in which leading representatives of the Christian churches came together with leaders of the non-Christian religions, prayed in common, spoke out freely with one another, and drew closer to one another.[36]

Catholic minorities in Asia, until then nervously isolated in their churches with their Latin liturgy, became vigorous, sprang to life, and entered into dialogue with the majority religions. And they were instrumental in bringing those religions to discussion among themselves.

In many Asian cities there are now regular meetings of leaders of the various religions and churches, for common prayer and study. There are also 'live-in' seminars at which young persons gather for a weekend and pray together, eat in common, learn from one another, and thereby discover that they are fundamentally much closer to one another than they thought.

All this touches, directly, only a modest number of the teeming millions of Asians. But a new road has opened up. A new note has been struck at the summit. It will have its repercussions.

By the same token it must be stressed that inter-Christian ecumenism in the present state of the world is not a luxury for a few enthusiasts, but a requirement of salvation history. It is not tolerable for Christ to be divided. It is not tolerable for the church of Christ to turn a fragmented, strife-torn visage to the non-Christian world.

One Worldwide Religion?

May one cherish the hope that after the long, long history of interchurch strife the time is at last coming when we may not only see ourselves as one church subsisting in the many churches but also as one religion subsisting in a plurality of religions?[37] The answer is yes and no. Christians in fact have very many elements in common, very much common ground; and rightly today we, Catholics and Protestants, no longer emphasize what separates us but what unites us.

Above all we may agree today that we all honour one and the same God. For wherever and whenever human beings raise their hearts to God and offer prayers and sacrifices to 'their' God, they attain to God in spite of polytheistic trappings. Whether God is called Mungu or Nzambi or Lesa (in Africa), or Allah or Brahma or Kame (in Asia), behind all those names there always stood the

50

one true God looking in love on all human beings, sending them, as always and everywhere, before and since, the Spirit, divine inspiration, prophets. The phenomenon of the Old and New Testament revelation does not, then, stand out like a stray outcrop on the field of the world religions, nor is it like a monopoly merger, but much more an exemplar in the interests of all. For God makes no distinctions. We may therefore be rightly impressed and gladdened by the religious fervour of Hindus in Benares, Buddhists in Bangkok, Shintoists in Tokyo. All religions are about the ultimate questions of life and death, and the meaning of life; and for that the one true God does not leave anyone high and dry. We are therefore in fact one human family — all God's children — and may not only put our hands to building a better world but also raise our hands together in prayer to the same God and Father/Mother. Our shared feeling for life should not be dissipated by extraneous differences.

We can go still further and say that even the historical Jesus, as he lived and taught, does not separate us; he unites us. His message and his life are everywhere accepted. The three countries in the world where the most bibles are sold annually are: the U.S.A., Japan, and India. Millions of Asian non-Christians love Jesus and read the gospels. Depictions of him are frequently to be found in their homes. Jesus came not to separate but to unite. He announced God's kingdom, which is as universal as is God. The visible church has no monopoly over God's kingdom but, as its embodiment and sign, should represent and proclaim the kingdom.

What does separate us, then, is the Christ of the creeds, of the dogmas, of the claims to uniqueness and exclusiveness. That is something Christians cannot abandon if they are to remain Christians, even though they must always continue to scrutinize those dogmas, searching for a better understanding. Is the Word simply God self-revealed to all religions, as Asians maintain, or is the Word fully and exclusively to be identified with Jesus of Nazareth, as Christians believe? After, unfortunately, having insisted on Christian exclusivism in the past, they ought now rather hold back and say: 'Wait and see; we shall know in time'.

In a letter I received from a very busy Hindu doctor I had made friends with in India, he had this to say:

My personal philosophy is founded on the universality of all religions. I believe Christ, Krishna, Zoroaster, Buddha and Muhammed

51

were all one and the same person, coming in flesh at different periods and announcing the same message with the differences belonging to the various cultures and periods. There could still be many other such manifestations of the 'Ancient of Days' about which we do not know anything exactly. I should be happy to be called a Christian or a Zoroastrian or a Muslim or a Hindu or simply one who is seeking and loving God. That is the truth so far as I see it. [The infinite] God cannot be comprehended by a limited human being. The reality of God cannot be experienced.

It seems to me that not a few Christian theologians too are thinking along these lines.

We are further divided by the church as institution; in the past it was too closely identified with Christ and the kingdom of God. This phase of exaggerated ecclesiology can now be considered behind us. It also seems to me that christology is being displaced as the focal point of present-day theological research. At the centre of interest stands simply theology as such or pneumatology — namely, the question what, when all is said and done, God ultimately intends for the human race.

After stressing the common foundation of all religions, I should like to warn against dreaming of a false universalism. We must also be aware of what specifically differentiates and particularizes us. The richness of humanity does not lie solely in the basic similarity of all human beings, but also in their ineffaceable individualness, each with their own personal characteristics and charisms. The Holy Spirit does not favour carbon copies but originals. It is not only for individual Christians but also for members of all religions that St. Paul's word holds good, when he speaks about the many different charisms, which all nevertheless come from the same Spirit (1 Cor. 12). No religion, not even the Christian religion, can express the full richness of God's creativity. We need one another and should fulfill one another. All should love their own religion and live according to it, while also being acquainted with and appreciating other religions — and leave the rest to the guidance of God's Spirit.

In this meeting with other religions, we are, *nolens volens*, making a great leap forward in dogmatic development. Throughout the course of history there has always been organic development, and now and then a leap forward — for example, when Thomas Aquinas took over the philosophy of the 'pagan' Aristotle and put it to the service of theology, which for many was truly a scandal.

Today a still greater leap forward is under way, but only in order to throw more light on the cosmic dimension of the Word. If it was possible and useful to produce a christology with the aid of Greek philosophy, then it must also be possible and useful to do the same with the aid of Hindu philosophy.

I have already said that after *Mysterium Salutis* there should be *Mysterium Liberationis* and *Mysterium Incarnationis*. I should like to draw this concept out further and give expression to the hope that Asia may in time have its own theology on the theme of *Mysterium Revelationis*. It would show how the eternal and mysterious God has already, in all times and places, made a self-revelation to humanity, how God has already always and everywhere called forth mystics and seers, how today a new sphere of revelation is opening up, like the outer space being explored by courageous astronauts. All theologians together would then give some faint idea of the riches of the world of theology, in discovering which we are always only at the beginning.

Small minds may reel at such prospects. For someone who knows and accepts only the traditional Western scholastic theology, contemporary theology looks suspect. It is inevitable that books by Asian theologians will come into conflict with Roman censors. Sebastian Kappen, who finds himself in this position, has posed the fundamental question of whether Western theologians are qualified to judge Indian theology. He said he would accept censure only from theologians knowing Hinduism from within and who like himself live among the poor.[38] Is he entirely in the wrong?

Dialogue with the Poor

Anyone visiting some of the eight hundred thousand villages of India — which still house 81 percent of the Indian population — and seeing the slum areas bordering the central boulevards with their hotels, banks, and supermarkets, will feel, like a hot wind blowing in the face, the shameful poverty of the masses. That human poverty, in all Asian countries, coexists with small elites of shrewd, powerful, and very wealthy nationals. *Contextual theology* takes upon itself to unmask just this state of things, hold it up to criticism, and change it in the strength of the gospel.

This is all the more needed in that Asian religions, with their caste concept and their view of divine providence, as well as the

53

Western 'Christian' capitalist system, have contributed not a little to creating this state of things and hardening it. Today these religions must together make every attempt for secular history — the striving of the masses for freedom, dignity, development — to be understood as part of salvation history. As at the exodus of the people of Israel out of Egypt, God's religious call of the people and the 'secular' yearning for liberation from slavery coincided, so today religion must not merely be supportive of, but a powerful force within, the struggle to overcome poverty, sickness, ignorance, oppression, and exploitation.

At the first meeting of the Federation of Asian Bishops' Conferences in Manila in 1970 the leaders responsible for the Catholic Church in Asia took account of this situation and its challenge. They first of all recognized that it is not enough to practice charity and maintain schools and hospitals for the affluent sector of society, but that it is a question of enabling the countless poor to lead a fully human life. It became evident that such a hope could be realized only through working together with all persons of good will. Therefore the bishops resolved to inaugurate 'on open, honest, continuing dialogue with our brothers of the other great religions in Asia', aiming at more effective cooperation for development but also 'so that we can learn from one another how to become better persons'.

In the same year, 1970, the World Conference of Religions for Peace took place in Kyoto, Japan, at which two hundred and fifty participants from thirty-nine countries and ten religions, with the accompaniment of a considerable media presence, strove to work together for justice and peace. Out of this arose a standing body with its international secretariat at the U.N. in New York and with continental secretariats.

After dialogue with fellow Christians and with members of non-Christian religions, the way must be opened for dialogue with human beings as such, whether religious or secular — a dialogue not merely of words but of living together with the poor and like the poor, struggling with them against a poverty that must be termed destitution. In this field, religious and secular persons can reach out to each other and go forward together. And at the Last Judgement it will be made clear 'secular' concerns were religious concerns too, because everything done for God's poor was done for Jesus himself.

The Task of Christendom

Having lingered too long in isolation from history, by reason of their exodus from the rest of humanity, forming an exclusive club that passed judgement on everyone else, today Christians must start back to an 'eisodus' and incorporate themselves again into the whole of humanity with its other faiths.[39] Christianity and the other world religions, as organized systems, have failed humanity through exclusivism and thereby done harm to religion as such, so that Radhakrishna could say, 'The world could be a much more religious place if all the religions were taken out of it'. In redirecting themselves back to humanity at large, Christians will in no way sacrifice their identity. On the contrary, the Christian task can henceforth be described as a threefold mission to the world:

● *To interpret the world.* To all the nations, to all persons of whatsoever religion or worldview, Christians should, by personal witness and by all the means of social communication, interpret created reality in terms of the all-embracing love of God. Thanks to Jesus, Christians have been given an insight into God as the good shepherd seeking every lost lamb and bringing it home with joy; they understand that God has the sun rise on the good and the bad alike, and lets the rain fall on sinners and the just; that God opens the door of salvation to all those who knock. To pass this on to others is to evangelize the world, irrigating it with the good news of the gospel, 'shalomizing' it by gifting it with peace and salvation. The church must understand itself not as a powerful institution but as an outspoken interpreter, as that body of persons who in faith and joy, without a great flurry of ifs and buts, make God's salvation known to the world.

● *To transform the world.* God is not content with mere words; God's self-manifestation is in deed and in truth. The church should bear witness to this dynamic love of God and, more than any other body, engage in 'word-and-deed' dialogue with the poor. This is *the* Christian privilege. Christians are called to be standard-bearers in the efforts for a more just and humane world as an approach toward eschatological fulness.

● *To christianize the world.* In the past, Christians went 'on the missions', in Asia too, to baptize as quickly as possible as many 'heathen' as possible, and make Christians of them. In this they were radically unsuccessful, at least in Asia, with the exception of the Philippines. In future they will have to make committed, credible efforts to first interpret and transform the world, as outlined just above. If, at the same time, by genuine fellowship, they succeed in breaking down the anti-Western feeling resulting from Western 'Christian' behaviour in the past; if they overcome the divisions among the Christian churches, develop a stronger base of mystical prayer, and wipe out the stigma of an imported religion by radical inculturation — then there will be some Asians who will be attracted to their witness.[40] They will want to know more about Christians and Christ. Some may become catechumens and may perhaps be baptized, but not 'to save their souls', as if otherwise they would be damned, but to become full members of the 'Jesus movement' and take full part in its mission. And the whole process starts again from the beginning: interpreting, transforming, christianizing.

In this fashion Christianity and the other world religions will finally be interrelated as in God's ultimate purposes. God will rejoice over the entry of the 'chosen peoples' into the promised land flowing with milk and honey, where justice and peace will be the norm, not the exception.

Chapter Five

Justice and the Writing of History

The message of Jesus, always the same, has been accented differently in the course of the centuries. Anyone with a finger on the pulse of today knows that justice, peace, hope, and fellowship are on the forefront of interest. Anyone speaking on these topics can generally count on attentive ears. I want to examine the gospel under these four perspectives, beginning with the subject of justice.

In outlining the three continental churches of Latin America, Africa, and Asia, the perspective of justice has already been emphasized strongly. It must be admitted that the West has erred grievously in this respect in the past. We do not, however, utterly condemn our forebears and the courageous missionaries of former times. We would have done the same in their place. But we are glad that today there is another way of thinking and a sharper instinct for justice. I do not agree with those who praise 'the good old days' beyond all measure, and see only ruin in the world today. But we should not be too quick to dissociate ourselves from the past. Mistakes should be honestly recognized, humbly admitted, and rectified.

I shall, then, expressly take up the theme of justice and set it in a new perspective, perhaps at first sight a strange one, but one that is very interesting: the writing of history. Anticipating the outcome of my exposé, it must be admitted that injustice has been done in the way that the history of the Third World has been written. What we had was a colonial and missionary history written from the viewpoint of the centre, the Western church and world, locked into a position of injustice toward the periphery, Third World peoples. It is a good thing that this period of historical writing has now come to an end.

Eurocentric Apologetic History

In the long period before the advent of critical scientific history, nations as well as the church adopted a decidedly triumphalistic interpretation of history. The heroes of the past were idealized. Their failures were glossed over, their burdens exaggerated. Damaging records were suppressed, favourable reports emphasized. Everything served the purpose of presenting church and state to the next generation as something great, something to which unconditional dedication was due.[41]

In church history there was in addition an apologetic aim. It was to adduce from the vast extent of the church, from its holiness, its victory over foes, proof of its divine institution. Behind all this there was the concept of the kingdom, *Christianitas*. That is, once the church had christianized the power of the Roman empire from within, had itself become the established religion and been endowed with lands and privileges, the unencumbered Jesus movement became more and more an institution. The tent city on a hill became a citadel with fortifications and moats; Peter's little boat on the high seas became a rock, the waves breaking against it; the church mystical became the church imperial. Within this *Christianitas* was authentic culture, the only true religion, the way to salvation and heaven. Without was seen only barbarism, heathenism, the way to damnation and hell. What was once said, with at least a grain of truth, about nations could also have been said about the church: 'A nation is a group of persons united by a common misconception of their forebears and a common disdain of their neighbours'.

Let me illustrate this state of affairs with one classic case out of many possible examples.

The classic model of a missionary

Without a doubt St. Francis Xavier, patron of Catholic missions, his image systematically put together, was, so to speak, 'hagiographized' as the ideal for missionaries. We read of his holiness and union with God, his wonderful gift for languages, as his preaching and baptizing went from one success to another. But then the critical edition of his biography by Schurhammer put the picture in something of a new light. The English Jesuit Alban Goodier even wrote a tract with the subtitle, 'The Failure of St. Francis Xavier'.[42] We know today that Francis Xavier complained in his letters that he did not know languages and could not talk with the people; that now and again as superior of the missions in Goa he was so psychologically depressed that he would cut himself off from the community for days at a time and shut himself up in the gatehouse; that in his last letter to St. Ignatius, which arrived after his death, he asked if he could be transferred to Ethiopia, in the hope of finding at least one people open to the gospel. All this does not deny that he had enormous zeal, set the tone for the missionary enterprise in Asia, and was an outstanding figure. But he was clearly not so far removed from human problems and trials as apologetic hagiography for long would have had us believe.[43]

Classic mission literature

Missionaries all had an interest in informing their friends at home about their work and encouraging them to help the missions. The classic collection of such 'informative and edifying letters' (*Lettres édifiantes et curieuses*) was published by the Jesuits from 1714 to 1782. The many volumes went through at least six editions. In the Preface they were dedicated in style to the king of France: 'Your Majesty will see herein how greatly the name of the King of France is loved and revered to the ends of the earth'. By missionaries? By the missionized? With considerable self-condemnation there was continual reference in the reports to 'our missions', the 'good we are able to do', the 'zeal for souls, for the honour of God, and for the good name of the Society', as 'we, following the example of Jesus, heal spiritual and bodily diseases and for our recompense have to suffer ill-treatment at the hands of these ingrates'.

In response to the eighteenth-century Enlightenment, which despised the church and saw it as an enemy to culture and literature, Chateaubriand described in his work *Le génie du Christianism*, in poetic language and from an idealistic viewpoint, the greatness and beauty of Christianity and its mission in the world. It soon came to be called 'the most important book of the nineteenth century' (Lesourd). Translated into several languages, it made a great contribution to the revival of the Catholic missions.

Le génie gave voice to the convictions of missionaries that the other religions were only idol worship, that only in the Catholic Church were healing and salvation to be found, that all non-Christians were not only heathen but also uncivilized savages, that the Christian messengers of the gospel spent themselves for them and did not fear even to shed their blood. Young missionaries who then went off to the missions, drawn by such a soul-stirring picture, fell soon enough from the clouds of their idealistic outlook to the harsh reality of everyday life on the missions, and did not easily forgive not being told the truth about it beforehand.

Classic mission histories

The newly aroused missionary enterprises of the nineteenth century were quickly reflected in the histories of the missions in several volumes by Henrion (French), Marshall (English), Wittman and Hahn (German). They all drew, in utterly unecumenical fashion, a very one-sided picture: with Catholics all was light; with Protestants, on the other hand, all was shadow. Prof. J. Schmidlin, who wrote the first critical history of the missions in 1924, says of these works:

> Produced out of warm sympathy and borne along by an attractive enthusiasm, typical of the Romantic period of Catholic Idealism, they devotedly plunged into a presentation of the great exploits of the church in the field of the world apostolate; but they lacked what belongs to a scientific writing of history and detailed research, and had therefore too great a tendency to use more apologetic panegyric, inherited from earlier narrative literature, than would be allowed in our sober, critical present, which in such matters applies much stricter standards.[44]

These examples, which could be multiplied ad nauseam, are quite sufficient to support my working hypothesis — namely, that in the great missionary centuries homage was paid to a European-centred apologetic in the writing of history. With the mission histories of Schmidlin, Mulders, and Latourette, there was considerable improvement. But still they were written from a centrist standpoint. They depicted the heroic deeds of missionaries and the growth of the church in other continents without ever asking themselves how those peoples reacted to the massive European presence and how they were living and forming a history of their own, parallel to the European.

Something similar and worse could be said of the colonial histories in which conquerors' savagery was toned down to become heroism and, when faced with the basic questions of colonialism and everything that went with it, was always seen to be in the right. Blatant indications of this are the towns and countries arrogantly christened with European names — Stanleyville, Elizabethville, Leopoldville in Zaire; the 'newly discovered' continent named America after the voyager Amerigo Vespucci, its inhabitants incorrectly designated 'Indians' (putative inhabitants of India), and its southern half called *Latin* America after the invaders, as though there had not been an indigenous population.

This Western way of writing history must today be judged defective, prone to racist temptations and to treating other peoples as if they were solely objects of European history, not subjects of their own.[45] Gustavo Gutiérrez rightly says that colonial peoples were 'absent from history'. But to ignore and repress the historical consciousness of a people is to rob it of more than land and natural resources.

Passionate, Polarized History

This state of affairs had to change. It started in the 1950s, just when Asians, Africans, and Latin Americans began taking up the pen themselves and writing history from their standpoint.

Asia

In 1953 K. M. Pannikar brought out his impressive work *Asia and Western Dominance* (London). The author did not take his task lightly. He worked on it for nearly twenty-five years, drawing his material from several archives. Meanwhile — a sign of the times — India achieved independence (1947) and all Western powers withdrew from China (1949). Now the first chapter of a real history of the world was beginning.

Pannikar was objective and gave a sympathetic treatment of, for example, the activity of St. Francis Xavier, 'that greatest of the figures in the history of Christianity in Asia'. But for all that he held up a mirror of history in which colonial powers could see what they had in fact done: how they were driven by greed for gain (above all through the spice trade) as the strongest motivation in their undertakings; how they acted with dishonest rivalry (Genoese vying with Venetians, the Portuguese with the Dutch and English); how they used tensions between Hindus and Muslims to their own advantage

— how, for example, the viceregent Albuquerque, in order to gain the favour of Hindu princes, enticed Muslims into a town and then set fire to it; how they had little success with the aid of Bible pictures but more by selling pictures of naked women, and so forth. He showed how missionaries for four hundred and fifty years had projected a disgusting sense of superiority, in contrast with the universality and tolerance of Asian mores; how they went along hand in hand with Western expansion and so were thought of by the people as enemies; how they took up a very prejudiced stand in their reports and books, and wrote only negatively about Asiatic cultures and religions. For these reasons the attempt by the West to bring Asia to Christ was never realistic.

For the first time missionaries were taken to task and their work became the object of serious research. At that same period, with much less objectivity and much more severity, missionary activity was pilloried in the people's courts and the press in communist China.[46] Now Westerners were the ones without power or rights, as Asians had been before.

Africa

In 1952 the Protestant historian Nosipho Majeke from South Africa brought out a book that was harsh in its judgement of missionaries.[47] He recommended, as part of the liberation process, correcting the errors of Western historiography. Until then, he said, whites had not only subjugated blacks but, to bolster their power, taught, from primary school to university, that blacks were inferior, with the result that they were ashamed of their own culture and history. The missions had shown themselves willing cohorts in those tactics. In mission schools children developed inferiority complexes. But now Africans had seen through this game. Now the heroes of the earlier histories had been exposed and stood defenceless and humiliated.

Somewhat later, in 1956, and much more reservedly, a group of black priests joined in the argument.[48] In the Preface of their book they summed up their experience: missionaries had thought out and solved problems beforehand 'for us, without us, and even against us' — that is, decisions had been made even over the heads of the African clergy. In a publication entitled *Propaganda and Truth* the complaint was levelled that missionaries had publicized in the West a false and degrading picture of the African so as to arouse sympathy and augment almsgiving. Other publications brought to light African values that had been virtually unknown in the West.

Since then and to the present day, more and more powerful and eloquent voices have been raised in Africa, which I have collected and annotated in two publications.[49] For it is after all part of the duty of reparation to become aware of such voices and show understanding.

Latin America

Here I shall not go into detail, but only point to the monumental undertaking that has been going on since the mid-1970s, the 10-volume Latin American church history to which a hundred history specialists from the whole continent are contributing. The first three volumes have appeared already.[50] The achievements of conquistadors and missionaries are fittingly recognized, but interest is centred on the reaction of the Latin American peoples. The two volumes on Brazil carry the expressive title: 'The church history of Brazil as seen by the oppressed'. It is shown how the church entered into an alliance with the political and sociological power structures; how it played its part in forming a patriarchal and even militant Catholicism; how in many a townhall the council chamber was situated in the splendid upper building, below was the prison, and outside on the open plaza before it was the platform on which once a week incarcerated slaves were flogged; how the masses in their popular piety, in art and music, and in messianic movements, reacted to the harshness of their lives. In all objectivity, it must be said that this church history does take up a one-sided position, and so is to be evaluated as an intermediate stage, an exercise in *audiatur et altera pars* (letting the other side of the question be heard).

This short outline of an eloquent, polarized history may leave the impression that it is not entirely free of bias or, in certain cases, of racist ideology. This can be admitted without turning it into a reproach. Biased as we others have been, we have the least cause to point the finger of reproach. We have to recognize these voices and let them work upon us, without trying to set them right. They are the expressions of peoples who have suffered and had much reason to hold up the other side of the picture to us. The task remains of achieving a history that will be synthetic and universalist.

63

Synthetic, Universalist History

This is the task set before us. There is hope for its success; it is already on the way. It will be achieved only in dialogue and friendliness, when all participants are willing to listen, learn, forgive; when there is no more fighting and the stronger no longer lord it over the weaker, whether by gunfire or the pen; when all parties see that their interests have been presented with exactitude, with understanding, with sympathy even, so that they can stand by the presentations given.

A good preparation for this is already to hand. Westerners no longer think of Asians, Africans, and Latin Americans as 'the other side', the ones who point out their faults to them. Westerners have since learned to discover their own faults and humbly admit them. Let me cite one outstanding example for each continent.

For Asia there is Thomas Ohm's *Asiens Nein und Ja zum westlichen Christentum* ['Asia's no and yes to Western Christendom'] (Munich, 1960). The author brings together a great number of Asian voices and admits that many Asians live closer to the teaching of the Sermon on the Mount than do many Christians; that for many Christians the athlete is better known than the saint; that many Christians have no time to pray and live life to the full, but only to work and keep running. For Africa there is H. W. Mobley's *The Ghanaian Image of the Missionary* (Leiden, 1970), in which is shown that not only in recent years but as long ago as the first decade of the twentieth century African Christians spoke very critically of missionaries, in marked contrast to the romantic descriptions popularized in missionary magazines. For Latin America there is J. Höffner's *Christentum und Menschenwürd: Das Anliegen der spanischen Kolonialethik im Goldenen Zeitalter* ['Christianity and human dignity: the purpose of the Spanish colonial ethic in the "golden age"'] (Trier, 1947).[51] Höffner writes: 'The New World experienced such an appalling enslavement and extermination of its peoples as to make one's blood run cold'.

So we do not throw stones at each other any longer, but become our own accusers. That bodes well for the writing of history in the future. Next I should like to turn to a case study, that of African colonialism, to point out how in a short space of time great strides have been made. Africa was unspeakably humiliated by the presence and bearing of Westerners, but now it is experiencing a reinstatement. Since 1970 no other history has attracted so much interest as that of Africa.

In 1970 Henri Deschamps brought out, as editor, a 2-volume history of Africa.[52] In the Introduction he rightly emphasizes that eurocentricity is an anachronism to be overcome, that previous French historians had taken up a hagiographic, heroic, and patriotic stance, and by that very attitude triggered the anticolonial reaction that could speak of 'white devils and exploiters'. But the pity of it was, though, that of his twenty collaborators all without exception were French, English, and Belgian. It was an amusing quirk of history when two years later the African, J. Ki-Zerbo, on his own wrote a 700-page history of Africa that stood up to every criticism, and so supplied the proof that African collaborators were to be had.[53] However, the authors of the 8-volume *Cambridge History of Africa*, irreproachable as a work of scholarship, included only two Africans.[54]

Against this as a pattern of collaboration can be taken the UNESCO history of Africa project. Two-thirds of its writers and researchers are African. They have at their disposal the resources of the world organization and the competence of the other, Western, scholars. Of the eight volumes foreseen, two were published in 1980.[55] It is emphasized in the Introduction that African history long remained buried under myth and prejudice. In practise, 'white and black' stood for 'overlord and underling', and at the same time it was thought that Africa had had no history. Now it is known that the history of Africa goes back three million years, and that hominization probably took place in Africa. But dogmatizing is to be avoided in this project; no 'revenge history' is to be written.

Burning issues, such as slavery and colonialism, are to be approached calmly, with objectivity and historical discipline. It was hoped that this history, which would also be translated into the main African languages, would in addition be instrumental in restoring to Africa its memory and enabling it to be united within itself and with the world. May this hope become a reality!

In the area of church history the 10-volume Latin American project mentioned above is an important undertaking, although crimped by its emphasis on anticolonialism. The 13,000-page work by Hans-Jürgen Prien also deserves to be mentioned here.[56] Although its author is a German, he makes a conscious and successful effort to overcome the eurocentric outlook and to adopt the standpoint of Latin America. And so a universalist writing of history, exonerating and binding peoples together, is slowly coming about. Only when the past has been studied and worked out can the present and the future be given a fully informed structuration.

In conclusion, and as a toast to the birth of the universalist writing of history. I should like to describe its significance and range under four aspects. First of all it is a *sophia*, a science, intently drawing elements together and projecting an objective picture of de facto history. But beware of those who pass days and years ferreting out old documents and deciphering them, and nothing more.

Universalist historiography reaches a fuller value when it becomes *koinonia*, the impetus to build community, in the strength of which a people and the whole of humanity can build a future. Basically it is not past history but history as it happens which is decisive. History lying dead and buried in the dust of archives can no longer be changed, and changes nothing in us. But history passing through our hands day by day, which we have the opportunity of shaping, is of burning interest and has existential significance. Here we cannot overemphasize our responsibility to ourselves and to the community of which we are a member. Here we sense that history is more than the sum of many destinies, that it is indivisible, my interests concurring with the interests of the community that challenges me wholly. The church has hardly any greater task than to act as a leaven for unity and to motivate persons to community responsibility.

The writing of history must go yet a step further and also become *kerygma*, message. There is little interest today in the truths of the catechism. But everyone is looking for the meaning of life and history. So suddenly we find that there is much more to history than a science that leaves us cold. If the writing of history has not something kerygmatic about it, thinks of itself as only a strictly scientific presentation of a course of events, then it falls short of its special purpose. History becomes one of the humanities only when it lets us observe the relationships between events, the lives of others, and the divine intention, so that it may be understood to be a call and a challenge, and will encourage us to take a hand in God's history with humanity. Without reference to God and to existential truth, history would be little more than natural science.[57]

All this remains dead theorizing if the writing of history does not courageously dare to leap into real life and also become *diakonia*, service. Looking at the thick volumes of missionary and colonial history one cannot but smile. Such an outlay in terms of time, money, and acrimony in the service of the past! The centre of interest today has clearly shifted to forming the present and the future. It is not enough to *predict* the meaning of history. One must get beyond that entirely and be committed to meaningful history in the here and now. Thus our enquiry into justice and the *writing* of history (the title of this chapter) turns into the challenge of justice and the *formation* of history, to which we are all called. The theme of justice and the writing of history will no longer betoken the path toward fault-finding, but become a sign of hope in the Third World centre of conflict.

Chapter Six

Mission in the Service of Peace

We live in a time of uneasy 'peace', the quiet before the storm. We have only very brittle guarantees that there will not follow on Hiroshima a Euroshima or a Globoshima. Those who are concerned about this possibility take to the streets in favour of peace. In the 1960s they did it for revolution, in the 1970s for ecology, now for peace. Anyone with a finger on the pulse of the times feels the threat to peace and suspects that a third world war could and in all probability would mean the end of the world.

It is a good thing that activist groups in various countries are protesting such a prospect and that the world with its peace demonstrations is pushing the church to take action, although motivation for peace efforts should really be given to the world by the church. For the church was sent from the beginning to speak peace and to make peace. And the more peace is threatened, the more the church is obliged to seek peace. It remains to be seen whether the church will measure up to its responsibilities in this regard.

Have Christians, on the basis of the gospel, anything particular to say on the subject of peace, and what are the particular facets and requirements that they ought to advocate?

Theology of Peace

Peace as Messianic Promise

It does not require proving, because it is such an obvious fact, that almost everyone, deep down, longs for peace. But at the same time the whole of history teaches us that humankind clearly has not been able to secure and maintain peace. So the peoples, and in particular Israel, came to understand that peace is a gift of God.[58]

The Greeks and Romans defined peace as *tranquilitas ordinis*, the tranquility order, and they believed they could procure this peace by

68

overthrowing the enemy with the help of arms and the gods. Israel could trust far less to arms and so besought God the more for the gift of peace, expecting it as the fruit of the covenant with Yahweh (Isa. 48:22, 54:10, 57:20; Num. 6:22 ff., 25:12). Peace becomes the central concept of the prophetic message and a key word for the expectation of salvation in the messianic age (Isa. 57:19, 66:12; Jer. 33:6; Ezek. 34:25, 37:26).

In Jesus of Nazareth this promise of peace is fulfilled. Already at his birth, peace is announced for all those whom God loves (Luke 2:14). With a greeting of peace Jesus heals the sick and forgives sins (Luke 7:50, 8:48). He calls peacemakers blessed for they will be called God's offspring (Matt. 5:9), and he leaves to the disciples who have followed him, as their most treasured heritage, his peace, a peace that the world cannot give (John 14:27). After the resurrection he comforts the downcast disciples with his greeting of peace (John 20:19,26) and finally sends them out on the great mission of peace, to make the kingdom of God known everywhere, drive out devils, heal the sick, and bring peace to every house, every person (Luke 10:5 f.).

Obviously there was strife as well, and even Jesus could use harsh words about the Pharisees and the scribes. Exegetes today incline to the view that such angry talk was clearly not used so forcefully by the historical Jesus, but was formulated later by the evangelists from their bitter experience with the synagogue and Hellenism — in other words, that the evangelists projected their resentment and strong reaction back onto Jesus. At any rate, the heart of the gospel is to be found in the announcement of God's kingdom, the year of the Lord (Mark 1:15; Luke 4:19), the parables of the good Samaritan, the lost sheep, the lost son (Luke 10:25–37, 15:3–7, 11–32) — in short, in the teaching on the heavenly Father, rich in mercy, who will not quench the smoking flax or break the bruised reed, who looks after the flowers of the field and the birds of the air, and how much more all humankind.

If the word 'pacifist' did not have political overtones, we would have to say that Jesus was a thoroughgoing pacifist, who never used violence against anyone; an idealist who, believing in God's goodness, believed also in the goodness of humankind; a utopian who prescribed a different pattern of life for humanity and carried it out in his own life.

His disciples, in accordance with their commission, took the peace of Christ everywhere. They said that their message was, in brief, 'the gospel of Jesus' (Acts 10:36; Eph. 6:15); they began their letters with the greeting 'grace and peace' (Rom. 1:7; 1 Cor. 1:3); for them, peace was the characteristic gift of the Spirit of Jesus (Rom. 8:6, 14:17; Gal. 5:22).

The Hebrew word *shalom*, peace, is inherently what Jesus meant by the coming of the kingdom and what Paul expressed by the concept of redemption and salvation. It is the heart of the Christian message, the particular gift of Jesus to the human race.

Mission History as a Caricature of Peace-making

The church was left by Jesus in the world with a sublime peace mission. It should cry shalom in all times and places, 'shalomize' the world, interpret the world in the light of God's peace and love.

But here the opponents of the church could say 'Look what it has been in practice!' And we have to admit that Christ's peace mission degenerated all too quickly. Instead of being a sign of salvation for all, as was belatedly emphasized in Vatican II, the church became in the course of history an ark of salvation for the privileged few. True, there was always in the church a great weight of holiness and love, pardon and redemption, charity and culture. But in its relations with those outside — the Jews and heathen, heretics and schismatics — the church became absolutist and exclusivist. In this respect, the church lived contrary to Jesus' message.

From the fourth century onward, the church made an alliance with power and became the established church with privileges and lands. It set Christ triumphant in line with emperor worship, viewing him as pantocrator, imperator. It developed the concept of Christendom, a closed religious, cultural, and political bloc, within which was the true religion, true culture, and the road to heaven; outside was only barbarism, idolatry, and the road to hell.

On the basis of this worldview there was no hesitation at incorporating Saxons and Wends into the empire by force. Able-bodied men were summed to the crusades against Saracens and Muslims. Held at the time to be the highest expression of faith, today it is termed 'a heretical fantasy'.[59] Pope Alexander VI divided the New World between Spain and Portugal 'so as to subjugate the barbarian peoples and spread the Catholic faith there'. Beginning in the nineteenth century, it is true, colonialism and missionary effort were kept

70

more, though not entirely, separate, but well into the twentieth century the idea prevailed that for nonbelievers there was only conversion or damnation.

As I have said, this is only one side, the ugly side, of the story. But it is still part of the whole. If we were to continue producing apologetical mission history, wanting to show only the attractive side,[60] then Africans and Asians would come and tell the other side.[61] We cannot deny this history but we should take care that it is not carried on further and that we return to the true peace mission of Christ. When looking at history, we all have reason to say *mea culpa*, and renew our faith in the peace of the gospel.

On the Track of Peace again

To those who bemoan the present state of the church, I say: 'What sort of gloomy talk is that? Don't you see how the church, in what concerns her externals, is in a much better state than ever before since the first centuries?' In fact, since the mid-1960s, thanks to Pope John XXIII and the council he summoned, Catholics have been making their way out of a long tunnel, as it were, and today freely associate with those with whom they had long been at odds — Jews, Protestants, non-Christians, nonbelievers — and hold dialogue and prayer groups in common with them.

Not only has the way of peace been opened up again, but the whole content of peace has been rediscovered afresh. Shalom means peace, fulfillment, blessing, wholeness, soundness, completeness — personal and communal. Concretely: bodily health, psychological well-being, economic prosperity. In short, a kind of return to paradisal happiness.

Instead of all-embracing biblical peace, an ersatz shalom was worked out. Messianic peace was linked with the beyond, with what comes after death. There was talk of *eternal* peace. Because peace on earth corresponded so little to the messianic promises, it was sited in the world to come — and an alibi was invented for noncommitment to peace on earth. Peace was also situated in interiority. There was talk of *interior* peace, which was not to be disturbed even if the whole world were torn with strife.

I do not mean to suggest that the Catholic Church has not always practised charity, furthered civilization, and undertaken in mission fields what was later to be called development. But in thought, in the catechism, in spiritual writings, in sermons, it was an otherworldly peace that was prominent — so much so that slavery could be condoned, and the only care shown to slaves was that they be baptized in preparation for their journey across the ocean so that at least their souls could be saved. Eschatological peace was privatized, spiritualized. A disincarnate salvation, outside history and time, was preached. But it was not this alone that Yahweh, the God of history, wanted for the chosen people, or that Jesus lived and taught. Jesus did indeed want his followers to set their hope heavenward, but he was also concerned about the shoe that pinched.

The new understanding of integral salvation — shalom in the original and broad sense — was first developed in Latin America, in that 'Catholic continent' where land and wealth were concentrated in the hands of a few, a thorn in God's side, whereas the many, closer to God's heart, spent their lives in the search for mere survival. Increasingly, lay persons, priests, and bishops demanded that this unchristian scandal be terminated. If the eucharistic bread is to be broken, daily bread must also be shared. So the poor were educated, conscientized, inspired with the courage to do what was necessary and possible to free themselves of this state of affairs, and construct for themselves a life fit for human beings, as is God's plan and intention. Religion could suddenly be seen to be no longer an opium, but rather a stimulus for striving to form a better life in concert with others.

In the bishops' synod of 1971 on justice in the world, under the influence especially of the Latin American bishops, the classic proposition was formulated that justice is an essential part of evangelization itself and so a requirement to be taken seriously by those who would carry out Jesus' mandate to evangelize the world. Until then, work in schools, hospitals, and social service centres was thought of as preevangelization. It was taken to be a means to an end. With it the ground was to be prepared for acceptance of 'full evangelization', the Christian faith. But now this was no longer thinkable, for it was an essential part of evangelization itself. Whenever and however we help human beings to understand themselves better, better fulfill their legitimate aspirations, is already a means to the salvation that God wills to send to one person through another; and it is already *Christian* salvation, for since Christ became incarnate there is nothing human that has not to do with him and no human beings with whom he does not identify. The bishops' synod of 1974 on evangelization in the world affirmed this concept and affirmed the two dimensions of salvation — the eschatologico-transcendental and the historico-immanent — as being both component parts of God's salvation.

It is surprising and heartening how much the sense of justice and peace has grown since Pope Paul VI set up the Pontifical Commission Justitia et Pax in 1967. Pope John Paul II, the bishops' conferences of several countries, and the World Council of Churches repeatedly raise their voices in the struggle for peace and its prerequirement, justice. The religious institutes, too, have turned outward from their introverted spirituality toward the world and today no longer emphasize renouncing the world, denial of the world, flight from the world, but rather 'flight ahead with the world'.[62] For they have become conscious that God is revealed only to those who seek to discover God in the least of their fellows (Matt. 25:31–46).

Peace and the Third World

I begin with some preliminary remarks. 'Peace and the Third World' will introduce socio-economic and political problems. It can be asked what they have to do with theology. Ever since, beginning in the Third World, 'contextual theology' has been pursued, there is little interest shown for 'universal theology', one that applies everywhere but fits nowhere. Interest today is shown for local theology, studying real situations, casting on them the light of the gospel and giving a particular people the courage and strength to change what needs to be changed. To read the reports of the Ecumenical Association of Third World Theologians is to be struck by how often they deal more with politics than with theology. But perhaps that is the new way of pursuing a theology that will be relevant.[63]

I say 'Third World', not 'the missions'. First, because 'the missions' are now, ecclesially speaking, local churches and it is for this very reason psychologically hurtful to go on talking of 'the missions', and still more of *our* missions'. Secondly, because the church is not its own justification, it has not as its first priority to extend and strengthen itself, but to serve humanity, speaking as an advocate, acting as a prophet, and so to mediate integral salvation.

I could here cite a comprehensive and basic text, the synodal document on the contribution of the West German Catholic Church to development and peace. To be sure, from the mid-1970s to the mid-1980s the situation in the Third World worsened in some respects, because of rampant corruption, worsening conditions of world trade, and the oil crisis, which has hit the poor countries much harder than the wealthy. Although the poor countries, taken together, cut back their oil imports by 25 percent from 1978 to 1980, they nonetheless had to pay out $3.3 milliard (billion) instead of $2.1 milliard.

The peace problematic in the Third World has to do principally with the many ethnic and national wars, which the First World takes calmly because they are far away. But I hope that in time they will dissipate and the realization will finally dawn everywhere that civilized countries do not go to war with one another. I see peace in the Third World in the long run not so much from out of the past, which still threatens to unleash monstrous racial discord, but in view of a future becoming ever bleaker, specifically in three wide-ranging areas of conflict.

Worldwide ecological conflict. This will come about, for example, because mass tourism in the tropical zones is destroying the very surroundings that attract tourists. In Hawaii 80 percent of the original bird species are already extinct. Again, the export, economically welcome to buyers and sellers, of timber from Indonesia, Zaire, and Brazil is leaving whole districts deforested and the ecological balance disturbed. Rapidly increasing urbanization is creating unhealthy urban conditions and leaving the countryside forsaken, so that more and more food supplies have to be imported.

Furthermore we have to agree with the reports of the Club of Rome and Global 2000 that what nature built up in the course of millions of years has been madly exploited in three decades. In the foreseeable future, shortages of oil and of many other raw materials important for life will set in, and then the great powers will fight over their share, like nomads of yore over grazing lands, and will take over the more helpless nations of the Third World, putting them under their guardianship and economic dictatorship.

North-South economic conflict. Since the first development decade, 1960 to 1970, there has been talk about bridging the gap between the rich and the poor countries. Instead, it is becoming wider all the time. Within the poor countries themselves, a small elite of the newly rich has been forming, whereas the bulk of the population has barely enough to live on. North-South dialogue and the famous Brandt Report do scarcely more than confirm the dire state of affairs, and the West bemoans its economic crisis and is no longer prepared to play fairy godmother. Third World countries, however, by the year

74

2000 will make up 80 percent of the world population, and so a growing revolt of the massed poor against the scattered rich edges more and more toward the realm of possibility and probability, and North-South dialogue threatens to turn into North-South conflict.

Militarist East-West conflict. Here we touch on the root of the matter. We have been witnesses in our lifetime of the greatest scandal in human history. Scarcely were the horrors of the Second World War at an end when the senseless, baleful arms race for the Third World War broke out. Humankind is like a madman setting out to smash everything to pieces and destroy the world itself. The Stockholm International Peace Institute made known in 1980 that approximately 400,000 scientists, 40 percent of all scientists in the world, are working on armaments, and that annually $25 milliard (billion) are spent on military research, four times more than on medical research. The U.S.A. poured out $285 milliard for 1983, the largest military budget in world history. And all this is in addition to the 60,000 atomic warheads that the U.S.A. and the U.S.S.R. already have in position, which is equivalent to a million Hiroshima atomic bombs, with which the U.S.S.R. can destroy every American city of more than 100,000 inhabitants 28 times over, and the U.S.A. in turn every Soviet city 34 times over. For this the Americans have coined the world 'overkill'.

It might be said that this is a problem for the two superpowers, which are perhaps on the way to bringing about the ruin of East and West. But at the same time there are also the 110 young nations that, instead of contenting themselves with a domestic police force, have been equipped militarily, and so everyone shares in the responsibility for the more than 130 small wars that have broken out in the Third World since the Second World War: the Third World provides the corpses; the First World and Second World provide the weapons. This ludicrous turn of events cannot be condemned too strongly. Here are a few examples of sick, and sickening, statistics:

● The outlay for military budgets the world over was running at $152 milliard in 1956, and in 1980 (reckoning at the same dollar value) $700 milliard. The Third World share of this in 1971 was 9 percent, but by 1980 it was 16 percent.

● The sum total of military personnel in the world doubles the combined total of teachers, doctors, and nurses.

● To pay for this military expenditure all citizens must in their lifetime sacrifice the income of from three to four years.

75

• For the cost of a modern tank there could be built classrooms for 30,000 children. The cost of a Trident submarine would pay for schooling for 16 million children in developing countries.[64]

One must fully agree with 'The Holy See and Disarmament', a Vatican study presented to the UNO, that this arms race, even under the guise of legitimate self-defence, is nonsense: it is nothing other than the legitimation of fear-mongering.[65] It also constitutes robbery, alienation of funds, because the astronomical sums used for weapons should be employed to create better survival opportunities for the poor. Such madness will not escape judgement before the court of history.

We still have to ask ourselves what, in spite of all the odds, we should do, in this seemingly helpless and hopeless state of affairs, to create a saner and more peaceful world.

Building a World Peace Community

I should like to be able to postulate a utopian peace, with all the forces of history converging toward it. In the wider historical context, however, it looks more like this: for thousands of centuries humanity wandered in scattered nomadic groups over a thinly populated earth and made war only in a sporadic and minor way over cattle, pasture, and wife-stealing. The tribe was the world at that time.

Some ten thousand years ago our ancestors turned from nomadic animal husbandry to agriculture, then went on to urban culture, then to nation-building. Now the nation was the world with which to be identified. History was until recently under the banner of nationalism.

It would seem today that this stage of nationalism has to pass on to a new and final stage under the pressure of communication and information technology. The heroes of the future will identify with the whole of humanity and be committed to it. For if unity and fellowship are no longer feasible, we are all threatened with going under in nuclear death. 'We must all hang together, or assuredly we shall all hang separately' (Benjamin Franklin).

Sacred scripture gives us a more profound basis and stresses that we are called to unity. We should go back to the story of God's first love, the first eleven chapters of Genesis, where God always deals with humanity as a whole. The word 'man' is to be found there 539 times as a collective noun: the human being, all humankind. Then

76

with chapter 12 we zoom in on one individual picked out against the human horizon and set in the foreground: Abraham. After that the history of salvation continues for 3,500 years in the line of Abraham and his posterity, Moses and his people, Jesus and his church.

In the Old Testament history of Israel, the concept of election led to the abuses of isolationism and contempt of other peoples. It must here be added that today, with a better knowledge of ethnocentricity, we are discovering that every people is in practice convinced that it is the centre of the world, that it stands in a special relationship to God by its religion, and so is a special people, a people of God, implicitly or explicitly a chosen people.

We ought by now to have come far enough to affirm boldly that God in fact loves all peoples, that Christians represent not a monopoly but an example of God's love for all peoples. The eurocentric and ecclesiocentric worldview will have to be replaced by a creative, new worldview—the original worldview of Genesis 1–12. The bracketing out of other peoples will have to be suspended in favour of a return to 'the human being', humanity. We are approaching a final stage, but one designed from the beginning, in which it will be clear that in fact all peoples are chosen peoples, or that there is only one chosen people, one humanity, within which Christians have a special revelation and special task: to be speakers, interpreters, pioneers of humanity for salvation and for peace.

So viewed, the mission of the church has a long and compelling future, and we must now ask ourselves how we can hasten toward that future.

Practice of Peace

If the disciples of Jesus had to carry out, according to the Master's command, a mission of peace to an unpeaceful world, and in doing so, coordinating content and method, had to proceed by peaceful means, they gave us a model for our evangelization efforts. I should like in what follows to propound some arguments on the understanding and development of mission in the service of peace.

The Missionary as Messenger of Peace

Missionaries are the key figures in the mediation of God's peace to the world. On them depends whether evangelization takes place —

that is, whether the gospel message of peace and joy reaches to a new group of persons which do not yet expressly know that peace. Missionaries must say 'shalom' everywhere, not merely in greeting: their arrival in a particular area should be felt as an existential experiencing of peace. 'His peace' is such a reality that, if hearers are not receptive, it returns to the missionary again (Matt. 10:13).

In order to radiate this peace missionaries must themselves first be seized and filled by it. Only the evangelized can evangelize, and all the evangelized must evangelize in their turn. Today missionaries do not rely on 'the authority of the white man'. They rely on a mystery that has endured through all ages and is still worthy of credence today, whether missionaries be European, African, or Asian. Through them speaks the Spirit of God, the creator Spirit, the Spirit of Jesus, the Spirit of redemption, of a new creation. Certainly they must be open to this Spirit and believe in the Spirit's continuing inspiration. They will always draw from this Spirit in prayer. In this Spirit they will never be shaken in their self-confidence, and in all human uncertainties, in every 'fear and anxiety' (1 Cor. 2:3), they will be filled with an inner *dynamis* that is inexhaustible and indestructible, stronger than any nuclear force. It will uphold them in every difficulty.

In this way they will bring to others not a codified teaching, a system of verities, but a living witness, an alternative lifestyle that is credible and attractive, and they will always go on finding sympathizers and followers. In this way the missionary will not only be accepted by 'not-yet' Christians but will also find entry to already constituted local churches. No longer do missionaries live in an ecclesial no man's land as before. Today they will no longer be merely 'sent out' as before, but must be 'invited in' by a local church wanting and needing them. Whether or not they will continue to be welcome in a local church will depend on them. Their spirituality is therefore not merely a precondition of good works in general, but of their very existence as missionaries.

The Place for Missionary Proclamation Today: All Six Continents

Peace has become indivisible. It needs to be strengthened (pastoral activity) and taken to new recipients (missionary activity) in all three worlds and in all six continents. Earlier, the world was divided into church here, missions there. Today church is everywhere, *but* a church in a missionary situation. Wherever groups of persons are to be found who are far from Christ, a missionary situation is implicit, and so a missionary challenge. And whoever consciously goes out beyond the boundary of the Christian community and seeks to carry gospel values to those far from Christ is a missionary, regardless of whether it be in Africa, Asia, or Europe, and regardless of whether the gospel is being carried to 'not-yet Christians' or 'no-longer Christians'. Geographical distance, then, no longer counts in missionary activity but sociological and ecclesiological distance do.

I believe it very important for missionary institutes to help their home churches to be open to this missionary challenge. Further, they should, without taking anything from them or holding them back, be active as animators of this challenge, encouraging Christians to evangelize the areas where they live. Here we stand before virgin country. Most Christians are so very inward-looking and concerned only with their own souls. A new inspiration of the Spirit is needed for them to take Christ's message to others in a new language and with new methods. I think that, for example, teachers have a great opportunity to enter into pedagogical and religious conversation with the parents of their pupils. Also, members of basic Christian communities could now and again invite friends and acquaintances who are alienated from the church. They could discover a new kind of church and would perhaps allow their latent faith to revive. Among the many neocatechetical movements in Italy, for example, as many as half of those attending had not been to church for years.

When we speak of persons far from Christ that is only to say that they are far from him, not that he is far from them. Christ and his Spirit are near to all — Christians, 'not-yet Christians', and 'no-longer Christians' alike. Christ was ahead of his disciples when, weary with rowing, they reached the other side of the lake. In the same way he is always there ahead of all missionaries when they encounter persons who are 'far from Christ'. On this rests our hope that our efforts will not remain fruitless. We have to seek out those in whom Christ is already mysteriously at work, to lead them to familiarity with the mystery of Christ (*Redemptor Hominis*, 10).

For the mission of peace to the Third World, the churches of the West will not in the future be able to count on many vocations. Statistics show that of the 7,845 missionaries from Germany, 58 percent are over sixty years old and few young ones are coming along to take their place.[66] This seems to indicate a definite

79

missionary crisis. But it must be noted, first, that this crisis is decidedly a phenomenon of the Western church: taken as a whole, missionary activity is very much on the increase today, because not only does the West send out missionaries to other continents but *all* local churches in *all six* continents are actively missionary. Secondly, the missionary crisis of the West was in fact providentially necessary to break up its monopoly over the missions and create the atmosphere necessary for the young churches to realize their own responsibility and develop their own strengths. This is not resignation to the inevitable but, I believe, a prophetic indication of a new historical situation.

Announcing the Gospel and Changing the World: Proclamation and Transformation

We have already seen that the two dimensions of salvation, the transcendent and the immanent, together respond to the deepest aspirations of the human spirit, and neither may be left aside or denied without going contrary to human nature and so to God. The expressly religious, other-worldly, definitive dimension has an absoluteness not matched by the interior dimension. As such it will always retain a certain priority. Without peace with God there will be no true peace with one's fellows. Conversion of heart always remains a requirement for a better world. Otherwise the stage and the actors in the human drama will be endlessly changed but individuals will remain, as ever, hard, selfish, and grasping. 'There is no new humanity if there are not first new persons' (*Evangelii Nuntiandi*, 18). So there will always be the possibility and the need to speak of faith and prayer, church and sacraments, death and eternal life, as has always been the case.

But added now to that comes the emphasis on this-worldly salvation, which makes a greater impression and carries greater immediacy than transcendental salvation. The horizontal should not stand in opposition to the vertical but as a necessary complement in order to achieve synthesis and harmony. We have to take care that in religious instruction, in all parts of the world, it is made clear to the young and to adults that to be a Christian also means to take a stand for justice and not to suffer wrong done to the poor — they are identified with Christ!

This means that missionary institutes may no longer be content with mere distribution of alms, but must by every means of conscientization – preaching, lectures, the press — take care that our fellow citizens — for example, those with responsibility in economics and politics — take seriously their duties of justice and peace. North-South dialogue may not be allowed to stagnate. We must lend our voices to the reports of Global 2000 and A Plan for Survival (the Brandt Commission), which have found little response, and also take care that *Populorum Progressio* not fall into oblivion. We should leave others no peace! They may not go about their daily rounds, their consciences undisturbed! We should have no inhibitions at taking to the streets with the young and protesting environmental conditions or campaigning for a better lifestyle, for justice in the world.

We must spread the idea that not only should the developing countries make up lost ground but that, to this end, the industrial nations should shorten their lead: on ecological grounds, because the pillaging of nature may no longer be tolerated; on psychological grounds, because the countries with a high standard of living have the greatest incidence of psychologically maladjusted and frustrated individuals, as also a higher incidence of broken marriages and suicides; on grounds of solidarity, so as at last to bridge the gulf between rich and poor peoples. The book by A. Tévéodjiré, *La pauvreté, richesse des peuples* ['poverty, the wealth of nations'] (Paris, 1980), can give us inspiration for this. He insists that abject poverty, unworthy of human beings, should be eliminated by every means possible, but that a moderate, joyful poverty is the way to restore happiness to human life.

Transformation of the world, at the service of peace, will also mean that in the Third World, under the guidance of missionaries and local church personnel, Christians will become, by reason of their Christian outlook, the best animators of the work of development ('nation-building'). They will not wait for the government or the West to do something for them, but will lend a hand and, working together, do what they can do. And they will see in this their 'salvation history', their 'flight out of Egypt', and truly believe that God will free them from ignorance, sickness, and poverty, and lead them to a better life, a 'promised land'.

Conflicts and Nonviolence

Transformation of the world will not be achieved without conflict. Tensions between different temperaments, mentalities, outlooks, and interests belong to the dialectical course of history. We are sent into this history and have to conduct ourselves in it as guilelessly as lambs and as wisely as serpents (Matt. 10:16). It can also be said that we have to act from a prophetic, or sometimes a diplomatic, charism.

Ideally, these two charisms should co-exist evenly in a person, but often they do not. Each has its own self-justification and its own laws. The diplomatic person, in the good sense, seeks to speak the truth with smiles and love. Such a person knows that more bees are caught with a drop of honey than with a quart of vinegar. Sympathy radiated, trust given freely to others, bear in themselves their own power of reconciliation and persuasion. The whole of psychology advocates this way of acting. A person with this gift should use it to the full and speak in this way with those holding responsibility in church and world.

The prophet, on the other hand, strikes a different note. The prophet, like John the Baptist, denounces sins and injustices, and sets before the eyes of the impenitent the judgement of God and of history. The prophet sees the wrong in the world to be so great that it can no longer be spoken of smilingly, but only in a rage. Prophets know that what they say is not generally acceptable, that it will set up walls of opposition endangering their own lives. What makes prophets is that nevertheless they do speak out and they believe that what they are after will come to something — subsequent to, and because of, their death. In Jesus the fate and the victory of the prophet find their confirmation.

Even today they are in their hundreds, their thousands, speaking prophetically for what they are after, for justice, for shalom — and suffering death for it. We know today that there were not as many martyrs in the first centuries as the apologists would have us believe. But today there are far more martyrs than we know, martyrs not for orthodoxy, for an article of the creed, but for orthopraxis, for living up to the faith. Religious freedom is basically recognized everywhere today as a human right. Therefore persons are no longer put to death for voicing their credo. But if they want to translate that credo, then they risk torture and death. And nonetheless we are not at liberty to practise a harmless, a historical, privatized religion.

The prophet will, therefore, reproach oppressors, but by peaceful means. Even when the use of force can be justified in view of the need and defence of basic human rights, and even when great sympathy must be shown for those who in such situations use force as a last resort in good conscience, yet the gospel prophet will almost always eschew force rather than resort to it. In this way the escalation of violence is checked, its absurdity is exposed, and the ultimate meaning of history is made credible.

For the missionary it is a practical matter whether or not to assume the role of prophet as the guest of another country, another church. In most instances it would only lead to expulsion or silencing. The missionary should concentrate on inspiring a local church to take action where it is inclined to inaction because of conformism, diplomacy, or fear. I am thinking of the example of the White Fathers, who left Mozambique in a body as a protest, because the Portuguese bishops, out of chauvinism and financial interests, supported a repressive government.

Dialogical Kerygma

'Dialogical kerygma' seems a contradiction in terms. And yet the two elements must go together.

Kerygma is the convinced, confident, outspoken, proclamation of the message — not discussion, questioning, listening, but teaching. The Gospel mandates us to spread the message of the crucified and risen Lord in season and out of season (2 Tim. 4:2). To refuse belief will bring down judgement on a person.

Missionaries have for centuries evangelized in this way and accordingly felled sacred oaks, destroyed places of sacrifice, disputed with the votaries of other religions. They were convinced they had a monopoly on Jesus Christ, they had the one and only truth. Heretics and schismatics in mission lands were accorded the same (mis)treatment as in Europe.

Today we are appalled by this antiecumenical past. We now call 'heretics' Christian brethren, and 'unbelievers' believers of other religions. We accept that the Lord of lords and the Holy Spirit were already present in other churches and religions, too, and sending their adherents peace and salvation, prophets and inspiration.

Suddenly dialogue comes to the forefront. Before we can teach, we must learn; before we speak, we must listen; before we preach Christ, we must recognize him already present. Dialogue has its own motivation. It should not be thought of merely as a handmaid of conversion. It is correct to think well of members of other religions, to talk and pray with them, to read their religious books and offer them the Bible in a dialogical exchange — and leave the rest to God.

Both dialogue and kerygma, then, have their own place. How they go together, how they can be seen in synthesis, unfortunately we have no major work to tell us. Perhaps they interrelate as mysteriously as does the almighty power of God with human freedom and responsibility. We can only stand in veneration before the freedom of God and the freedom of human beings, scrutinize the signs of the times, and try to discern in the Spirit when and where we ought rather to practise dialogue or kerygma.

We ought therefore to interpret the world in the light of God's love and try to change it by dedicated commitment. There will always be those who will show interest in what we are doing and will perhaps come to love Jesus too and want to be baptized — not in order to 'save their souls', as though this was not possible before, but in order to become full members of the church and take part in its mission of world salvation.

A Clear Stand on the Question of Armaments

I know this is a controversial subject. The Central Committee for German Catholics published a position paper in 1981 on current peace discussions and even spoke of 'an insane competition'. But then, after long consideration, it came to the conclusion that 'political reason and moral responsibility for the common good require setting up and maintaining a balance of power'.[67]

More recent communications from the bishops' conferences of Germany, Austria, Switzerland, and above all the U.S.A. have spoken more perceptively and more courageously on the matter. Basically they say that peace must be assured through human cooperation, that a 'balance of terror' is unworthy of humanity, and at most (!) for the present (!) can be tolerated (!) as a lesser evil (!). From Roman times to the present, homage has been paid to the principle *Si vis pacem, para bellum* — 'if you want peace, prepare for war'. This principle has in fact been adhered to, and there has been one war after another. Long overdue is the attempt to implement a new principle: *Si vis pacem, para pacem* — 'if you want peace, prepare for peace'. There must be some way to at last break out of the senseless spiral of militarization, which threatens never to come to an end.

84

Christians should bring something other than merely political considerations to this discussion. We all shudder at what a nuclear war could mean. We have no guarantee at all that what is possible for unpredictable human nature will not some day become a reality. We have come to the point where another war is unthinkable, where the nonviolence of the Sermon on the Mount is no longer a postulate for idealists but a practical demand of realistic politics. Military power, trigger-happy on both sides as it has become, and intensified by counterarming on the part of NATO and counter-counterarming on the part of the U.S.S.R., is enough to make many want to be six foot underground.

Anyone who thinks such considerations are procommunist should read *Gaudium et Spes*, 79–81, and the whole documentation contained in 'The Holy See and Disarmament' mentioned above. Christians must take to the streets along with scientists, the young, those of other faiths, and exert pressure on governments to seriously undertake steps towards disarmament. If there is no right to drop H-bombs, there is also no right to produce them! 'One cannot serve God and militarism' (Dorothee Sölle). From various surveys in the U.S.A. it becomes clear that Christians are more war-minded than non-Christians, call more for nuclear weapons, and are more likely to see war as a means to ending conflict — and indeed Catholics more than Protestants, and Protestants more than unbelievers.[68] How does that square with the gospel of peace?

We ought above all to promote creative alternatives, for even military disarmament remains useless if not matched with spiritual rearmament, if persons are not helped to a new experience of life in the framework of a meaningful design for life. We ought to encourage those who live in the First World to put their intelligence and their technical ability, their money and their pride, into carrying out development programmes on a grand scale — irrigating the Sahara, eliminating tropical diseases, conserving natural resources. The Roman principle could be recast: 'If you want peace, struggle for justice'.

So long as humanity has not the courage to turn about and foster priorities such as these, it is headed toward an abyss, and can sooner or later be annihilated, surprised by catastrophe as though by a thunderbolt. The church as herald of peace cannot give forewarning too loudly while there is still time.

85

In the midst of this age without peace, holy scripture exhorts us that with messianic times has come the moment 'to set our feet on the way of peace' (Luke 1:79). If we are unwilling to give up hope of peace, we have to carry out the work of peace in small steps.[69]

We must in our own daily life, in our dealings with others, let it be seen that aggressiveness can be unlearned, that to share the majority opinion is not necessarily the correct point of view, that we should not distinguish between white and nonwhite, between believers and atheists, between rich and poor, between 'right' and 'left'. Unfortunately 'politics' easily lends itself to polarization and can divide a community. One side sees violence and injustice only in the East, the other only in the West. Objectivity and impartiality would be steps toward peace.

We must in company with other groups promote the extension of peaceful moves and initiatives. There is still a great work of conscientization to be done! Newly acquired concepts and insights have now to be brought to wider circles.

We may also note with satisfaction that the concept of justice and peace (*iustitia et pax*) is well on the way, and that a new spirituality is being elaborated in which there is not talk so much any more of humility, obedience, and personal sanctification but of courage, taking risks, commitment, transforming the world. Moral theology no longer deals merely with individual virtues and sins, but emphasizes strongly the duties of a Christian in reference to ecology, peace, and justice in the world.[70] Peace has become a science in its own right, and is pursued in 78 institutes of higher learning and four hundred and eighty-three journals and publications. At more than five hundred other schools lectures and courses are given.[71] This is still in no way comparable with what is done for war. But the movement is gaining momentum and the snowball can perhaps — thanks also to small contributions — become an avalanche.

There will be opposition: Pope John Paul II repeatedly warns priests and religious not to get mixed up in politics. Yet he himself engages in politics to a considerable degree. We might think of his Angelus exhortations and his official speeches before the UNO and to the diplomatic corps in various countries, his interventions in behalf of Poland, and so on. Obviously, someone who is an official representative of the church should not practise party politics and take one side against another, to say nothing about taking up arms for political goals. But no one should be dissuaded from caring about questions of justice and peace.

Five Levels of Koinonia

In earlier times the oneness of the Catholic Church was thought of primarily in terms of church structure and juridical subordination to Rome. Today we understand better that this unity is not founded on human structures but on faith in the one Lord Jesus Christ, one baptism, one mutual love, one mission — namely, the service of world peace.

The church today has nothing to do with European hegemony. It lives today in all six continents. Since 1970 it has shifted its centre of gravity to the Third World. The church must therefore speak everywhere for peace. We all have an interest in mutually strengthening the continental churches and, by an exchange of values, becoming a *koinonia* (community) of the one church.

This exchange takes place on different levels.[72] Monetary aid, though of considerable importance, I would assign to the lowest level, because it is a one-way street (distorted relationships can easily develop between sending and receiving) and because money, for all its usefulness, does not approach the heart of ecclesiality.

On the second rung I would see an exchange of personnel. Here one-sidedness is surpassed. Today missionaries go to and from all six continents. Even though there are increasingly more countries no longer granting visas for missionaries and more and more local chuches with no need for more missionaries, yet God will always give the missionary vocation to individuals and they will always find 'missionary situations' in which they can work, even if 'only' in the First World. Besides, the world of tomorrow is going to be racially mixed and so there must always be missionaries here and there as messengers of peace between churches and cultures.

The next higher step is that of an exchange of theology. Western theology monopolized the Third World until the mid-1960s. The whole church is now in the happy position of also receiving theology produced in the Third World.

Higher still, because not only academic but existential in import, would be an exchange of pastoral experiences with basic ecclesial communities, with groups without a priest, with spontaneous creative

87

liturgy. The continental churches should not try to keep in step with Roman policy but each make its own advances and experiments, and then contribute to a living church by means of exchange.

Finally, the highest stage would be an exchange of lifestyles, models of faithful Christian life, of saints, of martyrs for justice. Such examples show us what it means to lose our life so as to gain it. At a time when meaninglessness is so prevalent, such examples can not only help us keep above water but infuse us with courage to go on joyfully in the way of peace.

A church living thus in *koinonia* and continually renewing and enriching itself will see its principal interest no longer in institutional self-perpetuation but in its service to the world. The promise that nothing shall prevail against it was not given to the church by Christ for its own sake only but for the sake of the world, because the world will always need such a church. Today the church is to be the courageous advocate of all persons of good will, the one to initiate dialogue with other religions, a universal sacrament of peace. It must not tear itself apart in a plurality of internal opinions but must as a community pull itself together for its task of peace for the world. We do well to identify with this church, to shalomize with all in the church for the world, and so with Jesus to bear witness that our God is indeed the 'God of peace' (1 Thess. 5:23).

Chapter Seven

Hope for the Western Church from the Third World?

The more disturbing the political, economic, and ecclesiastical situation, the more we seek to hold fast to hope. Hope is the last thing we give up. Those who lose it write themselves off the list of those taking part in the discussion on shaping the world and the church.

The Austrian Katholikentag held in Vienna in 1983 adopted for its theme 'Live hope, give hope'. I should like to take up from the varied facets of this subject the question, whether hope has not perhaps something to do with the Third World too; whether perhaps in our times, weary of hope, a certain stimulus can be expected from the Third World.

The title of this chapter is intentionally given a question mark, and for two reasons. First, it expresses surprise. For the very question implies a radical turning around of our previous world order. Hitherto it was Western Christianity that was held to be the source of all values. Those in the First World thought of themselves as possessors; they had something to give. Those in the Third World counted as the poor; they had everything to receive. The suggestion that the West could learn something of culture or religion from Third World have-nots would have been laughed at until very recently.

Meanwhile the cocky self-assurance of the First World has taken many a knock. So many symbols of hope were erected, but their enthusiasts are empty-handed today. In the 1960s there was hope in revolution. Che Guevara was idolized by many young persons, a saint for modern times. Nothing of that is left now. Hope was put in 'The American way of life', unlimited progress, prosperity for all. Instead, today the world faces a crisis with no solution in sight. Hope was put in decolonialization, that upsurge of over a hundred young nations with waving banners entering upon independence. But those hopeful multitudes soon experienced a sad awakening from their euphoria. Hope was put in the UNO, in a messianic age of peace. Instead, today the whole world is threatened by the possibility of the most frightful catastrophe in human history. Hope was put in the Second Vatican Council, that magnificent breakthrough that could only be compared with the Jesus Movement of almost two thousand years earlier. But instead there is disappointment at the withdrawal of young persons from the church and resignation to the tendency toward reinstitutionalization of the church. Can we honestly go along with that confident motto, 'Live hope, give hope'? Can it perhaps be true that the demoralized, once so proud, Western church can look to the Third World to escape drowning? In its lack of hope can it expect new hope from that direction?

But then doubt also arises — the second reason for the question-mark in the title — whether the Third World really is so full of idealism and hope that help can be expected of it. Let us admit that, basically, there is no holy world, no holy church, anywhere. All churches everywhere carry marks of human frailty. I often had the experience on my many travels of how persons in a particular place moaned over the poor conditions and were enthusiastic over another church, another country, another missionary institute, and thought everything there must be fine. But when I arrived there I noticed the same dissatisfaction. In fact, nowhere does the church give internal evidence of its divine character. It everywhere occasions hope against all hope.

Now we can approach the answer to the opening question. First I must, in order to be realistic, play the devil's advocate a little and one-sidedly — but not erroneously — point out the almost hopeless state of the Third World from which the First World nevertheless expects something hopeful.

Hope in Its Third World Context

The Almost Hopeless Situation of the Young Nations

What was dreamed of and expected from decolonialization has been in no way fulfilled. On the contrary, after the radiant morning of independence-day celebrations there quickly spread over those countries, as after a heavy storm, a general mood of despondency.

As to the social aspect, the old tribal order, guaranteeing authority, tradition, and continuity, fell apart under the influence especially of education, which imparted European knowledge but few life values, and paved the way to an interregnum of individualism and self-seeking, flight from the land and unchartered urbanization, mounting unemployment, crime, and terrorism.

From the economic point of view, production and export quotas were easily raised but they in no way kept pace with the simultaneous rise in population and world trade prices. These young countries have indeed won the right to 'fly their own flag' but, economically speaking, they are still entangled in the jaws of foreign marketing systems.

A new wave of hope swept through not a few poor countries, upon seizing power through communism, because of youth training programmes, land reform, and the change from capitalist trade patterns to cooperatives. But after a few years of the experiment, disappointment was as widespread as elsewhere, or more so. For years there was hope for something from a distinctively African socialism. President Julius Nyerere sought to create a model between the extremes of capitalism and communism, based neither on self-interest nor on restricted freedom, but on the insight and spirituality of a people animated by its religious leaders. That too remained a beautiful dream. There is in Tanzania just as much corruption and crime and economic ruin as elsewhere.

As for the political aspect, the tribal conflicts and revolutionary coups, the massacres and other abuses of human rights, the over-bureaucratization and administrative inefficiency speak for themselves. G. Scotese's film *Tomorrow's Cannibals* is a striking portrayal of how in the southern hemisphere human and ecological disasters on the largest scale are impending and how there is no funding for measures to prevent them, because it has all been put into militarization. A cry of protest echoes and reechoes around the modern world. It takes courage not to lose courage in such a state of affairs.

The Almost Hopeless Situation of the Young Churches

I repeat that what I am doing is playing devil's advocate and speaking one-sidedly. Let me, then, point out that the young churches, with all their vitality, suffer from three ills that should be taken seriously.

91

First is 'latinitis'. Latin as a liturgical language has been translated into the vernacular. But even so the young churches have scarcely freed themselves of the restrictions of the Latin church. As soon as they wanted to take any real steps in this direction, so as to become local churches with their own garb and character, it was made clear to them that this does not suit the Latin church. That Latin church has made itself into an absolute. But it ought to consider that before it existed there was a Jewish church and a Greek church and that therefore there could be, alongside it, a Latin American, an African, an Asian church — and indeed on the basis of the same historical logic by which in the third century it itself developed a new cultural and political ambience. We may well have to wait until the year 2000 for the young churches to recover from 'latinitis' and become themselves.

The second is 'clericalitis'. This disease goes along with the first. The Latin church clings adamantly to one priesthood type — male, at least eight years of training, celibate — stemming from the Council of Trent. This too has been made into an absolute: either this priest or no priest! But it is the need of the community that should be the absolute, and the priest-type should conform to it. 'Clericalitis' has as a result that the number of Catholics to every priest is at present increasing everywhere, less so in Europe (where older priests still in office are delaying the crisis), more so in Asia, even more in Africa, and to a catastrophic degree in Latin America, as can be seen in Table 1.

Table 1

Catholics per Priest

	1970	1975	1980
North America	794	793	854
Oceania	800	912	1,025
Europe	1,020	1,026	1,090
Asia	2,000	2,050	2,311
Africa	2,326	2,803	3,383
Latin America	5,263	5,945	6,910

No one can take pleasure in such a development. Communities are growing, the number of priests is declining. In order to retain this priest-type, tens of thousands of communities are condemned to remain without a priest and without the Eucharist.

Thirdly there is 'secularitis'. Even though Third World persons are naturally religious, nevertheless the tides of modernism, scepticism, and secularism are passing through every continent. Christians are leaving the institutional church, and non-Christians are giving up their religion — in the millions. Enormous numbers of human beings are living their lives without religion, often without any real life-purpose. This certainly poses a challenge to evangelization.

Hoping against Hope

In spite of this gloomy picture, most Third World persons go around with a happy face. They have a wonderful talent for accepting things as they are, managing somehow, finding a way out or a solution, surviving, even taking joy in the midst of all the troubles of life. Surrounded by meaninglessness, they still find a meaning, and even in tragic periods of their history they hold fast to an ultimate value. What keeps them up is not hope in a distant future. It is not so much that they live by hope as by the experience and fulfillment of the present moment.

At times of celebration and the rites of passage — birth, marriage, death; seedtime, harvest — they sing and dance in a blissful mood that lets all the hardships of life fall away. Such days are to be thoroughly enjoyed, they are stepping-stones across the torrent of life. Then when the festival is over, they take up life again just as it is, accepting it as ordained by God — others have often wrongly called it fatalism. Westerners wonder how they can squander so much time and money on celebrations. But they just smile and wonder what use money is if it brings no added joy to life. These are two ways of life that certainly could have something to learn from one another. But life seldom follows the lines of a clear-cut synthesis; it leads itself to variations, and we all have to find our own way.

Now that the hope of the peoples of the Third World is understood better, we can pose the question of how, perhaps, they can temper the mettle of First World hope.

Grounds for Hope in the Third World

A Wider Horizon

Humankind is growing, with wider aims, wider horizons. When the Third World comes into the sights of the First World, it too can grow accordingly. Most of us have a keener awareness of other countries, other continents, than did our ancestors. Our children will be one-world citizens. Ecclesially too we are looking beyond the shadow of our own church spire. Europeans are thinking more and more in terms of dioceses and countries, even of the Western church as a whole, though the Americas, Africa, and Asia have developed a stronger continental church consciousness than have Europeans.

It remains for the First World to widen its field of vision to the Third World — and then to 'the ends of the earth'. In the past the Catholic Church was the church of the West with missionaries in other continents. In the meantime it has become a church in six continents. At the beginning of this century over 70 percent of all Catholics lived in the West; by the year 2000 over 70 percent of all Catholics will be living in the South. The church of the West has become a side aisle in the great cathedral of the world church. It must think of itself as just one segment of a much more voluminous church.

The West must grow along with the rest of humankind. Until a few decades ago the world centred on Europe. Today we live in a polycentric world. We must take all the ends of the earth seriously — politically, economically, culturally, and religiously. For better or for worse, we are growing together into one humankind.

We already have our feet set on the road to this new horizon. There are Third World groups, Third World shops, Third World study centres and seminars, development volunteer societies, and more. We have further to go along this road. The West should understand and fortify its role today in the interests of political and ecclesial symbolism: no longer Christians versus Muslims, East versus West, but all for each so as to give common service to human beings, to humanity. All ecumenical effort in its widest sense should be given fresh impetus.

Theological Self-understanding

In this wider horizon we can also see theology better in its

94

relativity and at the same time in its magnitude. This is not to object to the *philosophia perennis* and the scholastic theology bound up with it as *one* historical form of theology. But that anyone would export this abstract theology, this thesis and sentence theology, these 'eternal principles', as the only theology for all times and places seems to me dishonourable.

In recent years this theology has itself been profoundly revised and revitalized. The sixteen volumes of Karl Rahner's *Schriften zur Theologie* are an eloquent proof. Since the mid-1960s Third World theologians have been working on their own 'contextual theology', addressed to diverse cultural, social, economic, and political situations so as to give local peoples, in their de facto circumstances, a helping hand to Christian action based on the gospel. Such theology develops on the frontiers of life. It does not hoist persons onto a tightrope of airborne theses and laws but helps them find meaning in life, joy in living, courage to persevere. Such theology is not an academic pursuit but an aid to living. This is an auspicious, hope-filled development.

It is advisable that we should take this Third World theology to heart so as to remain open to dialogue on the world level and profit from it ourselves. Adolf Exeler has rightly called for a 'comparative theology' instead of the North Atlantic missiology that prescribed how church should be realized elsewhere. Comparative studies have led to a revitalization and enrichment of other disciplines. It could also happen in theology.

The Catholic Church has long cherished the humanities. Humanism in the present-day context would no longer imply going back to the sources of Western culture but looking outward on the sea of cultures surrounding the West. Concretely, this means that in the study of literature some class time would be devoted to the literature of Latin America, Africa, or Asia. In theology seminars would be held on important works of Third World theology.

Above all, the core theme of theology, Christ, brings us into fresh contact with the young churches and their environment. We have today moved on from confrontation and arrived at a real meeting with other religions and mutual discovery. We can accept today that the Logos, God's self-revelation to the human race that took concrete form in Jesus of Nazareth, was already always at work in all followers of every religion. Jesus did not let his hands be tied and his activity restricted by the imperfect work of his apostles;

he was already there long before the missionaries, in every place to which they came. If we today feel ashamed at the faults of the church, we can draw new hope from Christ, who always rises above those faults.

Pastoral Self-determination

The church has not merely to understand itself and the world better and better, but above all to realize itself in and for the world. For this the young churches provide the older churches with a good counterbalance to the overearnestness of the Western work ethic and efficiency. Many Westerners have become robots, machine tenders, and in so doing have forgotten how to be human beings, how to live in community, take part in family life, be glad to be alive, have faith in the future, respect old age. The young Third World peoples, with their spontaneous, warm-hearted ways, their hospitality, their joy in life in the midst of poverty, can heal the West of its insensitivity. From the childhood experience of assurance in a mother's arms, they retain a sense of security on through to the experience of final assurance in death, which they accept peacefully and as a matter of course.

A second service lies on the ecclesial plane — namely, an exchange of pastoral experiences. In this regard each continent has made its own way and has its own values to offer.

Latin America provides a shining example of how an old-style, clericalized, sacramentalist church can renew itself profoundly in a short time, thanks above all to two new experiments. One is liberation theology, which stresses that the gospel not only frees the individual from individual sin but frees a whole people from the roots of sin, selfishness, social sin, from the effects of sin objectivized in hardened socio-political structures of injustice, whether in world trade or in dictatorships of right or left; frees us also for full freedom in Christ and courageous action in him. The Medellín and Puebla documents never expressly use the term 'liberation theology', but they hammer home repeatedly that all theology and pastoral care should be 'liberating', because we all in various ways live in a captive state. We know now that we should bring peace not only when we enter a house (Luke 10:5) but also when we enter the socio-economic and political world. To it too

96

we should bring peace by all legitimate and practical means and introduce experiential salvation.

Churches in Latin America, formerly part of the system, have done all this, and boldly. In so doing they have lost much in privileges and prestige, but for all that they have won over the people. They enjoy much greater credibility. With this perception of integral salvation and 'commitment to justice as an intrinsic part of the gospel' (Synod of Bishops 1971) it should be possible to clarify the meaning of the Bible and the church to young Christians, unless they are already lost to reactionary and world-shy groups.

This liberating theology is followed above all in the basic ecclesial communities, the second specifically Latin American experiment, mentioned above in chapter 2 (p. 21).

All this should certainly not be exaggerated, as though now everything in Latin America is fine. It is estimated that at most perhaps 5 percent of the population is affected by this new life. But to have brought about this beginning of a committed lay church is noteworthy. What is arising here out of a situation of need, in a process of 'ecclesiogenesis' (Leonardo Boff), is a new kind of church whose significance for the future we cannot yet foresee. At the 1974 synod of bishops this experiment was made known and recommended, a first contribution from a non-European church to the church as a whole. African bishops who were impressed by it introduced it to their dioceses, and gave reports on it to the 1977 synod of bishops.

In Europe there are a great number of similar attempts arising from various historical backgrounds and variously accented, but all aiming at the same goal, to build up true Christians in the power of the gospel and of community. They are all expression of *one* movement, the movement of the Spirit in the church. Ferdinand Klostermann told me about how, on his retirement, he had set about finding out what there was of such basic communities in Vienna. He discovered much more than he had expected. It is up to the local clergy to uncover such spontaneous groups in parishes, encourage them, and incorporate them into the parish. They are where the church is active and a sign of hope.

In Africa also the church has changed since the mid-1960s. At that time an unchristian, antiecumenical fight over schools was

97

going on. Each church tried to excel over others in filling school places. Enticing away each other's teachers and pupils, even setting fire to school buildings, was all part of the game plan. But since then dialogue was inaugurated, a common position was taken up vis-à-vis the government, joint social action was undertaken, and twenty years later eighty collaborative work projects were going on in translating, printing, and distributing the Bible.

Apart from this, the African example of spontaneous liturgy and gatherings without a priest can help the West. For too many Westerners a 'proper' Mass is one read from the printed page, from the first sign of the cross to the final blessing. They ought to go to Kinshasa, or to many other places in towns or in the country, where the liturgy lasts up to two hours, where the participants, young and old, fully take part in praying and singing, with gestures and swaying of the body — a drama, the weekly festive witness of the people. Here spontaneity and creativity come to bear as intrinsic elements of a healthy liturgy. More room should be made for spontaneity in Western parishes, for the young especially, if liturgy is not to become again merely the performance of a rite, the fulfillment of a duty, to which the majority of the young attach hardly any importance.

The West faces a crisis in the priesthood that is only now coming upon us to any radical extent. Church circles stand before this knowledge as though helpless, lame, blank. It could be, and I for one am sure of it, that the shortage of priests is a providential necessity to declericalize an all too clerical church.

The shortage of priests can certainly be the reason why Christian community life is falling apart. By the same token, it can be the occasion for lay persons, the people of God, to at last become aware that they too are church, that from being a 'cared-for community they must become a caring community' (Zulehner), and they must not merely keep church-goers together but also, from their own experience of grace, develop a pastoral missionary zeal, for which most priests apparently have neither the time nor the inspiration. Sunday services held without a priest in the Southern continents can set a good example. By this I do not mean to say that a celebration of the word without a priest is ideal. But it can be a useful interim stage for bringing out possibilities among the laity. A few years ago three bishops from West Malaysia organized a one-month refresher course for all priests, with the additional aim that their communities, prepared for it beforehand, would for once have to spend a 'priestless month' and have to meet together without a priest to pray, sing, and read the gospel. Such courageous initiatives could be an inspiration for the West.

From non-Christian Asia the Christian world can receive suggestions and techniques for meditation. This has already been done, but outside the church, in the many Yoga, Zen, and TM centres in larger towns. This should no longer be, and change is already in sight. Several Catholic monasteries and communities practise this kind of meditation and teach others how to engage in it. As long ago as the early 1960s Jean Daniélou foresaw that the church as a whole could expect from Africa a renewal of the liturgy, and from Asia a renewal of meditation and mysticism. We are now beginning to see this happen.

In matters of a wider ecumenism Asia also offers an example of renewal. In the 1960s the small Asian Catholic community lived as a ghetto, celebrated the Latin liturgy, and condemned other religions, not knowing them from the inside. At that time there were thousands of priests and sisters, foreign and indigenous, with academic degrees for teaching, but scarcely one home-produced scholar. Since then the door has been opened. There are now among Asian priests a great number of the best specialists in non-Christian religions. Congresses are held from the highest level downward in many places, attended by leaders of different religions, and on the local level there are regular meetings for dialogue and prayer in common. Obviously only a small fraction of the Asian masses is reached by this. But it is something to have made a beginning and to be starting out on a new road.

We could well learn from this not to let ourselves be discouraged by the thousands outside the church but simply start to enter into conversation with some of them, to awaken in them a certain longing after the transcendent, give them a word of hope, whether when talking with them about their children in our schools, at funerals, or working for the common concerns of the town and the area. Pastorally we should not let ourselves be led by the totalitarian principle of 'all or nothing'. We must also be able to be satisfied with less Moreover we could, under the influence of Asia, bring much more courage to ecumenism. If Asians ask themselves how to practise ecumenism with non-Christian religions and practise *communicatio in sacris* because that is after all the deepest means of communication, Westerners ought not to be so niggling in their ecumenical approaches to other Christian denominations, with persons of the same faith and the same baptism, and overcome at last their out-dated divisions. 'Live hope, give hope' is a maxim that calls all Catholics, all Christians, all persons, to a common mission to the world and a joint pledge to work together for the world.

These are some of the urgings, some of the grounds for hope, that can be expected from the Third World. It could be that many Christians in the school of Christ, each with their own charism, could pick out many more still. In any case there has been something of a change in the churches of the Third World in their relationship with Western Christianity. They have gone from a one-way system to mutuality. Out of mutual giving and receiving, out of a sense of being both wealthy and poor, there comes *koinonia*, community, between the churches. The many local churches of the six continents can fully develop in their own way and then make an enriching exchange with other churches.

In contrast with the complaints about the church common in many circles, I have the conviction that the church today in many respects is in a much better state than in the 'good old days'. It is well to become aware of these experiences of renewal, these signs of hope, not letting ourselves be crippled by negative aspects but doing what we can with enthusiasm, for the inspirations we need for the task ahead of us will not spring up save in a climate of hope.

What I could here only sketch in outline rather than develop at length are certainly not prescriptions that can simply be carried out elsewhere. No church should simply copy any other church. The Holy Spirit is so rich in possibilities, has something special to say to each church, does not want carbon copies but originals. The basic attitude we can learn from other churches is to be just as honest in our analysis of our own situation as they are of theirs, just as open to the Spirit and as ready to work for renewal as they are, that we too should have the courage to go on gradually and entrust the rest to God. Then we shall create new hope because we shall see then that no *situation* is hopeless so long as *we* are hopeful.

Chapter Eight

Francis, Brother to All

Today we are surfeited with words, theories, analyses, reports, addresses, books. The important thing is to take the step to praxis, to change reality. We should like to see credible examples of how individuals or groups have in fact followed the way of the gospel, examples that will encourage us to follow along the same way. Examples speak louder than words.

Therefore I should like to close part 1 of this book with an example to follow, Francis of Assisi. Even if he lived eight hundred years ago, his light still shines. He is loved and honoured not only by Catholics but also by Protestants, by adherents of other religions, even by the unchurched — by all those in whom his love of nature, his trust in the heavenly Father, his universal brotherhood, awakens a certain longing. Whoever feels attracted by these values is 'franciscan'.

The following considerations could also be entitled 'Francis, prophet of a new apostolic presence in the world of today'. The two titles clearly overlap, for the new apostolic presence we are seeking must above all be founded on fraternity toward all, offering the gospel message to all.

Until Vatican II the Catholic Church was a somewhat introverted church. Quite apart from the fact that Christians as a whole make up barely a third of the world population and at present have no likelihood whatever of exceeding this proportion, it is scarcely an exaggeration to say that in the so-called Christian West 80 percent of the priests are occupied with 20 percent of the laity, the churchgoers. Priests spend 95 percent of their time in preaching, religious instruction, saying Mass, dispensing the sacraments, pilgrimages, and private retreats for Catholics. These Catholics in the main are introverted Christians; they are not proselytizers, nor are

101

they prepared for dialogue, nor are they missionary disciples of Christ.

With a view to a new apostolic presence in the world, therefore, we have to ask ourselves how to carry the gospel mandate beyond churchgoers, how to train churchgoers to be missionary, make them into out-going Christians. Francis of Assisi has something to tell us about this.

Prophet of Universal Fellowship

On May 24, 1982, Brother Leonard Lehmann, at the Pontifical Antonianum University in Rome, defended a dissertation entitled 'The Universalism in the Prayers and Letters of St. Francis'. The question is why work on such an obvious and important theme had to wait until 1982. In his Testament, for example, Francis writes:

God gave me such faith in the church that I was accustomed to pray: We pray to Thee, Lord Jesus Christ, *here and in all the churches of the world*, and we praise Thee because by the holy Cross Thou hast redeemed the whole world.

To a prayer that was well known at that time, Francis added the words in italics: 'here and in all the churches of the world'. Thus he practised a geographical universalism and, upon entering a church, he always thought of the presence of Jesus throughout the world.

In the unapproved *Rule of 1221* (no. 23) he calls on every individual, clerical and lay, man and woman, child and adult, all people, races, families, and tongues, 'and all persons in every place, those in the present and those to come', to continue in the true faith and a life of penance. Elsewhere he speaks also of the 'saints who were, who are, and who will be'. This can be called historical universalism. Francis always has everyone in mind. His universalism, which could be much further developed, can be a help to us now in the context of the present day.

The Franciscans (meaning the friars of the First Order, the nuns and sisters of the Second and Third Orders, the priests, brothers, and lay persons of the Third Order) have no monopoly over Francis. He belongs to the whole church and the whole of humanity. There are in fact not a few persons who are not called

Franciscans but who live that way of life more closely than do some Franciscans. Franciscans must always be measuring themselves against Francis, and assessing and renewing their commitment. Otherwise it could happen that Francis would rise up and bear witness against them.

As regards method, there are two ways of interpreting Francis. *Hagiographical* interpretation presents the saint as an exemplar of all virtues, especially poverty, simplicity, and love. *Prophetic* interpretation shows how Francis recognized the signs of the times, understood them as the will of God; how he had the courage to act accordingly despite all difficulties; and how through this he was a messenger of God for his own time and for today.

I shall follow this second course, especially in view of the fact that Vatican II, in its decree on the renewal of the religious life, *Perfectae Caritatis*, set up, alongside the three well-established retrospective criteria — the spirit of the gospel; the spirit of founders; sound tradition — a new, forward-looking criterion — namely, accordance with the signs of the time. Contrary to an opinion held in some ecclesiastical circles (can. 576 of the new Canon Law refers only to tradition, and the spirit of founders), I do not believe that accordance with the signs of the time has now been achieved definitively and so can be ignored. Renewal in the light of the signs of the times is an ongoing process and hence remains an ongoing duty.

Prophetic Deeds

Something could be said about the prophetic words of St. Francis. We could consider, for example, his letters to all the guardians of Franciscan friaries, to all the faithful, to all rulers of the peoples. But I shall confine myself to his concrete prophetic actions, actions that changed his life and the lives of others. We have today too many 'prophetic words' and protests. What is convincing is deeds, life. What exactly is striking and typical in Francis is that he did not protest but simply acted.

He did not condemn the feudal system of his day, which divided society into various levels and discriminated against the lower classes. But he himself did not distinguish between clerics and lay folk, doctors of canon law and the illiterate; he linked all in one fellowship.

He did not reproach the authorities for punishing robbers, but he himself went into the forest, sought out his 'brother robbers', and took them bread and wine so that they should no longer be in any need to steal.

He did not expose the social order for ostracizing lepers, but he himself went to them, embraced them, and spent time with them.

He did not criticize the church for its preaching against the heretics of the day, Cathars, Waldenses, Albigensians, and for having recourse to the arm of the state, but in his writings there is not the least polemical element to be found. He was content to live the Christian faith, full and entire, and thus to renew the church.[73]

He did not question the Crusaders, with all that went with them, especially because a Crusade had been summoned by the Fourth Lateran Council. But he himself, by his visit to the sultan at Damietta, radically altered the undertaking and set for all time an example of how monolithic thinking should be countered.

After two vain attempts to reach the land of the Muslims, he succeeded the third time. In a crusader ship he reached Egypt, where Christian soldiers were besieging the town of Damietta. The spectacle there presented to the visitor from Assisi was anything but edifying: tension and quarreling among the soldiery of the different countries and cities, drunkenness, greed, sexual excesses, and cruelty. One day eight Mulsim prisoners had their ears, noses, lips, and arms cut off, and one eye torn out. When Francis spoke of peace he was taken for a fool, a dreamer, a dangerous pacifist. When he expressed the idea of paying a visit to the sultan, the papal legate, Cardinal Pelagius, opposed him vehemently. He only gave in when Francis begged over and over again, and after the Christians had in the meantime suffered a defeat. Francis then spent several days in the sultan's camp, won his friendship, and so admired the Muslims for their repeated daily prayer that he afterward wanted to introduce something similar in Italy. Finally the sultan let him go with great respect and gave him gifts.

If we are to judge by tangible results, we have to say the visit was a failure. Francis did not achieve his purpose. He sought martyrdom, as Thomas of Celano stresses. That grace was not for him. He tried to convert the sultan and his people, as Bonaventure writes. This satisfaction was not afforded him. He hoped to bring about peace, put an end to the unchristian war, as modern authors emphasize (Basett-Sani and de Beer). In that too he did not succeed. The war raged on and when fresh reinforcements arrived, Damietta was finally taken after all.

Nevertheless Francis hardly returned home giving the impression of having been a failure. He had won the sultan's friendship. In him the sultan, until then only experiencing the Crusaders at a distance as enemies, came upon a true Christian, a man of God, a brother. Francis did not let himself be blinkered and bound by prevailing thought patterns, but went before the sultan without prejudice, with no show of force, simply as man to man, convinced that the sultan too, like anyone else, was honestly seeking the way to salvation.[74]

Underlying Inspiration

Behind all the deeds mentioned above, one thing is evident: Francis is a prophet, a pioneer of universal fellowship. He always opens a way to the other, builds bridges to the other, to all, most especially to the marginalized, social outcasts, the illiterate, thieves, lepers, the excommunicated, heretics, and infidels. He rejected all exclusivism.

By doing this he was going against the current of his day. The church was then and for too long afterward — in fact until John XXIII — against Jews, against Muslims, against the heathen, against heretics, against schismatics. It condemned all these groups without knowing them from the inside and without having tried to dialogue with them. Francis was against no one but sought to speak to all as brothers and sisters.

How did he come to this exceptional insight? Apparently his earlier inspiration came from the Psalms, which often cry out: 'All you peoples clap your hands, all the islands praise God!' The Book of Revelation too speaks of all peoples, languages, and nations. But all other Christians of his day knew those texts without thereby having their horizons widened. With Francis a special 'divine inspiration' (a favourite thought in his spirituality) must also have entered in, so that suddenly, quite clearly, there came to him an understanding of the all-embracing love of the heavenly Father whose goodness to all peoples Francis could never praise enough, and for whose goodness therefore he could never thank

God enough. His directly mystical passages should be noted — for example, in the unapproved *Rule of 1221* (no. 23).

Now we have to ask ourselves: What does this prophetic attitude of St. Francis in favour of universal fellowship mean for our time?

Franciscans as Pioneers of Postconciliar Fellowship

I am not speaking here of postconciliar *renewal* — but not because it is unimportant; its importance is taken for granted. It must, however, be understood that this renewal is not its own end; it is a starting point for the credible witness of the church in the world as a whole. Throughout history the councils have frequently spoken of 'renewal of head and members'. But in practice it was an inward-looking aversion to the world. The church has been too concerned with itself. And yet it was supposed to be 'church for others'.

An 'opening out' to others, to the world as a whole, typified Vatican II. In this the council followed the spirituality of John XXIII who, in his first audience, said very simply, 'Do not be afraid of me, I am Joseph your brother'. Within a very short time he changed the atmosphere of the world, arousing joy among Catholics, Protestants, non-Christians, Marxists, and diffusing a new spirit of all-inclusive fellowship.

Have we as yet in our apostolate brought this opening-out to its completion? We certainly did not need to imitate St. Francis's particular example for this. All must discern their own path in faith and be open in their own way to the divine indwelling, to the signs of the times. If Francis were among us, he would not advise us to search in early Franciscan texts, to learn how he reacted then, but would far rather say: 'Keep your eyes open, look for the signs of the times, and act!'

The postconciliar breakthrough required of us can be translated into postconciliar fellowship and postconciliar ecumenism in the widest sense, which should be in practice in the First World as well as in the Third.

Oikoumene and Protestants

Since John XXIII, Catholics are no longer fixated on what separates them from others, but joyfully look for what unites them to others — something far more important. They are coming to understand that the differences of constituent elements and traditions that still remain scarcely any longer justify rifts between the churches and that in basic communities, for example, we are already living a practical unity. Francis would not in any case lay much stress on structures but on the one Spirit, the one gospel, the one Lord Jesus Christ, the one baptism. He would not argue with Protestants, but read and discern the gospel together with them, act with them for a joint propagation of the Bible, and for a more just, more human world.

The Capuchins, along with the Jesuits, have in this regard a special duty of reparation. In the wake of the Council of Trent, they were the protagonists of the Counter-Reformation in Germanic countries. Many of them preached polemical sermons and wrote virulent books against their brothers in the faith. They ought today, in the wake of Vatican II, to be protagonists of ecumenism. May we all in our turn succeed in stirring up ecumenism on the local level so that we may become, if not prophets, then at least pioneers of postconciliar ecumenism. All Catholic communities should promote fellowship with Protestant Christians.

Oikoumene and Non-Christians

If Protestants and Catholics can join in ecumenism, it is with the non-Christian two-thirds of humankind that they should pursue fellowship. Francis would have rejoiced at the new theology of religions that helps us understand that God has always, to all peoples and in all religions, given grace and favour, sent revelation and prophets, raised up saints and mystics; that consequently those religions are paths to salvation and that the Holy Spirit can be heard speaking in their holy books. Francis would probably also today have wanted to spend some time in a monastery of Hindus, praying along with them as he once did in Damietta with Muslims.

The Indian Jesuit Samuel Rayan has said dialogue with Hinduism would take place in 'franciscan' language or it would not take place at all. What a challenge for Franciscans in Asia! There are today in Asia and Oceania 2,700 Franciscans, of whom 65 percent are Asians. This massive Franciscan presence ought to have its effect on interreligious dialogue. Even though dialogue with Islam has grown more difficult at the present time, it cannot be more difficult than it was in the time of Francis. And yet Francis found the way to Muslims despite all the difficulties.

Oikoumene and the Nonreligious World

The new state of things for the church consists in this: that there is no longer church in Europe and the Americas, and missions in Africa and Asia. Church is to be found everywhere — and everywhere in a missionary situation. In Asia and Africa there are very many 'not-yet Christians', in Europe and America very many 'no-longer Christians', no longer practising, no longer believing. In both East and West there are very many convinced, militant atheists.

It is an essential part of the call to evangelize the world that every disciple of Christ should proclaim God's kingdom. To be missionary today has nothing to do with geographical distances. All communities are surrounded by missionary situations challenging us to a missionary response. With faith in divine inspiration we can find the right way.

Oikoumene and the Poor

Here it is not a question of dialogue in a multitude of studies, in fine words, but in faith-filled actions, in a dialogue of life as we live poor among the poor to overcome along with them poverty in the sense of destitution. Consciousness of justice and peace has developed strongly in the church in recent years. Christians have to learn that the option for justice, for development, for disarmament, is not the same thing as 'going in for politics', but an essential part of evangelization, as the bishops' synod of 1971 declared.

In the Vatican each of these four kinds of ecumenism has its own bureau — the Secretariat for Christian Unity, for Non-Christian Religions, for Unbelievers, and the Papal Commission Justitia et Pax. The ten older congregations (for the teaching of the Catholic faith, for the bishops, for the sacraments, and so on) are directed more to the church as church, to the sacramentalizing of the faithful; the new secretariats are more for the kingdom of God, which extends beyond the church, to evangelization of all peoples, to dialogue with all. It is an open secret that a certain tension exists between the two groups precisely on account of their different orientations. Those doing pioneer work in one of the new secretariats must expect occasional conflict with the church establishment. But that is part of the hazard of 'franciscan' life.

In this connection we could go on to speak of ecumenism with the hierarchy, how it is possible to combine the prophetic charism with obedience to those in authority in the church. And we could discuss inter-Franciscan ecumenism: how members of the different historical Franciscan groupings could work together still more in various areas, so that Francis would not be divided, and with undivided will they could inspire the world with his example.

Franciscans as Pioneers of the Postnationalist One World

What has been said up to now from the ecclesiastical and religious standpoint is confirmed and furthered by purely human considerations. All the signs of the times point to the fact that the West has no other choice but to begin an opening outward, dialogue fellowship. Communications and information techniques have shrunk the world. In every living room and out to the most far-flung bush, almost, the whole world is linked by telephone, radio, and television. We all stand today in a relationship of interdependence economically, politically, and strategically: common surmounting of a crisis or common helplessness before approaching problems; advancing together in the striving for peace, or overwhelmed together in nuclear death.

History until recently was conducted under the sign of nationalism. Every nation looked to its own interests. On the main squares of European capitals stand memorials to the heroes who 'served their country'. Not infrequently they did so by making war on other countries and conquering them, or building up a colonial empire around their own nation.

In St. Paul's (Anglican) Cathedral in London there rests in the crypt amidst the memorials to the heroes of Trafalgar and Waterloo a simple plaque with the inscription: Sir Alexander Fleming. During his many years of intense laboratory study he discovered penicillin and thereby served not only his own nation but the whole of humanity. He betokens the heroes of the one humanity now on its way. We are still standing at the beginning of the history of *global* humanity. We are just beginning; we have as yet no experience in planetary thinking. We need pioneers, models, animators, integrating personalities, for the one humanity. It would seem that so far each continent has produced one such figure, a person who lived passionately for peace and unity: Mahatma Gandhi for Asia, Albert Luthuli for Africa, Martin Luther King, Jr., for North America, Archbishop Oscar Romero for Latin America, Francis of Assisi for Europe.

But may we not see in Francis of Assisi a symbol for all humanity? By his brotherly understanding of the whole of creation, which led him to call all creatures 'brother' and 'sister', and by his intuitive interpretation of the course of history shown by his prophetic deeds, he became the model for the whole of humanity on its way to postnational oneness. With all his unstinted love for the distinctive features of salvation history, the event of Jesus Christ and the fact of the church, Francis with his whole spirituality yet stood close to the theology of the first eleven chapters of Genesis, which treat of humanity as a whole. From the call of Abraham until today covers only 3,500 years, whereas the first eleven chapters in Genesis embrace the whole of human history, and so around a million years. God's first love was for humanity as a whole.

Will Francis indeed work the miracle of a united humanity? If so, it will not be the result of magic worked from a distance but only through persons who think as he did, who see their sole privilege as Christians is to be in the forefront on the way to a unified humanity, involved, and in this sense acting as models, because of believing with Francis that all human beings are God's children, that they are all on the way to the one God who has the sun rise on the good and the bad, and lets love divine fall like rain on the just and on the unjust, for the very reason that he is the prodigal Father, of whose love Francis was a herald and, more than that, a personification.

Part Two

Prototypes for the Year 2000

Introduction

There are various ways of calculating the future of the church. One can open up horizons starting from biblical inspirations, or from historico-theological or dogmatic reflections, and thus sketch indications of the future. I leave such studies to competent specialists and concern myself from a pastoral standpoint in this book with the church as it is, immediately visible, tangible, ascertainable, understandable, whose successes and trials, joys and sorrows, we not only take cognizance of but for which we take our share of responsibility and accountability.

Those of us who have been on the way with this church in the last twenty years from 1965 to 1985 may not have fully participated in what was happening in it. So I should like to analyze the geographical, statistical, pastoral image of the church in those twenty years, then project for the next twenty years the trends and lines of development that were at work during this time, and ask what must be the consequences of such development. Thus all who are ready to work with the church can have an approximation of what to expect.

This procedure might be called 'near futurology' or church pastoral projection or inductive trend study or empirical ecclesial extrapolation. This last term comes from mathematics. It is a method of projecting the validity and course of a law of development beyond the boundaries of the realm of the verifiable. Concretely in our case: on the basis of firm data — the known trends of those twenty years — the corresponding curve will, hypothetically, be determined for the next twenty years also. This forecast offers no certain proof but it does offer a reasonable probability. It holds good on the supposition that the trends at work today are not going to break off suddenly. The prognosis would have to be tested every five years or so and adjusted accordingly.[75] Such an extrapolation is the only way to know something of the future in advance and prepare suitable measures in good time.

Many who experienced the increasing pace of the twenty years from 1965 to 1985 have not sufficiently realized what an enor-

113

mously interesting period of time they had the good fortune to pass through. History to be written in the future will describe this period in terms of a qualitative leap within the framework of evolving world events.

In this time span, first, decolonization was completed. In its course more than a hundred new states appeared on the world stage. With that the 500-year-long division of the world into a few colonial powers and many colonies could finally be consigned to past history. The young nations gained a two-thirds majority in the UNO and a share in the making of world politics. In addition so-called world history, which until then was basically European history, gave way to the first stage of genuine world history, and lies like an open book before us. This promising advance, with its messianic euphoria, was followed all too rapidly by growing disillusion. As a result of unjust world trade conditions, the harsh oil crisis and its horrendous cost, ethno-racial warfare, national uprisings, corruption, and government inefficiency, there was talk of the 'sad ending' of the two previous development decades, 1960/70 and 1970/80.

This same period saw, secondly, a similar change of climate in the Western world. After the excitement of the 'American way of life' — unlimited progress — warnings soon sounded from the Club of Rome and other sources, and the label was changed to 'limited progress', coupled with political and economic crisis world-wide in extent. The shifting ground of the crisis in the West can be read in demonstration slogans: in the 1960s they enjoined 'revolution', in the 1970s 'ecology', in the 1980s 'death to nuclear death'.

In this same period of time, thirdly, church history turned a corner. It began with the breakthrough undertaken by Pope John XXIII and the Vatican Council called by him. The enthusiasms it kindled were dampened by the forces of reactionism, giving rise to a pathetic witticism that the postconciliar expectation of 'joy and hope' (*Gaudium et Spes*, the Pastoral Constitution on the Church in the Modern World) had been changed to 'sadness and resignation'.[76]

Fourthly, there came about, almost imperceptibly, a transition that will set the church of the future before quite new dimensions and challenges — namely, the shift of the centre of gravity in the church from the Western to the Southern world. I shall in what follows concentrate on this phenomenon because it is of inestimable importance for the church as a whole on the threshold of the third millennium and because its implications have not yet sufficiently taken hold of church members at all levels. In the same way as Luke in the Acts of the Apostles gave a description of the state of the church of those days, with its wonderful expansion but also with its tensions between co-workers for the gospel, above all the tensions abounding in the transition from a Jewish to a gentile church, so too a similar 'Acts of the Apostles' could be composed for every century. Probably no century would offer so many similarities with the first as our own: on the one hand, a unique missionary expansion; on the other, tensions consequent on the liberation, not now from the 1,000-year-old law of Moses, but from the almost 2,000-year-old law of the church, as we shall soon see.

If indeed 1965 to 1985 carry so much historical weight, what about the next twenty years! They will give the church the form it will pass on to the third millennium. It is fascinating to think about these forty years, to predict their outcome, and above all to become involved in their shaping.

Forty years — it spontaneously recalls by association the forty years of the people of Israel in the desert. It would appear that a span of forty years has been operative again and again, in forming a new stage of development in the mission of the church. Such an idea might be thought too fanciful. It does *not* offer any historical *proof* of anything. But a closer perusal of the track of this intuition could perhaps be informative:

30–70 A.D. The first age of Christianity, still living by the Spirit and the oral traditions of the Apostles.

70–110 The four Gospels are written down and reach their canonical form. During this period the definitive foundational constitution of the church is arrived at. It also marks the transition from a Jewish church to a gentile church — a transition sealed by the destruction of Jerusalem in the year 70.

310–350 The time of the Constantinian 'turning point'; the church becomes a state church with all its consequences, lasting through the Middle Ages and, to some extent, to Vatican II.

115

1520–1560 Reformation and Counter-Reformation, from Witten-
berg to Trent.

1620–1660 Beginnings of the Congregation Propaganda Fide:
founded in 1622, set on course by Secretary Ingoli
in 1658.

1960–2000 Vatican II and the postconciliar period, in a world
experiencing messianic, apocalyptic times, with well-
founded fears of nuclear warfare and longings for a
new era of peace and fellowship for all.

Chapter Nine

New Presence of the Church

Restructuring of the Church as the People of God

Today, when we are at the end of a stage in church history, we are for the first time fully conscious of how long, and to what extent the church was tied to the West. Statistics speak eloquently.[77] They show that the church at the opening of the twentieth century still had its centre of gravity in the Northern, developed world (Europe and North America), and only a very small part in the Southern, less developed, later to be called Third World — Latin America, Africa, Asia, Oceania (see Table 2a).

Table 2

Population Distributions ca. 1900*

		Northern world	Southern world
a)	Total Christian population		
	millions	474	83
	%	85	15
b)	Catholic population		
	millions	204	62
	%	77	23

---

* These figures are from the first edition of C. Streit's *Atlas Hierarchicus* (Paderborn, 1913), and were reckoned in the year 1912. I make the assumption that differences between 1900 and 1912 were negligible.

117

For the Catholic Church alone the disproportion was somewhat less marked, because Latin America, with 56 million Catholics, had already at that time altered the balance somewhat in favour of the Southern world (see Table 2b).

European preponderance is explained by the fact that for some fifteen hundred years Europe was practically alone in having the gospel: the other continents came under evangelization only when 'discovered' by Europe or when access to them became easier and was desirable. But also in the time since then Europe took the lead over the rest of the world. It had colonies everywhere. All lines of world politics, world trade, world church met in Europe. The colonial powers enjoyed uninhibited authority and could apparently rule the world, their dictates unopposed. It is only books published recently that have brought to light the opposition that was always there in colonized lands, but at the time it was internalized; mouths were kept prudently shut.

This period of European supremacy reached its zenith, and its termination, in the middle of the twentieth century. During the Second World War, Africa and Asia could still be mobilized for Europe. Very quickly after that the colonial empires collapsed one after the other.

In this same period an upheaval was also going on in the ecclesiastical realm, which created just as much of a radically new condition for the world. That is to say, the quantitative lead of Northern Christendom was visibly reduced because the North Atlantic world was demographically becoming more and more static, whereas the Southern world, because of the population explosion, especially in Latin America, and new converts, especially in Africa and Asia-Oceania, showed a strong growth for the church. The corresponding growth increase among Christians in the period from 1970 to 1982 is, strikingly, 0.26 for Europe, 0.63 for North America, 2.66 for Latin America, 3.55 for southern Asia, 4.04 for East Africa.

As a result, the shortfall of the Southern continents was almost eliminated by 1960, and from 1970 on they could take the lead.

The changing proportion of Catholics in the Northern and Southern worlds is tabulated in Table 3. In the 1960–70 decade, the proportion of Catholics in the South (Table 3b) rose from 48 to 52 percent (a 4% increase); in the following decade it rose from 52 to 58 percent (a 6% increase). If we project this latter increase

Table 3

World Catholic Population, North/South Proportionalities

	1960	1970	1980
a) Catholics (millions)			
Europe	220	259	272
North America	47	55	61
The North	267	314	333
Latin America	192	245	324
Africa	23	40	59
Asia	33	50	63
Oceania	3	4	6
The South	251	339	452
b) World totals (%)			
The North	52	48	42
The South	48	52	58

over the next twenty years (6% + 6%), Catholics in the South would comprise 70 percent of the total Catholic world population. Supposing the expected increase would be half as much again (9% + 9%), which is not unlikely, Catholics in the South would comprise 76 percent of the total Catholic world population; the North would be reduced to 24 percent — the reverse of the proportionality obtaining at the beginning of this century (see Table 2b).

Since 1975 I have been estimating, on the basis of other, much less precise, calculations, that approximately 70 percent of all Catholics would be living in the Southern world in the year 2000.[78] My predictions, therefore, appear to be well founded.

As for Christians as a whole, the pattern is not exactly the same, but the same tendency is clear (Table 4).

Table 4

Christian World Population Distribution

Christians (%)	1970	1980	2000
The North	57	51	40
The South	43	49	60

We are therefore, almost without noticing it, witnesses of a dramatic change in the Christian church; the predominance of the Western church has been radically altered. From being the church of the West it has become a world church with an evident presence in all six continents. The church, which from the beginning had boldly attributed to itself with unheard-of self-assurance the name 'catholic', now is for the first time actually catholic, 'spread over the whole earth'. At the same time one must certainly remain aware of the relative nature of this statement, for in 30 of the 263 countries of the world all Christians taken together form less than 1 percent of the population; in 86 countries they constitute from 1 to 50 percent of the population; in 147 countries they are the majority.

Restructuring of the Hierarchy

Cardinals

Quite apart from any question of the historical and ecclesial merits of the college of cardinals, it has in fact to be reckoned with. Of major interest here is the extent to which the distribution within the cardinalate has kept pace with the shift of emphasis described in earlier chapters of this book.

At the beginning of 1960 there were three Asian cardinals but still no Africans. Then in the consistory of that year two more Asian and the first African cardinals were named, so that these two continents counted six of the eighty-five cardinals, or 7 percent. Then the number of cardinals was significantly increased. In 1970 it reached 126, eight being Asians and six Africans, 11 percent of the total. In 1980 the ten Asian and eleven African cardinals made up 17 percent of the college. Latin America was well represented with twenty-one cardinals in 1980.

As of the consistory held in February 1983, of the 120 cardinals, 59 (49%) were from Europe (29 from Italy, of whom 20 were members of the Roman Curia), 12 (10%) from North America, 20 (17%) from Latin America, 14 (12%) from Africa, 11 (9%) from Asia, and 4 (3%) from Oceania. The Southern continents counted 49 cardinals (41%). There was still one major blemish: Latin America, with more Catholics than in Europe, had fewer cardinals than did Italy. Greater efforts should be made to reduce 'payments' on this 'mortgage' from the past.

The consistory held in May 1985 showed a decline in the proportionality of cardinals from the Third World. Of the 152 cardinals, 82 (54%) were from Europe, 15 (10%) from North America, 23 (15%) from Latin America, 16 (10.5%) from Africa, 13 (8.5%) from Asia, and 3 (2%) from Oceania. Although the Southern continents counted 6 cardinals more than in 1983, their overall ratio declined from 41 to 36 percent, due to the increase of cardinals from the North, from 71 (59%) to 97 (64%) — a trend at odds with the patterns of the world Catholic population.

Nuncios

With the increase in young states the number of nunciatures has also increased. In 1960 there were 42 nunciatures and 17 apostolic delegations; in 1970, there were 67 and 15; in 1980 there were 97 and 20. It can only be surmised how the increase in buildings and personnel is affecting Vatican finances. Of the 117 posts, 89 are to be found in the Third World.

I shall not repeat here certain criticisms that can rightly be made of the institution of nunciatures.[79] I limit myself to the question of how far the Vatican has fulfilled the conciliar wish that 'papal legates should as far as possible be drawn on a more representative basis from the various regions of the Church, so that the offices or central agencies of the Church may have a truly universal spirit' (*Christus Dominus*, 10).

I realize that this cannot be done overnight. Not just anyone should be made a nuncio; qualifications and previous experience

121

are necessary. The restructuring, however, went forward so slowly that at the Synod of Bishops of 1984, Bishop James Sangu of Mbeya (Tanzania) felt obliged to return to the matter. He gave, as commissioned by the other African bishops, a report on the state of evangelization in that continent. In his English text he wrote: 'We African bishops humbly beg that the papal legations should display more of the universality of the church — governments often ask us whether our church is a church of Italians — and be more integrated into the local churches'. The translation into Latin, however, prepared by a Roman secretariat, changed his request into a statement: 'The papal legations display the universality of the church and are integrated into the local churches.' When he protested, the bishop was told that the pope had approved *this* text and he must read it, which he did.

In 1970, of the 65 papal legates, 49 were Italian (75%); in 1980, of the 72 legates, 52 were Italian (72%). In the ten years, therefore, during which the request of the council should have been complied with, the proportion had gone down by only 3 percent. Proceeding at the same rate, it would be necessary to wait another 60 years for non-Italians to fill 51 percent of the top posts in Vatican diplomacy. What is behind this disproportionately Italian position so stubbornly maintained?

Bishops

Rome must be given credit for going forward courageously with appointing indigenous bishops. After an understandably somewhat difficult warming-up stage (1923, consecration of the first Indian bishop; 1926, the first six Chinese bishops; 1927, the first Japanese bishops; 1939, the first two African bishops), rapid forward movement ensued (Table 5).

The 293 African bishops make up 65 percent, the 408 Asian bishops 76 percent, of the bishops in their respective continents. At the same time it should be noted that there are included a number of expatriate bishops who have in fact retired but continue to live in Africa or Asia. Otherwise the percentages would be still higher. In any case, in the not far distant future the generation of 'missionary bishops' will be part of history. But they will live on in memory, as the founders of new local churches.

Table 5

The Escalation of African and Asian Bishops

Year	African bishops	Asian bishops
1951	2	31
1961	38	75
1971	133	126
1981	293	408

Priests

Along with joy at the expansion of Christianity in the Southern continents, one is struck by the evidence that the number of priests is in no way keeping pace. Everywhere, with the exception of Asia and Africa, their overall number (diocesan and religious priests together) is falling slightly (Table 6).

Table 6

Number of Catholic Priests

	1960	1970	1980
Europe	255,800	255,336	243,319
North America	69,578	71,907	71,354
Latin America	46,524	49,652	48,778
Africa	17,172	17,314	17,346
Asia	25,060	25,632	27,136
Oceania	5,594	5,729	5,667
Totals	419,728	425,560	413,600

The result is that the ratio of Catholics per priest is growing everywhere, even in Asia, especially in Africa, and catastrophically in Latin America (see Table 1).

This state of affairs will clearly continue to worsen rapidly. Priests in the North and 'missionaries' in the South are largely older, nearing retirement, replaced by young men. Two startling thunderbolts in this situation: Catholic U.S. missionaries from 1968 to 1979 fell from 9,655 to 6,455 (33%); the 7,845 Catholic missionaries from Germany (fathers, brothers, sisters, lay volunteers) show an overwhelming preponderance of older age-groups (Table 7).[80]

Table 7

German Catholic Missionaries by Age-groupings

Age-group	Percentage of total
Over 70 years old	30.9
Between 60 and 70	27.5
Between 50 and 60	12.2
Between 40 and 50	19.7
Between 30 and 40	9.3
Between 20 and 30	0.4

Without the young lay volunteers the outlook would appear much worse. How this is to continue in the next ten years can easily be seen. The young churches all have trouble in filling the gaps left by departing missionaries. There can be no question of an immediate increase in the overall number of priests. In addition the fact must be reckoned with that, as of 1980, twenty-five countries of the Third World were completely closed to foreign missionaries, twenty-four were half-closed, and eighteen further countries made difficulties over issuing new visas. Hence, in sixty-seven countries, accounting for 3.1 milliard persons, it is difficult or impossible for foreign missionaries to preach the gospel.[81] The scarcity of priests is a problem that demands much more study.

Restructuring of Church and Mission

Church in Six Continents, Mission in Six Continents

By a 1969 instruction from the Congregation for the Evangelization of the Peoples, missionary institutes no longer carried full responsibility for 'their' missions; local churches, from being the object and aim of missionary activity, became the subject and carrier of the gospel to their locality. Missionaries are now in the service of these local churches. They are no longer the masters but the servants, no longer sent from a distant church but invited in by a local church. They had to make a psychological about-turn in order to pass from the one category to the other.

But, if *missions* have come to an end, *mission* continues — that is, preevangelization of groups far from Christ. What is new is the insight that this activity is pursued in all the countries of the world. Therefore along with 'church in six continents', there is also 'mission in six continents'. There is no longer today church *and* mission, but church *in* mission. Wherever the church is to be found, it faces a missionary situation, a missionary challenge.[82]

Africa is indeed well on the way also to becoming a Christian continent, as can be seen in Table 8, which includes the baptized, catechumens, and sympathizers. For black Africa (that is, not including North Africa) the proportion could rise to 57 percent by the year 2000.

	Table 8			
	Christian Populations (%)			
	1900	1970	1980	2000
Africa	9.2	40.5	44.2	48.4
Southern Asia	4.1	7.1	7.6	8.5
East Asia	0.4	1.4	1.8	2.4
World	34.4	33.7	32.8	32.2

For the giant continent of Asia, which accounts for almost 60 percent of the world population, the outlook is less favourable.

125

Even if we today have a different theological interpretation of religion and consequently also another method for mission,[83] the church must also now as then say with St. Paul: 'Woe to me if I do not preach the gospel!' (1 Cor. 9:16).

With the unlikelihood that the total world population will get much beyond the present 30 percent line (Table 8, 'World'), we must ask ourselves what indeed God's salvific intention may be in this historical situation. Does God truly will the church to be the 'ark of salvation' for the continually lessening privileged few to be found within it, as was thought in the past? Or should not the church far rather, as Vatican II emphasized (e.g., *Lumen Gentium*, 1, 5, 9, 48, 59), be the beginning and germ of the kingdom of God, sacrament and sign of salvation for all? Should not the church see its chief work in simply proclaiming the existence of God's kingdom as a free gift of God to all persons of good will?

We can use in this connection the well-known model of concentric circles representing degrees of church membership: around the innermost circle of the faithful are positioned the lax, then the nominal Christians who are no longer practising. Further off again, but nearer to Christ perhaps stand those not indeed baptized but in sympathy with the church. Many of them already live in the light of the church, rejoice in the gospel, but for various reasons will not and can not change their religious standpoint. They could be called 'Gandhi Christians' after Mahatma Gandhi, who admired Jesus and his gospel, and was inspired and led by the same Holy Spirit as were the Christian saints.[84] This conclusion may be drawn from the ever more widely accepted theological principle that all major world religions are a work of the Holy Spirit. Pope John Paul II emphasized this twice in *Redemptor Hominis* (6 and 12).

The number of these Gandhi-Christians or sympathizers cannot be determined, but there are certain indications of its size. Thus, in government censuses many nonbaptized classify themselves as Christian. According to Vatican sources there were in 1980 in Africa 58.7 million Catholics; by state reckoning, however, there were 76.8 million. In censuses in Japan, where all Christians together make up 1.2 percent of the population of 118 million, 5 percent of Japanese list themselves as Christians, 22 percent call themselves sympathizers, and 33 percent have visited a Christian church at least once.[85] This happens especially on the occasion of weddings, for 10 percent of young couples want to solemnize their union in a Christian church and experience, along with their relatives and friends, an intimate sharing in the half-hour religious service, with hymns, Bible reading, homily, prayers, and the exchange of vows.

Opportunities for Evangelization

Further out in a wider circle from the sympathizers are the 'evangelized', who do indeed possess a certain acquaintance with Christianity, Christ, and the gospel, but have not yet openly declared it. The growing presence of Christ in all the countries of the world, together with mass media techniques, produces incomparably better opportunities for such evangelization in the widest sense than was possible before. D. B. Barrett has calculated, on a vast scale, the degree of evangelization in each country, according to a coordinated system of indicators — for example, the number of Christians, how long Christianity has been present in the area, the number of preachers or evangelists, the extent to which the mass media are utilized for Christian purposes, the number of bibles sold.[86] The results are tabulated in Table 9.

Table 9

Extent of Preevangelization

	1900	1970	1980	2000
Europe	99.7	98.6	98.0	99.5
North America	99.8	99.6	99.8	99.9
Latin America	97.3	98.7	98.7	99.6
Africa	23.1	69.7	74.7	85.5
East Asia	27.0	27.8	37.5	62.7
Southern Asia	25.4	52.9	65.2	83.5
U.S.S.R.	97.0	64.0	71.0	94.0
Average	51.3	61.4	68.4	83.4

With the exception of East Asia (China), we are thus at the point of reaching the goal of preevangelization, though of course there is

127

still a distance from here to 'bringing full awareness of', 'witnessing in the power of', the Holy Spirit.

It should also not be overlooked that Christianity, by its missionary presence in Africa and Asia, has set in motion a kind of unconscious osmosis by which many Christian considerations, orientations, and values have entered into general ethical consciousness, legal processes, national constitutions, even non-Christian religions. Similarly, in the secularized West, there remain many Christian values that influence the general attitude toward non-Christian peoples.[87] What might there not be said about the opportunities for evangelization resulting from the growing presence of non-Christians in Western countries! In Germany there can be counted at present 1.8 million Muslims.[88] Something similar applies to other countries and other religions.

A Ground Swell of Unbelief

The somewhat optimistic overview of evangelization cannot allow us to neglect the meteoric rise in this century of secularism, agnosticism, and areligious or antireligious atheism.

It is difficult to take in this many-sided picture. Its causes lie in the Marxist critique of religion, as also in the scientific and psychological emancipation of 'humanity come of age', which boasts that it can solve all the problems of this world and get along better without faith than with it. Dietrich Bonhoeffer believed we were entering on a fully religionless period, when God would no longer be a 'stopgap' figure, when we would no longer need God 'as a working hypothesis', when God would no longer 'stand on the outer edge of our lives but in their centre, in the fullness of life, in interpersonal relationships'.[89]

T. Moser has something radical to say on the subject when, in an imaginary conversation, he accuses God of making persons long for divine consolation, keeping them clinging and childish, threatening them with the pains of hell and the gnashing of teeth, giving them a taste for sadism. He breathes again at having got over God, 'that great sickness', at being free of this 'giant crutch', letting him have 'a sense of power'. With understanding he, a psychiatrist, takes this stand:

> Insofar as others may need you so as not to suffer any further, I will not say anything against you. It is enough for me that I no longer need you. . . . Human countenances will take the place of

128

yours because yours was inhuman. My eyes are learning to see, since you no longer darken my horizon.[90]

Concrete manifestations of unbelief vary in urban and rural environments, and from one country to another. There also seems to be a countermovement at work that gives the lie to the theory of total secularization. P. M. Zaehner affirms that in Austria 34 percent still continue to call themselves very religious, 27 percent religious, 21 percent a little religious, and 18 percent nonreligious. In the city of Vienna certainly, he thinks, the proportion would be reversed. He speaks also of secularization being checked, to the extent that from 1970 to 1980 the number of the 'this-worldly', who do not believe in God, who say that everything finishes with death, came down from 21 to 16 percent, while the section of the 'other-worldly' has risen slightly, from 44 to 46 percent.[91] For 'Catholic' Munich it came as a shock when statistics confirmed that 52 percent of the marriages with both parties Catholic were no longer celebrated in church, that 42 percent of the newborn were no longer baptized, that in one year more persons left the church (6,079) than were baptized into it.[92]

In the U.S.A., surveys have shown that 50 million 'unchurched people' must be reckoned with, even though a strong religious upsurge has also been registered; six out of ten Americans hold religion to be 'very important'; a third of all adults claim to have newly discovered religion in recent years, feeling themselves reborn in faith.[93]

Concerning the spread of disbelief and substitute religions worldwide, D. M. Barrett, the expert with the best overall view, maintains:

From a minimum presence in 1900, scarcely 0.2% of the world population, these cults have shot up to 20.8% of world population in 1980. They are currently growing at the unusual rate of 8.5 million new 'converts' every year and will apparently in 1984 already have one milliard adherents. A large section of these members are the children and grandchildren of people who have practised the faith at some time in their lives. No Christian tactician in the year 1900 would have conceived of such a massive falling away from Christianity in his own country from what it was in the nineteenth century.

This fate has not befallen only Christianity but all religions.

129

Buddhism, for example, has indeed, thanks to an intensive missionary activity, expanded in recent years in eighty-four countries, but at the same time is losing annually around nine hundred thousand adherents to agnosticism.[94]

Who will take the necessary steps from insight to corrective action? The Christian West of old has become the most difficult of mission lands and remains almost helpless before the new challenge. France and the U.S.A. were ahead of other countries by a few years in regard to missionary pastoral work.[95] The symposium of the European Bishops' Conferences, October 4–8, 1982, in Rome, was willing to grasp the nettle, but did not go much further than passing a resolution to devote another longer, better-prepared symposium to this subject. Will the inspiration come from the missionary churches of the Third World?

Although this has not been an exhaustive survey of the new church presence, one thing clearly emerges: the church stands before a new historical epoch, its world epoch, with as many opportunities as hazards. Extraordinary times such as these are the hour of the Spirit. Just as, at the beginning of creation, when the earth lay bare and formless, the Spirit of God moved over the waters, and chaos became cosmos (Gen. 1:11–2). Just as when the young church had to dare the leap into the pagan world but did not know how, the Holy Spirit went into action and spoke to the church of Antioch, given over to prayer and fasting, 'Separate for me Barnabas and Saul for the work to which I have called them' (Acts 13:3), and the triumphant course of the gospel began. Just as in the Middle Ages, when the church was caught up in power and wealth, Francis of Assisi and other reformers realized 'in the divine indwelling' what the church should be and do, and once more restored its force to the gospel. Just as in the nineteenth century, when the need for general education arose and the European colonization of Africa and Asia had come about, men and women, filled with the Spirit, arrived on the scene and founded educational, medical, and missionary institutes. Who and where are the leaders, the prophets, those drawn by the Spirit, who have ears to hear what the Spirit has to say to the church on the road to the third millennium? (Rev. 2:7).

Chapter Ten

New Structure of the Church

Motives and Models

The preceding chapter, with all its statistics, poses questions with respect to church structures. A grown-up cannot wear the clothing of childhood. A church of six continents cannot wear the attire and insignia of the Western church. What was acceptable when the church was commensurate with the Christian West looks odd, anachronistic, imperialistic even, in other continents. There is no hobbling on one leg into the new world epoch, the other leg chained with the weight of Western tradition.

Structures are not the most important thing for the church. They are secondary. They could even be called a necessary evil. What Jesus wanted most was not structure, organization, authority, by which persons should attain salvation; it was groups of followers scattered over the world who lived his gospel, exemplified it to the world, and in this way extended the circle of disciples. But wherever groups are formed, there needs to be a certain order. It was Jesus' intention, and was brought about by the Spirit of Jesus, that various charisms, various offices of leadership, develop in the communities, which lent the young church, along with all its freedom in the Spirit, a certain structuration.[96]

Then, in the Constantinian era, these *ministri*, servants of the community, became a social class with privileges, titles, and lands, monopolized more and more all the offices in the church, in practice identified themselves with the church, and downgraded the laity to merely passive membership. When the Reformation called such a church into question, the Counter-Reformation defended these offices all the more, and this continued right up to the eve of the Second Vatican Council. In the well-known Tanquerey dogmatic textbook, on which many generations of priests were brought up in many countries, sixty-two pages are devoted to demonstrating that Christ founded the church as a true society, a

131

hierarchical society, a monarchical society; as a kind of after-thought, two more pages treat of the church as the Body of Christ and Bride of Christ.

Then the council broke over the church like a new pentecostal storm. Catholics could again be inspired by the image of the early church. As the fruit of authentic dialogue between renewal-minded bishops and theologians came *Lumen Gentium*, which 'declerical-ized' the church and, against great opposition, completed the shift of emphasis from a juridical, apologetic to a charismatic, com-munal church image.[97] Much that is fine and hopeful has since been said and written to show how this image became a new reality in living communities, renewal groups, basic communities, all over the world.[98]

The Vatican II rejuvenation has not permeated the whole church. In a novel, Anton Seipolt has Dionysius of Ephesus, a martyr from the third century, come back to life and wander through our period in the church. He is surprised and distressed to find how much is said in a Sunday sermon on morals and money but how little on Christ, and how below the pulpit there are no happy faces to be seen. He says to the archbishop, 'They preached to us in our day about what it means to be baptized. After that, commandments and prohibitions were no longer necessary'. To which the arch-bishop replies, 'We know we have to break new ground. But we are afraid'. Dionysius comes to the realization that 'the world is full of good persons, only they do not always get along together. They think each other hopeless. That takes the shine off their goodness'. His message is always the same: 'Rejoice!' Churchmen remark: 'Is that all?' When Dionysius falls asleep again and dies, they think, 'Sleep on, Dionysius, sleep more soundly this time! What did you wake up for?'[99]

In other words, despite Vatican II, not everything is right with the church. The interests of the church as a church of the Spirit, of love, of the good news, continually conflict with the interests of the institutional church, which has resisted change. The problem for the contemporary period in the church consists precisely in that the concepts having to do with the new image of the church — con-cepts propounded in many conciliar and postconciliar documents — have not yet been translated into structures. To that extent it is still very important to speak about structures.

Our knowledge of history awakens a certain anxious foreboding that threatens to rob us of confidence. How hard it was for the church to replace the mythological, biblical, geocentric worldview with a scientific, Galilean, heliocentric worldview; to acknowledge the good intentions of 'heretics' in the Middle Ages and today and not stigmatize them too hastily, without dialoguing; to fully accept modern, liberated, critical, scientific thinkers as co-workers and come to terms with the new age.[100]

Father Alfred Delp, who died a martyr under the Nazi regime, wrote prophetically:

> The churches, because of the lifestyle they have developed to cope with problems in the past, handicap themselves. I believe that whenever we will not willingly break away from this lifestyle for the sake of life itself, history as it unfolds will cut us off like a thunderbolt.[101]

For the last hundred years the church has lost one social class after another in the Western world, not as a whole, but the majority certainly: first the workers, because it did not take their problems seriously enough; then the intellectuals, because it would not accept the autonomy of science; then the men, because they grew tired of being treated like children; then the young, because they had no patience with the ecclesiastical mentality; and finally the women, because they form the main contingent at the basis of the church but have no voice at the top. There are still the elderly left; they will remain true to the church. But how can the church fulfill its historical mission with only *their* help?

Now the Third Church is rising as a new hope. Much will depend on whether the Northern church can be magnanimous enough to allow this Southern church to become itself and not remain merely a duplicate of the 'mother church'.

Meanwhile, here too the process of liberation is running into snags. Slamming on the brakes is no way to get moving. M. Singleton, referring to Moses' words to the pharaoh, 'Let my people go...' (Ex. 5:11), sums up his study of the church is West Africa:

> The priests want to go ahead but the bishops will not allow it. The seminarians want to go ahead but the staff will not allow it. The women want to go ahead but the men will not allow it. The young want to go ahead but the old will not allow it. The Nigerians want to go ahead but the expatriates will not allow it. The Protestants want to go ahead but the Catholics will not allow it. All of whom met in the course of this enquiry want to go ahead but power groups will not allow it.[102]

133

There may be some exaggeration here, but there is truth also. In the end these groups will go ahead, for the gospel of liberation will not be held back.

The whole of history teaches that to survive is to change. The history of evolution shows how plants, animals, and human groupings that do not adapt to their changing environment go under, whereas others, alert to the best opportunities for survival and development, reacted at the right time — and not just by taking small steps but to some extent even sizable leaps — and found an opening to new horizons. The same is to be seen in the history of civilization: cultures that did not know how to read their times, did not write along the lines of their times, became illiterate again, and had to leave the stage. This is why the experts of the Club of Rome exhort world leaders to take up the challenge of the present time by creative, innovative study. They must come to realize that, given the de facto resources of the world, unlimited human demands can no longer be entertained as they were in past decades.[103]

Under pressure from such signs of the times, a great number of national and international church congresses have been held in recent years in a feverish race to offer more understanding to the young churches and to enable them to find their way to be free. The crux of the matter is how the Catholic Church, at present the greatest 'world empire', is to hold its scattered and divergent masses of members together in unity and at the same time uphold their right to individuality. Perhaps we could learn something about this from other world empires in history.

It remains a matter of astonishment how ancient Rome, with the transportation and communication systems of the time, could hold under its yoke the whole of the then known world. Roman wisdom for centuries understood how to hold in balance a few basic centripetal formulas — a military presence, common coinage, ultimate judicial authority — with the centrifugal claims of a relative autonomy in the provinces. Local religions and languages, customs, usages, and laws, were left untouched so long as they did not conflict with the Roman will for power. A spontaneous process of free assimilation went on — for example, the romanizing of Germanic tribes, but equally the germanizing of the Romans. When the empire finally came apart, it was not due to its structures but to a biological factor. As a result of the growing standard of living and the corresponding relaxation in morals among the

Roman populace, there appeared an increasing fall in the birthrate. The dwindling ruling class no longer kept up with the 'barbarian' masses.[104]

The British empire, which reached from Gibraltar to Cape Town, from Suez to Singapore, was sustained by quite similar principles. A system of so-called indirect rule was followed: rulers and customs already in place were given recognition; only an over-all superintendence was established. So from one territory to another, considerable judicial and cultural diversity existed. Local governors enjoyed almost unlimited freedom of control and took decisions on the spot as seemed best to them.[105]

The present-day 'world empire' of the United Nations, with allied organizations — UNESCO, FAO, WHO, and others — had to learn from bitter experience the need for decentralized policies. At first, grandiose world plans were elaborated with a vast output of surveys and reports. But they lost sight of reality and changed nothing at the control centres of real life. Then there was a changeover to national projects, and again later to grassroots-level projects. Initiatives were left to local communities, with a U.N. agency to supply help in the form of money and expertise, and only insisting on certain general principles for lessening the gap between rich and poor: the needs of the people come before exports; the people should be allowed to share in decision-making and responsibility, and the like.[106]

The church can certainly learn something from all these experiences. John Naisbitt, in his *Megatrends: Ten New Directions Transforming Our Lives*, points out how on the secular level in the U.S.A. new tendencies are setting in: from a national to a world economy; from centralization to decentralization; from representative democracy to direct democracy; from hierarchical leadership to group efforts; from either-or attitude to the multiple-choice option.[107] He notes that such tendencies are like a drove of horses: it is easier to ride in the direction they are running — that is, politicians should take note of such tendencies, otherwise they risk losing votes. In the church the 'politicians' responsible have no need to fear losing votes, but should they not take seriously the tendencies, the signs of the times, they would be partially to blame if the gulf between people and hierarchy widens yet more.

Looking at the new state of the church in six continents, Karl Rahner has spoken of the pressing need for a pastoral strategy for

135

a world church.[108] He does not mean that all churches should now be tailored to the same pattern but that certain basic thrusts should be applied and certain fundamental structures formed so that within the context of a 'world pastoral strategy' all churches should recognize and develop their own initiatives. Pastoral care is an applied science. It has to start from the concrete situation, which differs from country to country, from one continent to another. Most of the Latin American countries have each their own pastoral plan with certain basic points in common, taking their inspiration from Medellín and Puebla: evangelization before sacramentalization; option for the poor; church in the framework of local culture, and so forth, which are concretely suited to the situation in each country and to which clergy and laity are committed.

Among the most important basic elements for a world church are decentralization and pluriformity. A generalized framework of guidelines such as these should not have to be fought for by a local church in a sort of defiant revolt but be recognized by Rome as requirements and signs of the times, to be legitimized with the calm acceptance that unity in the church will not be imposed through human force, but that one Lord, one gospel, one baptism, one faith, one love (Eph. 4:5) are in the end sufficient to hold a world church together.

When I develop these basic proposals in what follows, it will appear to some to be futuristic, utopian wishful thinking. In the present era, which follows rather the tendency toward rootage and consolidation, no great strides toward this utopia are to be expected. That does not prevent us from thinking that at the proper time the wind will blow again from another quarter, that the Eastern churches at least in the twenty-first century will achieve what they are seeking, and that therefore minds should be directed toward such possible models. Rightly is it said: one person's utopia remains a dream; when ten join in, it becomes feasible; with a thousand it becomes reality.

Constructive criticism out of love for the church is surely more helpful and more according to the gospel than is indifference or apathy. I appeal to a favourite expression of St. Paul, with which his biographer Luke also closes the Acts of the Apostles, as a clue to the whole of succeeding church history — namely, that Paul committed himself to the kingdom of God 'in all sincerity' (Acts 28:1).

Decentralization: a Postulate

The trend of contemporary history runs entirely in the direction of a united human race. After the long centuries of history under the aegis of nationalism, we are today faced with the alternative: either more universality, more fellowship, on the world level, or we risk the revolt of the poor against the rich, and nuclear war between the superpowers. All aspects of politics, economics, and strategy have taken on today a planetary dimension, quite apart from the fact that mass tourism is flooding the world and heavy technology covering it with motorways and concrete slabs.

As though in reaction to this, so as not to be swallowed up in an anonymous world, a new nationalism is appearing, a return to one's own culture, one's own language, one's own history, with a somewhat exaggerated but understandable emphasis on national identity. Similarly, as an interim phase, there has also been for some time a conscious macro-regionalism: the various continents are exercising continental consciousness, however fragile as yet, and so too the Arab bloc, the Eastern and Western blocs, and the Southern bloc. Thus, after the long period of monocentrism coterminous with eurocentrism, the new age of polycentrism has dawned.

Similar developments took place also within the church. Following on the frontline local churches and patriarchates of the first millennium, the papacy then increasingly extended its political and ecclesiastical power. With the loss of the papal states, its political significance declined but it strengthened its ecclesial standing all the more through the Vatican I definition of infallibility and universal primacy. We should not forget that this council was interrupted by the entry of the Piedmontese troops into Rome and as a result a further document, on the bishops (today we would say on the local churches), was not forthcoming. To that extent the council was unfinished, remaining one-sided. Only one pillar of ecclesiology was erected, that of central monarchical power, which was to lead to an overriding centralism.

After a delay of almost a century, Vatican II then erected the second pillar by filling in the teaching on the bishops, the local churches, collegiality. That led to various new structures such as the national conferences of bishops, the symposia of continental bishops' conferences, the Roman Synod of Bishops. These bodies have already contributed much in exchanging useful information, giving new directives, conscientizing bishops and people, uniting the church. Clearly, however, the required balance between the two councils has not yet been struck, between the central primatial authority and peripheral collegial authority. Collegial structures are still seen too much as being at the service of the primacy, instead of the other way round. At an international and interconfessional colloquium in Bologna in 1980, a critical balance sheet of the postconciliar period was drawn up. It was unanimously affirmed that the preconciliar image of the church was still too much in effect, and ecclesiastical office, the primacy, the universal church plainly overemphasized to the neglect of community, collegiality, the local church.[109]

Pentarchate

The first step toward ecclesial macro-regionalization has already been taken. The Latin American bishops were the first to take the initiative; in 1956 they founded the Latin American Episcopal Council (CELAM), which for a long time gave unprecedented stimulus toward renewal of the Latin American church. Analogously Africa has SECAM (Symposium of Episcopal Conferences of Africa and Madagascar), and Asia FABC (Federation of Asian Bishops' Conferences). The Council of the European Bishops' Conferences (CCEE) has — like Europe itself — the greatest difficulty in overcoming divisive structures rooted in history in order to create a continental consciousness and give new impetus to overcoming the threat of secularism. All the while the bishops together with the pope have been at great pains to revive reflection on the Christian heritage of Europe.[110]

Each continental church has its own character and its own problems with which to contend. At the Synod of Bishops in 1974 Cardinal Karol Wojtyla gave an account of the state of evangelization, saying that in Africa the subject of the africanization of Christianity held the foreground; in India, dialogue with other religions; in Latin America, liberation; in Europe and America, secularization.[111] The various continental churches are spurring one another on in a healthy rivalry. It could, however, turn to animosity. At international conferences it has been felt that the Latin Americans, with 'their own' theology and pastoral experimentation, give an impression of superiority and were leaning in the direction

138

of a new ecclesiastical hegemony and imperialism, something that easily provokes a defensive counterreaction.

These continental bishops' conferences may acquire wider powers in the future and be allowed to decide many questions arising from the specific viewpoint and situation of their particular continent — for example, the appointment of bishops, liturgical regulations, beatification and canonization processes. In this way the system of pentarchy, which regulated the relationships among the churches in the first Christian millennium, would appear again in a more contemporary form.

At that time churches that had been founded by Apostles or had acquired a special significance because of their political situation, adopted a leadership role and developed into metropolitan and patriarchal churches. It was virtually impossible for all bishops to maintain contact with all the others but the patriarchs at least did so among themselves and thus formed one church through an extended autonomy. These five patriarchates (the *pentarchia*) were Jerusalem, Antioch, Alexandria, Constantinople, and Rome.

The Roman patriarchate, meaning the Western church, then acquired a commanding position and, although earlier every episcopal see was 'catholic and apostolic', actually came to identify catholicity with 'romanicity'. But neither the classic ecclesiology nor the ecclesiology renewed by Vatican II canonizes this identification.[112]

A second step toward macro-regionalism may very well come about when existent continental ecclesiastical structures will be enhanced and permitted to settle continental problems within a universal legal framework not so detailed as the present codex. The bishop of Rome still carries today as one of his official titles 'patriarch of the West'. It is conceivable that in the future other continents too could have a kind of patriarchate.

A special case in this sphere is that of China. A church calling itself catholic cannot overlook the most populous nation in the world, which has topped the one milliard mark and constitutes 22 percent of the world population. Pope John Paul II, even more than Paul VI, seeks to make contact with China.[113] A precondition for acceptance would be — along with breaking off diplomatic relations with Taiwan — recognition of the Patriotic Chinese (Catholic) Church and its bishops. Certainly we cannot expect that these bishops, with their strongly nationalist consciousness, would

139

align themselves with Rome exactly as other Catholic bishops do. Why should Rome not be prepared for a magnanimous compromise and make China into a patriarchate with all the corresponding privileges?

At the first meeting between leading Christians from China and the West in October 1981 in Montreal one Chinese bishop said:

> We think of ourselves as an experimental laboratory. We are testing out what the churches in other continents are also seeking and will eventually achieve, an autonomous local church in unity with all the churches, but without the outdated dependence on Rome for everything.[114]

Certainly in this connection the danger of state-established churches, completely subservient to the state and not daring to speak freely, is not to be overlooked. Recourse to Rome and its moral authority will always be to the good.

Continental Councils

Conciliar history gives us valuable information on this apparently utopian suggestion. There were in the past so many ecclesiastical assemblies on various levels that it is far from easy to distinguish between ecumenical councils and regional synods. The latter often acquired quite as great an importance as the former. They not only promulgated pastoral directives but rendered decisions in matters of faith and discipline. The synods of China, Japan, and Korea, for example, bear witness to the concern for the founding and growth of local, popular, individual churches within their own cultures. The Congregation Propaganda Fide, knowing that a living expression of Christ's universal message could not be achieved from Rome, did not stop such synods but rather encouraged them. Quite frequently decrees of such synods have become directives for universal church law.[115]

In this light we can recognize that present-day synods on different levels, with their purely advisory character, are far from being in line with history. They are too much imbued with fear from on high, fear of Rome; and fear from below, fear for the autonomy of individual bishops. The truly synodal character that has continued in the Eastern churches from the beginning — and was also found in Rome at its beginnings — has not yet come to birth in the Latin church, which overemphasized the monarchical style of governance.

At present there is above all in Africa talk of a desire for an African council so as to break out of the vicious circle of the theory and the practice of inculturation.[116] According to some sources, however, leading African bishops are setting the idea aside. Are they afraid of taking responsibility?

The Appointment of Bishops

From the time when bishops were chosen by public acclamation, and when later courts and states exercised their influence by a veto, is a long way to the present-day system whereby Rome has the whole matter exclusively in hand. Although this no doubt has many advantages, yet many objections can be made to it on theological and pastoral grounds.[117] The appointment of a bishop is certainly by its very nature a thorny problem in many respects and one on which it is hard to pass fair judgement from outside. But, in the first place, everything is now done with the greatest secrecy. The local church as such has little say in the matter. In some cases the appointee has not been consulted. The apostolic nuncio can ask advice from whom he wills and then 'touch up' the candidate's profile with an airbrush. Then he sends the recommendation to Rome with the matter basically decided in advance. Secondly, because of this procedure, an appointment is often long delayed. Thirdly, Rome thereby practises a kind of ecclesiastical inbreeding, selecting only candidates who are completely 'in line', beyond the dictates of necessity. Thus a stop is put to the emergence of new ideas in the church.

If, however, bishops subsequently act according to their prophetic charism and are no longer a paragon of conformity, or if even an episcopal conference goes its own way too doggedly, Rome can play another card, packing such conferences with young bishops of inflexible loyalty, and therefore taking care that the church should everywhere be Roman, never Dutch, Brazilian, or Indonesian. After Vatican I there was no denying Rome the right to appoint all bishops. Whether that should still be done after Vatican II and in this manner is another question.

Like an islet in the open sea stands Switzerland, the sole instance in the Western church where bishops, according to a long-standing vested right, are collegially chosen by the cathedral chapter and

141

confirmed by Rome. In the Eastern churches in communion with Rome, the synod chooses a bishop. Will anyone venture to say that this system is not ecclesiastical or has not proved itself of pastoral value?

The Roman Synod of Bishops

Before Vatican II came to an end, some bishops were already apprehensive about the implementation of the council. They circulated the idea that some kind of postconciliar body should be set up to assist the pope and the Roman congregations in their legislative activity. Some thought it should be in a deliberate capacity (Cardinal Alfrink); others, merely advisory (Nuncio Oddi). Even a deliberative function would not, of course, annull papal prerogatives, as every council has shown. With the motu *Apostolica solicitudo* of September 15, 1965, Pope Paul VI instituted the Synod of Bishops and gave it an advisory character.

Since then, this synod addresses every three years the main events in the life of the church. So far so good. But questions remain. Why only advisory? Would it not be a more genuine expression of collegiality if the bishops not only reviewed pastoral questions but also, together with the pope, shared in ultimate decision-making for the church as a whole? Did not Paul VI almost break down under the cross of his lonely responsibility? What sort of a civil government would it be that always showed a tendency to conservatism and concern for salaries and careers if it had not a parliament alongside it, transmitting to it new suggestions and assignments? Why must in Rome alone the executive be coupled with the legislative in one and the same authority, and standing above the Synod of Bishops?

It is easy to diagnose at present a certain unease in the Roman Synod of Bishops. It springs from the fact that the final document of the synod of 1980, *Familiaris Consortio*, not only did not take cognizance of some findings of individual discussion groups but even of the synod as a whole, as a careful study has shown.[118] Further, the American bishops were openly so chided by a representative of the Roman Curia that they got up in protest and left the aula. But in the end some representatives were chosen for the synodal commission who were known for their frank and courageous attitudes, standing in contrast to the mentality of the Roman

142

Curia. This is a sign of hope. It can be taken that such reactions will bear fruit in time.

For the Second Vatican Council, 2,757 bishops were invited. To coordinate such a multitude into a dynamic grouping was a gigantic task that could not be done perfectly. By 1983 there were 4,393 bishops, and their number will increase still further. Is a council in the traditional manner still to be thought of for the future? Should not, therefore, the Synod of Bishops *with* legislative power, become a kind of perennial mini-council continually channeling oxygen and fresh blood from the base of the church? No such idea is current in Rome and the new Canon Law does not foresee it.[119] But that is not the final word on the subject: the 1917 code was revised when the need for it was recognized. Before the year 2000 there will be many opportunities for such a change, and more especially from then on. It would enable Rome to react more speedily to new situations, and could open the door to other suggestions for decentralization.

Kenosis in the Latin Church

Until Vatican II, Catholics commonly called their church 'Roman Catholic'. It was understood to be identical with the 'one, holy, catholic, and apostolic church', and was so understood in the preliminary draught of *Lumen Gentium*. The bishops in the council, however, introduced two changes. First, they did not say that the church of Christ 'is' the Roman Catholic Church but that the church is 'realized in' (subsistet), 'subsists in' the Catholic Church. They made no claim to an exclusive monopoly of all that 'church' implies. Secondly, they omitted the adjective 'Roman', on the grounds that the 'Roman Church' is a concrete local church, one part of the church universal, although its bishop is at the same time head of all the other bishops of the Catholic Church (*Lumen Gentium*, 8).

This 'deromanizing' has yet to enter the Roman vocabulary. As before, how things are done in Rome constitutes the sole legitimate exemplar for the Catholic Church. Think of the 'Roman Missal'. The nonuse of Latin is mourned over and it is emphasized that the 'Roman Church' (meaning the whole Catholic Church) should show particular care for this noble language of ancient Rome.[120] As before, there is talk in Rome of 'priests of the Latin Roman Church', of 'priestly consecration in the Latin Church', of

143

'the celibacy that priests of the Latin Church knowingly and freely undertake'.[121] Not only the theological deliberations of the council but also the new church presence in six continents demand a thorough investigation of this 'Latin Roman Church', which apparently has become an untouchable absolute. Even the new code commences short and sweet: 'The canons of this code concern only the Latin Church' (can. 1), by which is meant the church in six continents.

Before the Latin church there was a Jewish and a Greek church. Consequently, there could be other churches after, or rather alongside, it now. We know what great trouble the first church, the Jewish church, had in getting out of itself so as not to impose the Mosaic law on gentiles who wanted to embrace the gospel.[122] But the apostolic college, with unprecedented courage, took the step and made known: 'It is the decision of the Holy Spirit, and our decision, to lay no further burden upon you beyond these essentials' (Acts 15:28). A freedom charter such as this has seldom seen its like in history! The gentile church, the Greek church, could then develop in the pure faith of Jesus Christ.

There were Greek churches in first-century Rome. Greek was spoken and written; Latin was held to be a heathen language and not suitable for theology. Only in the middle of the second century did the need appear to have the Bible in Latin also, from the third century on, Latin gradually made its way, but not until the beginning of the fifth century was the use of the Latin language and culture consolidated in the church.

From the fourth century onward the split between East and West went on widening. At first there had been one empire and one church. But then conflict arose, sides were taken, and unity was sundered. Each culture became accustomed to having, as well as its own language, its own theology and outlook. The Eastern church concerned itself with christological and trinitarian teaching, lived in the light of faith in the Holy Spirit and the risen Lord, followed a synodal form of government and through its monks celebrated an elaborate otherworldly liturgy. The Western church was strongly inspired by Roman legal thinking, developed a monarchical form of government, remained open to the world, and in liturgy stressed exact formulation, accurate expressions, clearly defined rites. As time went on, in the vacuum left by geographical, cultural, and political collapse, the Latin church took over from the Greek.[123]

From this it is clear that there have been and there should be different models of church, different churches, different outlooks. Hence, it is not clear why the lengthy process of ecclesiogenesis should be broken off at a certain point and not go on further as a continuing process, just as creation still continues ceaselessly in evolution. The Latin church is rightly credited with a major achievement in that, on the foundation of Greco-Latin-Germanic culture, it built the Middle Ages, and also, since the discovery of the New World during the era of European hegemony, it helped form eurocentric history. But that era has now finally ended. It has been brought to a close by political and cultural autonomy in every country and every continent. The Latin church can, therefor, no longer go on acting as though nothing has changed.

Citizens of these young nations are asking themselves today: By what right does Rome expect that in Africa and Asia too, having nothing in common with Roman civilization, the church must be Latin? Cannot other cultures be as worthy a vehicle for the message of the gospel as the ancient traditions of Europe? Should there not develop today, alongside the Latin church — according to the same logic of history by which once the Jewish church, the Greek church, the Latin church, came into being — in areas geographically, culturally, and politically distinct, a Latin American church, an African church, an Asian church? The Latin Roman church would indeed always have preeminence, but otherwise be one among a number of other legitimate forms in the truly catholic — that is, worldwide — church that finds expression in all cultures. If the Eastern and the Roman churches have pursued such diverse emphases in theology, spirituality, and discipline, why should the same opportunity be denied to the young Southern continental churches? No one church can exhaust the fullness of ecclesial being. Only together can the various continental churches, each in their various ways, give witness to its fullness.

These questions are being asked more and more loudly in Africa because that continent was, for a long time, more despised and culturally repressed than the others, and therefore today seeks all the more energetically to have its own cultural and ecclesial identity and authenticity recognized. Let us listen to a few speakers on the subject. J. M. Ela: 'We feel ourselves still completely dependent on the Western church, a by-product of the Christian West. The young churches have been born with the symptoms of

145

premature senility. The church as the structure of Christendom must be demolished so as to discover a new creativity that can do justice to the shock-effect of the gospel in the African ambient'.[124] P. E. Mveng: 'We must at last move on from sub-mission to our inheritance' (de la sous-mission à la succession).[125] M. P. Hebga: 'What we want as a minimum is a long moratorium in which we can be left alone with ourselves and God, so that the Spirit can visit us too without having to ask leave of an external authority; so that the light of the Spirit can permeate us without first passing through the prism of a foreign culture'.[126] E. A. Ayandele: 'With respect to doctrine, culture, and church, we still bear a colonial or neocolonial image, which will not be got rid of so long as the church in Africa looks to London or Rome or New York or Richmond instead of looking to reach heaven from Africa'.[127]

Criticisms can be made of these statements, but they should not be ignored. In them can be recognized the signs of the times, in them can be seen and heard the thunder and lightning of history. We might even see Paul in them, this time fighting for freedom from Western law. It has to be admitted that these speakers have the gospel and Vatican II on their side and should therefore find a suitable solution trusting in the Holy Spirit and in humanity. The 'Latin church' should in this *kairos* of history meditate much on Philippians 2:5–11, not wanting to hold fast to its 'Latin Christian' being but enter with Christ into his *kenosis*, emptying itself and allowing all peoples to fulfill their discipleship in their own way under the one rule of Christ the Lord.

All these problems have a lot to do with ecumenism. Anglicans and Protestants are continually asking, in view of possible future union, whether the pope really acts along with the other bishops, or simply overrules them and gives orders. They would like to be assured that they would not be swallowed up by Roman centralization. Most churches today are longing for unity. They would adopt as a sign of unity the primacy of the bishop of Rome, but not in the way it was practised a hundred years ago.

In the famous Malines Conversations of 1921 to 1926 between representatives of the Catholic and the Anglican Churches, far-sighted Cardinal Mercier prophetically coined the phrase that the Anglican Church should be 'united with but not absorbed by Rome'.[128] He meant that the Anglican Church should again accept the bishop of Rome as head of all the churches, but for the rest to keep its traditions and privileges after the fashion of a patriarchate. Fifty years later Pope Paul VI declared to Dr. Coggan, archbishop of Canterbury and primate of the Anglican Church, 'These words of hope from Cardinal Mercier are no longer merely a dream'.[129]

When will the breakthrough occur? Where will it first take place? In the intrachurch sphere, when Rome grants the Catholic Churches of the various continents a greater legitimate independence? That would deepen credibility and have a great influence on ecumenism. Or will it take place in the interchurch sphere, when non-Catholic Christian churches unite with Rome on the basis of true decentralization and pluriformity? That would have an impact on local Catholic Churches. It is the fate of the churches today to be dependent on one another.

Pluriformity: a Consequence

Basic Premises

If true decentralization takes concrete shape in the world church, its natural consequence would be the emergence of a broad pluriformity. We would then have in the church a divinely willed reflection of creation, where we are met by an almost unending multiplicity of types, shapes, and colours in one sublime unity.

Until Vatican II, uniformity was a preoccupation of the Catholic Church. Throughout the world there was one catechism, the one Latin Mass, the one detailed Canon Law. A century of overstressed central authority resulted in a 'profound institutionalization of Christianity', 'churchification' (F. X. Kaufmann). In marked contrast with the prevailing values of society in general, which were more and more directed toward freedom, church authorities imposed strict order and uniformity, and tried the obedience of the harassed faithful until they finally found a solution: they obeyed outwardly, but in their inward belief and attitude they went their own way. Kaufmann concludes: 'The church today needs poets rather than thinkers, and mystics rather than vicars general or nuncios'.[130]

During Vatican II, for the first time and therefore very cautiously, there began to be talk of legitimate pluriformity (*Lumen Gentium*, 13, 23; *Sacrosanctum Concilium*, 37–40). Certain features

147

of the Eastern churches were singled out for admiration, almost envy, and there was hope that in the Latin church, too, local differences could again be developed (*Orientalium Ecclesiarum*, 6; *Unitatis Redintegratio*, 14, 17). Ten years later *Evangelii Nuntiandi*, after the 1974 Synod of Bishops, spoke with more courage and self-assurance of pluriformity, and suggested translating the gospel not only into other languages but into other cultures, and not merely as a right but as a duty. This would correspond with contemporary human experience and enrich the church (*Evangelii Nuntiandi*, 62, 63).

Ecclesiology has been elaborated from a number of different perspectives: kerygmatic, Rudolf Bultmann; eucharistic, Jérôme Hamer; ecumenical, Yves Congar; sacramental, Otto Semmelroth, Karl Rahner, Joseph Ratzinger; pneumatic, Hans Küng, H. Mühlen.[131] I think there is room for an incarnational ecclesiology. It would bring out what the incarnation of Christ means for the church: not a puppetlike repetition of the particular things that Jesus did, but acting in each particular case according to the dictates of the given situation, in all obedience to the positive commands of God, as Jesus did in his context.

The theme of the inculturation, indigenization, incarnation of Christianity has been dealt with in books and congresses, as also in papal utterances, and so is generally accepted. But its translation into practice encounters many difficulties. On the one hand most local churches have too little courage, too little creative imagination. And on the other hand the Roman Curia, out of fear of disaster, still holds too firmly to traditional uniformity.

In 1980 a bishops' conference in the Third World asked for approval of a eucharistic liturgy incorporating some features of a national holiday. Many non-Christians in the government and the military would be attending the ceremony; such a liturgy would make a deep impression on them. Rome replied in the negative. Then the bishops asked whether they might separate All Souls' Day from All Saints' Day, celebrating them two weeks apart, because the people had more devotion to deceased ancestors than to the Christian saints, and on All Saints' Day visited the cemetery, bringing flowers and candles. Again Rome said no. The third time permission was not asked but it was decided that in that tropical climate a white cassock or habit could take the place of an alb. Rome let it be known that the bishops had overstepped their authority. Is this really what the conciliar fathers had in mind when they spoke of collegiality and legitimate pluriformity?

This discrepancy between theory and practice shows up in other areas as well. Leonardo Boff points out, for example, how with reference to human rights in the church there is a discrepancy between what is preached and what is practised. Nor is it only a failing of given individuals; it has to do also with the image of the church based on centralization and authoritarianism. This gap between preaching and practice brings a burden to the lives of individual Christians, and brings suffering to the church in this postconciliar age.[132]

There is a similar discrepancy between the content of the encyclical *Dives in Misericordia,* where John Paul II describes the task of the church to make God's mercy visible and effective on earth, and the practice by which repentant priests who left the priesthood on grounds of conscience are denied reconciliation with the church.

A similar want of feeling is shown in the practice of general absolution. A very favourable opportunity was lost on the occasion of the Austrian Katholikentag in 1983. The events of the day had been imaginatively conceived and splendidly executed. At the opening ceremony on St. Stephen's Square, where thirty thousand persons stood for three hours, listening, singing, praying, and then celebrating together an inspiring penitential service, it was expected that Cardinal König, who was presiding, would grant general absolution. But he very pointedly avoided it, and did not grant even conditional absolution. Instead, he made the general statement that God is merciful and we too should pardon one another. Why must the church dispense its graces so grudgingly?

As regards inculturation, tension springs from the very principles that, according to John Paul II, must govern it — namely, 'the compatibility of a given culture with the gospel, and harmony with the church universal.'[133] Does this not come close to squaring the circle? Much that is consistent with the gospel is not practised in the church universal, and much that the church practises is not an inculturated datum in many parts of the world. In any case the essence of the gospel is better preserved when inculturated than when it is kept foreign.

In this whole complex matter it is not merely a question of inculturation into a culture transmitted from the past, but also

149

into a culture that is so contemporary. It applies, therefore, to the Northern world as much as to the Southern. The church must always and everywhere ask itself to what extent it can give an evangelical interpretation of modern culture and its values, such as love, trust, hope, responsibility, human rights, and so on, and on the other hand, faced with contemporary secularism, emphasize an opening up to the transcendental as a human value. With an outdated understanding of Christianity, we shall not get very far. The Third Church, with its more courageous advance in matters of pluriformity, could perhaps also encourage the Second Church and be supportive.

There is still need of earnest and constructive dialogue between the two poles of the church, between the Vatican and local churches, dialogue in which both groups would stand up for their different opinions, and in the end come to a sensible compromise. There is no way to avoid all conflict. Differences are a part of human life and are meant to be overcome. The bishops should never be against Rome but they should sometimes stand up to Rome. In any case North-South dialogue should not degenerate into permanent North-South conflict. It should no longer be true, as someone once said, 'If you take inculturation seriously, you will clash with Rome'. It is to be hoped that pioneers of inculturation will no longer have to wait four hundred years like Matteo Ricci until they are recognized in the church. Ricci's public recognition by Pope John Paul II has not indeed solved the fundamental problems, unfortunately. Karl Rahner said, 'The real rites controversy lies in the future'.[134]

Amid all the tension, many priests and faithful simply follow the way of the gospel, the council, and their courage. For them it is an obligation, and they want to remain part of a group. In large parishes, which today usually show evidence of a left and a right wing, the rules must be followed so that no one can have anything to complain of. In the basic groups there is no need to fear polarization. Such homogeneous groups are distinguished by their openness to the Spirit and their ability for spontaneity and creativity. They are the place for inculturation in the concrete. With all due respect for the norms of the church, new theological, liturgical, and disciplinary traditions are created by them, which can later find entry into the mainline church, as has often happened in the history of the church.[135] We have only to think of the groups around Romano Guardini; in the 1960s, to the anxiety of many bishops and other Christians, they celebrated a new, more meaningful liturgy, and from many points of view were pathfinders for Vatican II.

Areas of Application

In the Liturgy. Liturgy is not so much the fulfillment of a duty under pain of serious sin as the deepest expression of faith, the heart of Christian living. The Constitution on the Sacred Liturgy, *Sacrosanctum Concilium,* was the best prepared of the texts at the time and was therefore the first conciliar document to be accepted without difficulty, and it led to far-reaching consequences. The liturgists behind the document, spearheaded by Archbishop Bugnini, were unanimous that liturgical renewal must follow three stages: first, the drawing up of a simpler, more lucid form conducive to active participation; secondly translating it into the various languages; thirdly, incarnating this new liturgy in the various cultures (*Sacrosanctum Concilium,* 37–40). This broad concept utilization was subsequently narrowed down by various curial instructions on the liturgy in which the specialists had no say, and finally an authoritative halt was called to the liturgical movement and adaptation.

In India a liturgy more in keeping with the language, symbols, rites, and genius of the Indian spiritual patrimony had been worked on for several years. In 1975 the episcopal conference received from the Roman Congregation for the Sacraments a categorical order to stop. The fact that conservative groups of lay persons, priests, and bishops backed the order does not make it any the less a tragedy. Once again harm was done to the church of Asia; a halt was called as soon as a few practical steps were taken toward becoming a local church.

The Roman Curia wants it to be understood that all instructions from Rome are national guidelines and that everything must be done accordingly to the last iota. Thus, for example, the Confiteor must be recited, not sung; the Gloria and Credo may not be paraphrased but must be recited word for word. The close of the liturgy may not be phrased as a wish: 'Let us go in peace', but as a command: 'Go in peace', so as to underline once again the difference between priest and people, and so on.

151

Africa, with its sense of the holy, of community, of song and rhythm, was well suited especially to the possibilities of a renewed liturgy. Jean Daniélou had said many years earlier that the church could expect to receive from Asia a renewal of meditation, and from Africa a renewal of the liturgy. But the postconciliar Roman universal liturgy aroused disillusionment in Africa. However right the dry, objective style might be for Europe, it did not correspond to the feelings of Africans, to their song, movement, and spontaneous prayer. The liturgical calendar too, with all its European saints, found little response. It would have been far better to concentrate on the Christ Mystery and on biblical saints with a few others for Africa. In other words, liturgy for Africa should not have been made in Rome but allowed to grow up in charismatic communities, under the supervision of the bishops.[136]

The bishops of Zaire were more successful. They commissioned specialists to compose a Zairian eucharistic rite, and in 1974 sent the text to Rome, along with tapes and slides. Rome gave it approval only *ad experimentum*: only for small groups, without publicity, and for a set period. From these conditions it could easily be concluded that shortly, as in India, another brief would follow, declaring the experimental period at an end. But instead, the Zairian liturgy spread like a bush fire in many dioceses and in large parishes. It developed into a drama lasting two hours, during which children and grown-ups, men and women, fully participate with song, mime, dancing, and gesture, a real celebration of liturgy. It attracts everyone, including non-Christians. They are happy to go to church and go back happy to their daily lives.

Rome does not like this development, but knows also that it cannot now be reversed. This shows how, *per viam facti*, something can be carried through into action and into history. Rome ought to say yes with a full heart to such developments. But if it does not, there always remains the classic solution: like a flash stream, life will take its own course.

An even thornier problem is that of the eucharistic elements. When Jesus used bread and wine at the Last Supper as a sign of his enduring presence, he did indeed follow the Jewish tradition of the Pasch. But on the basis of the incarnational principle mentioned above, it could scarcely be concluded — as has, nevertheless, been done throughout history — that this was always and everywhere the only possible way to do it. Of all the elements used in the sacraments, only water is obtainable and meaningful everywhere. Bread and wine and olive oil are typical Mediterranean products. Wine imported from Europe and altar breads baked from imported flour have no symbolic value in Africa and Asia, nor are they 'fruit of the earth and of human labour' in a local sense. A solution to the problem could be, for communities mature in the faith, to use bread and wine most of the time, as a link with salvation history and the symbolism of the Old and New Testaments. But for younger communities, especially those for whom bread and wine seem to have magical qualities, and in cases of necessity, palm wine, and manioc, for example, could be additional legitimate possibilities.

In a particular diocese in Africa certain priests, on occasion, under special circumstances, used these African substances for the Eucharist. The nuncio heard of it and wrote a sharp letter to their bishop. The bishop went off to Rome and wanted to discuss the matter with the pope. He was told that he should consult with the relevant curial congregation. Well knowing what sort of an answer the congregation would give, he again requested a meeting with the pope. It was again refused. As a bishop, he could not accept this, and handed in his resignation although he was only fifty-six years old. His resignation was accepted. This happened in 1975. By the year 2000 will there be a more flexible way of proceeding with questions that do not involve unchangeable dogmas? When it is realized that most of the non-Christian religions have a great number of sacramentally symbolic rites (B. P. H. Hochegger has analyzed 2,606 ritual actions that have religious meaning in Zaire), it must be admitted that we are only at the very beginning of liturgical inculturation.[137]

In Theology. If there is much that is alive in theology today, it only shows that, after a period of static scholastic philosophy and theology, we have again found access to the best periods of theological history. Not only theology was always in flux, but revelation too was experienced in historical, dynamic, self-unfolding progress. From the Old to the New Testament, from the preaching of Jesus to the preaching on Jesus, from the Epistles to Acts, it was a question of not only handing on the message but actualizing it at all times. There was the desire to proclaim Jesus Christ reigning *now*. The New Testament was written with a view to specific situations. The synoptic Gospels in no sense merely copied each other, but presented the same material, interpreting it afresh to meet the needs of a particular community, drawing out particular emphases. The New Testament scriptures are thus not simply an unchanging doctrinal system fixed once and for all, but rather a seed that was meant to grow, an impetus that calls to faith in Christ in a variety of spiritual spheres, and so a variety of theologies as yet to be developed. There is then no *philosophia perennis*, only an *evangelium perenne*.[138]

At present we are experiencing an enormous and sudden development of theology not only quantitatively, in the production of articles and books, but also qualitatively, in the sense of a much more dynamic and down-to-earth theology. Also the fact that now thousands of lay persons are studying theology changes the theological scene drastically. In the winter term 1982–83 there were in West Germany alone 15,300 students enrolled in theological faculties; only 10 percent of them were candidates for the priesthood. What the thirteen thousand lay theologians will do later on is another question, because there are only around three thousand positions available to them. How they will influence the theological thinking and the quality of church life is another and very important question. That the bishops in the 1930s, when there was an excess of candidates for the priesthood, simply refused more than half of them, seems today a deplorably short-sighted policy. And how will our era be judged, and the opportunities given the church by the number of lay theologians?[139]

What wonder, then, if also in the young Third World churches, a theological breakthrough is now taking place! They were until now the readers, the consumers, of Northern religious thought, from catechism to theological textbooks. Their own theological silence, which in Latin America lasted four centuries, was an expression of colonialism. But meanwhile, in all three Southern continents, theological colleges and theological periodicals were founded. Theologians deserving of the name proclaimed the gospel to their spiritual and cultural milieu and produced a local, 'contextual' theology. They were dissatisfied with a universal and therefore abstract theology, which was supposed to suit exerywhere and really fitted nowhere. They believed that God's word enters into every concrete historical situation and will work liberation and salvation there. They believed that a *local theology* is an important prerequisite for a *local church*. Of course they were not going to ignore Northern theology, but neither would they merely imitate it. There was to be continuity, not severance.

Third World theology is distinguished by three special features: it is ecumenical, dialogical, and tolerant. In contrast to the closed Christianity of the Middle Ages, sufficient unto itself, in possession of the fullness of truth, most African and Asian Christians live as a minority. They are therefore open not only to ecumenism with other churches but also to ecumenism with other religions. They are willing to be inspired by typical Asian or African thought, and realize that there are positive values to be found in all religions, that they can be enriching, and that therefore they should study them in a spirit of reconciliation, toleration, harmony, and cooperation. In Hinduism and Buddhism religious figures have never been cast out as 'heretics', much less put to death. Life is more valuable than doctrine.[140] It is remarkable that the growing presence of Asian churches in the World Council of Churches followed closely on the decline of the exclusive, dialectical theology of Karl Barth. To be sure, institutional Christianity professes a teaching that is and must be given expression and, in certain circumstances, must be differentiated from 'heresy'. But this is consistent with a realization that we can learn from others, even from 'opponents', and that the eternal light of all-embracing truth has a future, not only a past.

It is not merely dialogue with other religions that is sought by Third World theology but still more dialogue with the poor. Third World peoples live in a zone of death, a zone of ignorance, sickness, and poverty. These theologians do not want to practise theology in air-conditioned lecture halls, with access to million-volume libraries, hermetically sealed off from the malaise of everyday life, a theology for the elite; they want to proclaim the gospel in its revolutionary power to the people and give the people courage to change a wrongful situation. The first act of such a theology is therefore to produce an analysis of the concrete socio-politico-economic situation, to get to brute facts and the veiled causes of poverty. The second act is to ask oneself how the God of history and of life wants to free humanity from this state, not by 'miracles' but by a committed Christian life in the service of one's neighbour.

Third World theologians do not claim to have a monopoly over theology. On the contrary they want only to be animators of

155

dynamic communities, the basic ecclesial groups. As in the liturgy, so too in theology, active participation of the laity is desired. In this too lies the third mark of this theology — that it is not written by individual theologians isolated in their workrooms, but is borne along by living communities, produced in the course of life lived in response to the gospel, and is therefore as many-sided as life itself. This 'theology from below' is passing like a warm, spring breeze through the Third World, working wonders, changing life, mirroring the joys and sorrows, the power and wisdom, of the people. It is building up a new, credible church.[141]

Will contextual theology, based on concrete situations, lead corporate creativity in the various continental churches to a distinctive, continental, theological movement? As mentioned in earlier chapters, theology under the sign of *mysterium salutis* was at one time thought to be postconciliar theology for the entire world, although all its authors were from the North Atlantic world and it was centred on the Western, pragmatic base of 'my salvation'. Latin American theologians are working on a continental theology under the sign of *mysterium incarnationis*, and an Asian theology under the sign of *mysterium revelationis* has also been suggested. Taken all together, four such theologies, even worked out in great detail, would convey only a glimmer of the richness of Christian theology that could unfold within the foreseeable future. We are on the threshold of the third millennium, which undoubtedly holds surprises for us.

For some Christians, this prospect arouses anxiety, especially when some Third World theologians are called into question by Rome. But theological research, by its very nature, is bound up with dangers and risks. Let it be remembered that Thomas Aquinas aroused astonishment and opposition when he adopted, to the extent he did, teachings of the 'pagan' Aristotle and Muslim philosophers. Anyone starting from the premise that theology is always 'on the way', that it — like the exploration of outer space — is at present making great strides, but for all that is fathoming only a small inlet of the ocean of the knowable, will follow these fascinating undertakings with interest and attention.

Third World theologians must be granted the 'right' to risk 'heresy'; it has been a constituent part of history. Mistakes will probably be corrected in the company, the *koinonia*, of other theologians and bishops. Can the Roman Congregation for the

Teaching of the Catholic Faith do justice to all these theologies? Outright denial of a dogma of the faith is one thing, but exploration, the discovery of hidden dimensions, is something else. If christology could make use of 'pagan' Greek concepts, how can the use of Hindu philosophy be excluded a priori? No one who understands the genius of Hinduism would think to question the orthodoxy of a christology incorporating Hindu elements.

In Church Discipline. Why is it that so many contemporary Christians find the church a burden, a stumbling block? Church officials complain of a decline in faith. But do they see everything? These Christians practise the 'fruits of the Spirit in love, joy, peace, patience, kindness, goodness, faithfulness' (Gal. 5:23). They rejoice in Jesus, whose mission is briefly summed up: 'He proclaimed the good news of the kingdom and healed every disease and every infirmity' (Matt. 9:35).

Many contemporary Christians have undergone a radical change in their moral consciousness. They see sin and virtue no longer principally in the sixth commandment, but ask themselves how far they have or have not shown and inspired courage, seriously accepted responsibility for others or not, seized upon hopeful initiatives for the good of humankind or not. They would accept from the church encouragement in matters of peace, justice, human values, ecology. But they cannot go along with the neolegalism more and more in evidence. They are convinced that some behavioural regulations insisted on by the church accord neither with real life, nor with the insights of medicine, psychology, and sociology.

The majority of contemporary Christians, especially in the Anglo-Saxon world, are 'empiricists'. They understand life from their concrete experience of it. They do not deny the existence of 'principles' and 'eternal, unchanging verities'. But they hold that such principles must be measured against lived experience. A practical understanding of such principles will set limits to their range, and difficulties and misunderstandings will be eliminated. These 'empiricists' are aware that the Roman mentality applies such principles injudiciously, that too little is learned from the history of the church, which shows that 'officially', in the name of 'eternal principles', new ideas have often and too hastily been condemned as unchristian — ideas that in time were seen to be entirely acceptable: democracy, trade unions, religious and con-

157

scientious freedom, modern scriptural exegesis, and the insights of the historical and natural sciences. The Synod of Toledo in 589 was so in favour of public confession that it condemned private confession, just then coming into practice, as an 'abominable arrogance' (*exsecrabilis praesumptio*), whereas the Fourth Lateran Council in 1215 imposed it under pain of grave sin.

Typical leaders of these two schools of thought opposed each other in the 1980 Synod of Bishops: Cardinal Hume spoke of a vision of a pilgrim church encouraging those on the way, radiating joy to them; he stressed the understanding of the faith found in the faithful (*sensus fidelium*), the experience of Christian married couples, who represented an authentic source of theology. On the other side stood Cardinal Felici who warned against being led astray by statistics and empirical data.[142] Fundamentally it is not those who dream of new ways of evangelical and Christian life who are utopian, but those who think that they can still keep things moving in the world with outmoded forms and regulations alien to life, or even that this is the way to proclaim the good news to the world, the primary task of the church.

It is high time the institutional church went further along the way of the council and learned how to accept historical reality, otherwise reality will escape it and the kingdom of God will increasingly be carried on without the church. I should like to illustrate the growing gap between the 'church from above' and the 'church from below' with three concrete examples.

Pope John Paul II lays great stress on the wearing of priestly and religious garb. Along with all the reasons for it, however, there are also weighty historical and psychological reasons against it. In Poland such dress is a sign of protest against the government; in Latin America on the other hand it is a sign of the identification of the traditional church with the government. Was not Jesus angered at the religious dress of the Pharisees (Matt. 23:5)? Did he not say, 'If there is love among you, then all will know that you are my disciples' (John 13:35), not by wearing a black soutane or a Roman collar? I gave some talks to a bishops' conference in the tropics; the bishops appeared one and all in shirt and trousers, the cardinal in a white soutane, the nuncio in black — and complained repeatedly of the stifling climate.

On October 19, 1982, at the opening of the academic year, by the authority of the pope, Cardinal Poletti, and the three Roman congregations for clerics, religious, and Catholic instruction, it was insisted that henceforth all priests and religious in Rome had always and everywhere to wear their distinctive garb.[143] By the end of the academic year, practically nothing had changed. As before, 70 to 80 percent of clerical students attended the papal universities in civvies. Why bring in the highest ecclesiastical authority to deal with such a secondary question?

Much more weighty are marriage questions. They bear on life itself. I am not now speaking of *Humanae Vitae* and the change it brought about. Until then, the axiom remained in force: *Roma locuta, causa finita.* But this time word from Rome did not put an end to debate; in fact, it started it, so that in time the great majority of married Catholics were quietly 'going their own way' and were therefore not upset when the 1980 Synod of Bishops once again put all the weight of its authority behind the document. Nor do I wish to address here the question of the divorced and remarried who, after *Familiaris Consortio*, could no longer be given the sacraments, which, however, many priests do as a 'pastoral solution'. In this matter certainly not a few seek not merely an ad hoc solution but a radical solution and, along with the theology of the Eastern churches, ask themselves whether completely broken, irremediable marriages have not dissolved themselves and whether a sacramental bond without love is not nonsense.[144]

I should like, however, to consider a particular African marriage problem. In view of the pastoral fact that in many places in Africa 70 percent of adult Christians remain excluded from the sacraments on account of marriages not recognized by the church (about the same holds true for Latin America), it is asked whether something is not wrong with such church discipline. The church is after all not there for an elite group but for the people as a whole.

In the greater part of Africa, among matriarchal agricultural peoples, marriage proceeds by stages. The two families negotiate, exchange first gifts, visit one another. Then the young man enters the girl's compound, builds himself a hut, and from a specified time onward lives with the girl. In the course of a few years he has to give proof that he can work, treat the girl well, honour the in-laws, and that they can have children by one another. When all this is clear, and meanwhile the dowry has been paid, the marriage is celebrated in the tribe. In the eyes of the church this is held to

159

be open concubinage, a state of mortal sin. Young Christians who have followed, as they must, the tradition of the tribe, are during the best years of their Christian maturity excluded from the sacraments — a fearful burden for the missionary, but also for the young Christian.

Eventually it came to be asked whether this African tradition was really so bad and so alien to the gospel. There and then the 'pastoral solution' began to be advocated: it was not announced from the pulpit that such persons were now allowed the sacraments, but their situation was explained as a special case pertaining to a local church. And the local church decided: 'These are fundamentally two good Christians, behaving according to the custom of their tribe; therefore they are allowed to receive the sacraments'.

At the 1980 Synod of Bishops, five African bishops, in the name of their episcopal conference, pleaded for an understanding of African-style marriage. It should not be termed 'concubinage, trial marriage, irregular union', but marriage by stages, progressive marriage. As the catechumenate leads step by step to baptism, so also this was a marriage catechumenate. It should not therefore be spoken of as a relationship 'out of marriage'. It should all be held to form part of marriage, which is not concluded in a brief ceremony but in a process of becoming. It was therefore asked that this procedure should be recognized and accompanied by suitable ceremonies.

In the final document of the synod, *Familiaris Consortio*, the pope appears to set African progressive marriage on a par with the growing problem in the West of trial marriage and to condemn them equally. Clearly, the last word has not been said.[143]

A more delicate problem is that of office in the church, not only in theological discussion but in its present pastoral practice.[144] Here again very much depends upon the image of the church: whether one thinks of it in preconciliar terms as predominantly clerical, administered from above, from without, from a distance, or whether one believes the church to be a witness to the Holy Spirit, a community of persons who devote themselves to the Jesus movement, a church growing and originating various offices from inner need and right as was the case originally in the Pauline communities — and in conformity with the teaching that office in the church rests on a commission from Christ and is not simply left to the 'democratic' whim of the hoi polloi.

The problem is very acute in the thousands of priestless communities in Latin America and Africa, and soon will be also in Europe. We have already reviewed this situation in chapter 9. The tragic state of affairs in Latin America has been known for a long time. We have now, however, to speak of a spreading 'latin americanization'. That fine student of Africa, Adrian Hastings, was of the opinion in 1967 — when there were 1,800 African Catholics per priest — that by the year 2000 there would certainly be 3,500. But this figure was reached in 1981. For the year 2000 there will be at least 5,500 Catholics per priest in Africa, and in Latin America 10,000. There can be no joy in this inequality of growth between the numbers of priests and believers.

Pastoral theologians and bishops' conferences are more and more suggesting the consecration to the priesthood of worthy married men, community leaders, hard workers, who have pursued some years of pastoral and theological study, and who can do everything, but — until now — may not pronounce two formulas: the words of consecration and sacramental absolution. Rome's answer remains always the same: 'No; and again, no. Be under no illusion. The Latin American church has remained true to the celibate priesthood and will continue to do so!'[149] In his prayer for priests on Maundy Thursday in 1982 the pope, in the form of a rhetorical question, stronger than a statement, imposed silence on the subject: 'Is it in place — contrary to the voice of the last Ecumenical Council and the Synod of Bishops — to continue demanding that the church must go back on this tradition and heritage?'[146]

With the present system there will be in Africa and Latin America no priests for the many outposts with a few hundred Christians; priests will be found only in urban centres. In every other type of administration there are lower, middle, and higher officials, each with their different levels of training, just as there are primary, secondary, and university teachers. Why in the church should there be only one, undifferentiated priesthood model?

As a Christian faithful to the church, one is faced here with a delicate situation: how to be loyal to the pope and to the people, to the church from above and the church from below? How to exercise obedience and prophecy? If no new way ahead is to be opened up to give priests to priestless communities, then in practice they are being made Protestant three times over: First, they have

161

only holy scripture and the creed — although that is already a great deal! Secondly, it is already happening that such communities on certain occasions 'celebrate the Eucharist' after their own fashion, the community deputizing someone to do this for the others. Anyone who has read Jungmann's *Missarum Sollemnia* knows under how many different forms in the course of history the Eucharist has been celebrated and consequently can be celebrated. Thirdly, the lay ministry is being widely developed now and confirms that the community is basically alive; that therefore the church, one way or another, with or without priests, can go forward. If the Tridentine model of the priesthood is overworked, it risks being lost altogether.

Pope John Paul II is convinced that thanks to his firmness and enthusiasm the crisis in the priesthood will be overcome. One must give him credit for acting according to his convictions. In certain countries, especially in the Third World, the number of candidates for the priesthood is noticeably on the increase and this for two reasons: because in an economic crisis the priestly calling offers security, and because in the basic community world and among the laity, devotedness to the apostolate can mature into a readiness to offer oneself to the service of the church, 'cost what it may'. We should not, however, allow ourselves to be deceived by this turn of events. We do not know how many candidates will have other ideas before reaching ordination, or whether later on many of them will not in their forties and fifties, on grounds of conscience, leave the priesthood and the questions raised above will be posed with renewed acuteness. Then, in ten or twenty years, we shall be discussing them again. Meanwhile, quite apart from the doubtful linkage of priestly celibacy with pastoral necessity and theological propriety, in the Western as in the Southern church the problems of the ordination of women and the consecration of well-tried married men have not been laid to rest.[147]

To most of the ideas and suggestions developed here it can be objected that they are contrary to the new code. Now, a new statute book tries — as far as it is able — to work through the present state of affairs and codify it. Then the law remains stationary, but life goes on. The law must, therefore, continually be renewed if it is to serve life and not fetter it. Ecclesiastical futurology has exactly this task of preparing ideas that could perhaps

162

be taken into consideration at a future revision of church law.

The new code clearly gives the impression over against the old that it is thinking more on the lines of a world church. Without expressly speaking of 'legitimate pluriformity' or of 'contextualization', many factors are nevertheless seen basically in this light. The dialogue with non-Christians is to help the message of the gospel to be understood in the character and the fashion of a given culture (can. 787); the pastoral training of students is to suit the needs of time and place (can. 255); in consideration of various circumstances there can be various kinds of seminaries (can. 233–38) and each nation can have its own scheme studies (can. 242); there are to be courses of study in comparative religion (can. 821); the episcopal conferences are to regulate the apostolate of the church in such a way that it is suited to the circumstances of time and place (can. 447); the liturgy of the local church is to be adapted to the spiritual circumstances of the people (can. 837, 899). So far, so good.

On the other side, however, it is tirelessly repeated that all liturgical matters must be approved by Rome (can. 826, 928); that all curricula for seminaries must be approved by Rome (can. 242); that all decrees of episcopal conferences must be put before the Holy See for approval (can. 455–56), and so on. This means that Rome still in practice continues to be concerned with strict uniformity after the Roman model, as earlier experience has shown. Sometime in the future a revision of Canon Law will no doubt be necessary and local churches may be given more scope for action, and the assertion that the bishops as leaders of local churches are successors to the apostles may be taken more seriously (can. 375).[148]

The church has far more power over itself that it thinks. It could in many cases agree to new ideas, but almost always says no. It is concerned to faithfully uphold backward-looking, dust-covered traditions and thinks too little of projecting a forward-looking, creative, tradition in an ongoing process which corresponds to life. Is it lacking in courage? In ability? In insight into the signs of the times? What, then, is this 'church' that blocks everything by the way it works?

Rome Measured against the New Understanding of Church

The Danger of Schism

I have had several occasions to note that the church from above and the church from below, church as hierarchy and church as people of God, are more and more drawing apart, although Vatican II had again brought to the fore the fundamental unity of the church at its deepest level. Anyone who, for example, conducts premarriage courses and religious instruction in the upper classes of school could say a thing or two about a gaping rift. It is all one can do to uphold church teaching; and that not merely in matters of sex and marriage but also for the Sunday obligation, the ordination of women, the traditional understanding of the Virgin Birth, Mary's assumption body and soul into heaven, transubstantiation, heaven and hell, and so forth.[149] Anyone making a systematic study of the prevailing discordance, and taking up the question of how far the teaching that the church proposes and the values it inculcates harmonize with the thinking and values of the people, will come to the conclusion that the church does not fit in with our times. The various forms of enticement, requirement, or force used in the past will no longer succeed. Faith and religion today can grow only on the basis of freedom.[150] Anyone who supports bureaucratization and authoritarianism, distance instead of dialogue, confirms the opinion that the church, according to a saying of Anton Exeler, 'is not only *losing* the young and the working class but actually driving them out'.[151]

Just as today there is already considerable unity in practice with Protestant Christians, even if structures still remain separate, so conversely within the Catholic Church a schism is more and more a fact, even though the structure officially still remains intact. In the Constantinian era, the leaders of both sides would have been hauled up and a judgement of schism and heresy pronounced. But today the official leadership of the church is ignored by increasingly larger groups as irrelevant. The high command remains in its headquarters issuing orders, but the troops have gone off in search of freedom.

The monolith that was Christendom has in the meantime broken up into three segments:

• The religionless, the secularized, the practical or militant atheists, with whom now there is only one ground of communication left: the longing for justice and peace. There can be dialogue on this. There is an opportunity here for believers and nonbelievers, for whatever different motives, to work hand in hand for a better world. Nonbelievers will be informed at the Last Judgement that what they did was 'Christian' (Matt. 25:37–40).

• The pious Christians, the remnant, the 10, 20, or 30 percent of churchgoers who give pastors the impression that all is not yet over with the church. Among them are to be found younger persons and adults who honestly try to be disciples of Jesus today. But others of these 'faithful churchgoers' have never been in agreement with the council or with the gospel. They are the 'sí-sí-no-no Catholics' in Italy, 'Rock of Peter Catholics' in Germany, 'Lefebvre Catholics' in France and Switzerland, and all the pious egotists who use the church as a service station for their religious and social needs, whose religion has been called 'folk religion',[152] 'middle-class religion',[153] 'old-style religion'.[154] What a lamentable picture of the church of Jesus these circles present to the world! Jesus could well see in many of them the 'self-justified Pharisees' of today, who — one might almost say, unfortunately — know of no disturbance to their faith and think themselves without sin. For that reason, however, they see sin all round them and look disdainfully on sinners, instead of having understanding for them, and in spite of sin radiating hope, and so overpowering sin. There is more joy in heaven and on earth over one sinner who pardons others than over ninety-nine who throw stones.

• Critical Christians who say: Jesus yes, church no; who live according to the gospel and their conscience, often in basic communities; who rejoice in their freedom but suffer from the church as it is; the protestors, the utopians, the prophets who were thrust out from the church, to be recognized later on. In the church of old the prophets held first place among those endowed with various charisms; they were usually named straight after the successors of the Apostles (1 Cor. 12:28; Eph. 2:30, 3:5, 4:11). We all know today who the successors of the Apostles are, but who and where are the successors of the prophets? [155] They are all those who courageously take their stand for pluriformity, for justice, for freedom, for full recognition of the laity and of women, for the gospel pure and simple.[156]

Looking at the Third World, one cannot help seeing that at certain places, in certain circles, there is a danger that latent tension will turn to open schism. At Catholic pan-African congresses there is strikingly often talk of the attraction of the 'independent churches', which number in their thousands, go their own way, are entirely African and also believe themselves to be entirely Christian. Rome is understandably anxious about this phenomenon and its attractiveness to African Catholics. They will not be held back by tightened reins, but only through wise give and take, by a genuine recognition of pluriformity. Suppose that a national church, in the interests of full africanization, were to secede from Rome and under the guidance of its bishops were to seek a healthy middle course between the universally uniform Catholic Church and the 'independent churches'. At a later date it would be said of it, too, as of the Reformation today, that it took a rightful place in salvation history, having actualized genuine values that the Catholic Church was not courageous enough to bring out.

The Roman Curia

If today we think back nostagically to Pope John XXIII, to his bold opening address to the council, to the Conciliar period itself, and if many Catholics today have to struggle not to give way to resignation, much of this change of mood is due to the part played by the Roman Curia since then.

No one can deny the historical facts of church history that the Curia was tricked into the idea of a council by the wily — or better, Spirit-filled — pope; that the schemata worked out in the spirit of the Curia had then to be reworked into new ones by the council in order to be in keeping with the times; that the Curia later on, 'when the storm was over', reinstated itself and tried to channel the initiatives of the council so that they might be re-inserted as harmlessly as possible into earlier practices of the church and not — even under the challenge of new situations — have the effect obviously intended by the council.

At the end of the council the bishops remained with the anxious,

166

unanswered question: 'What will become of the Curia?' There had been so much criticism, so much desire for its reform. Was all that to die away in the aula? Pope Paul VI took up all the questions, challenges, and proposals when, in an address shortly before the close of the council, he defended the Curia against exaggerations alleging that it was 'outdated, unproductive, egotistic, corrupt'. At the same time he agreed that a reform was necessary. He promised that he would take responsibility for it. It would take a long time, and its results would not appear all at once.[157]

What came from the reform decree, *Regimini Ecclesiae*, of 1967, and from the implementation directives of 1968, in no way fulfilled the promise and was in fact all for nothing. A few responsibilities were divided differently, a few titles altered. There were also more non-Italian cardinals named to head Roman congregations, though always only one at a time. But one man cannot change a whole system; he has to fall in with it or remain an outsider. In addition new appointees were often more 'Roman' than the Italian cardinals.

The religious orders and institutes went to work in a much more radical way. They held renewal chapters, studied the council proposals, then chose new leadership, taking the best elements from ground level and putting them in the lead. They could give their communities postconciliar direction. Such a radical change of staff was unfortunately never forthcoming in the Vatican.

As a result the Roman Curia, with the best will in the world on the part of individual officials, was experienced not as an accelerator but as a brake, a weight, a power structure, almost as the executive board of a multinational corporation with the dioceses as affiliates. Right-wing circles, their complaints and letters, were given a hearing. There were attempts to bring conservative forces into the various kinds of synodal bodies by introducing members named by Rome so as to ensure a majority with similar leanings. In the Roman congregations the commissions of experts called for by the council were indeed set up, but they were without function or hearing. Unity and uniformity, authority and obedience, were continually stressed, and the bishops were left under no misapprehension: no departure from the official line would be tolerated. So in many areas of church life a humanly and ecclesially unhealthy state of affairs could be diagnosed: if and to the extent that there was any reference downward, any taking into account of the realities of life, any listening to the understanding of the faith

167

shown by the people of God, yes could be said to many proposals, but on referring them upward, the yes would be changed to a no. Prophetic figures were conspicuous by their rarity.

Two examples, one a century ago and one from the present, can serve as illustrations. Wilhelm Massaia (1809–1889), a Capuchin, first vicar apostolic to the Galla in Ethiopia, later a cardinal, had to come to his own decisions in many matters — for example, building up a native clergy, publishing a very simplified catechism. He always kept Rome informed. When Rome, without further consultation, repeatedly disavowed him and condemned his actions, Massaia uttered prophetic words:

> This is now the fourth time Rome has taken a decision without me. It is impossible for me to live in peace with such an institution. I am handing in my resignation. I will not prostitute holy things, neither from fear nor from ambition. . . . In matters of faith I obey Rome, but in pastoral matters I am the bishop; I mount and lead into battle. If a king tries to conduct a campaign from his palace, it is lost from the start.[158]

In the present too, such voices are heard. A 33-member episcopal conference presented in 1980 on its *ad limina* visit to Rome the following views and requests:

> So long as the Roman Curia holds fast to outdated structures and practices inherited from an earlier age, its credibility and its service to the church are put into question. . . . We propose that a critical study be made of the present structure and exercise of authority of the Roman Curia so as to determine what is essential for it to be of service and what is only outmoded form; to learn how authority can be exercised as service and not as power, more with pastoral than with juridical motivation, more in accord with a prophetic than with a merely repressive form of leadership, and how differences of opinion can be settled by recourse to dialogue rather than to authoritarian dictates.[159]

The best solution would be for the pope to send half the curial officials to parish work for three years where they would come into contact with the realities of life, with the thinking of the people of God, and with the pastoral work of good priests, and could adopt a new attitude; and then the other half the same, so that in the end those still necessary for a strongly decentralized and therefore greatly reduced Curia could be selected.

Clearly Pope John Paul II must have taken into account that in this connection there was much that was long overdue and that it was expected of him, as the first non-Italian pope for four and a half centuries, to bring the matter at last to a good conclusion. A year after taking office he called all the cardinals together, with the renewal of the structures of the church and above all of the Roman Curia as the main subject of discussion. At the close he asked these, his nearest advisers, to hand him at the end of three months their suggestions on the matter in writing.[160] Since then we have been waiting and hoping, hoping against hope, excited over the second meeting of the cardinals in November 1982, where however there was only talk on the subject of 'possible changes in the direction of collegiality and pastoral action'. Otherwise only a strange silence reigned: the silence before a storm.[161] In the early summer of 1983 there were rumours that the pope would use the October 1983 Synod of Bishops to make the great attempt. Nothing happened. So we go on waiting and hoping.

An Abiding Papal Function

In the hope-strained years for the Jews of the exilic and post-exilic period, Isaiah arose, prophet of expectation, of messianic hope. The present depressing state of things also stirs up dreams, together with a great number of novels, visions, films of a pope and a church to come.[162] Remarkably, two themes are repeated: the pope, a prophetic figure, gets into difficulties with the Curia and loses out; and he has as trusted friend a biblical scholar.

There is no doubt the church is in need of a sign of unity, especially today when it is spread over six continents and must commit itself to a radical decentralization and pluriformity. I shall later address the matter of *horizontal koinonia*, which binds the church together. Here, however, I cannot disregard *vertical koinonia*, the community of all churches under a final head. Even the churches of the Reformation long for unity. According to some sources, the question for them is not: Pope or no pope? The only question is: What kind of pope? [163]

Pope John Paul II, everyone will grant, has an enormous influence. He can fascinate great crowds, even of youth. Wherever he goes he is a success. In part this rests on the fact that he remains the sole outstanding figure in a world that not so long ago still had great men like Kennedy, de Gaulle, Adenauer, de Gasperi, Nehru. The UNO and the World Council of Churches are unity organizations but they lack a sign of unity. The churches and all humanity, striving after unity today, need a representative speaker. Pope John Paul II fills the gap spontaneously and providentially.

He and his successors should extend this function further. But they should not at the same time be head of the gigantic machinery of the Roman Curia. The more the pope declines juridically, the more he will grow spiritually and evangelically. The less Rome is Rome, the more the pope can be pope or, speaking ecumenically, the better he can exercise the function of Peter.

Before the election of John Paul II, rumours were going around that the Vatican was interested in acquiring buildings in Jerusalem and that the city would be declared an international city because the pope could set up his residence there surrounded by a dozen or so experts, and leave a 'deputy' behind in Rome to administer local affairs. In view of Christian ecumenism, history favours neither Rome nor Geneva as a world centre, but Jerusalem could be such. A utopian dream, which yet — given radical decentralization — could suddenly appear viable.

In any case the popes are in the service of the world church and as such are given permanent functions, which may seem much reduced in comparison with the papacy of the last hundred years but can in no way put in question the teaching of the First Vatican Council — and I leave dogmatic aspects aside here. In view of Vatican II, in view of the history of the first century, in view of biblical *kenosis*, and finally in view of the new church presence in six continents, this outlook could be very well thought of.

The Task of Evangelization. The special task of Peter, to which he was called by the express bidding of the Lord, was to spread the gospel and strengthen the brethren in the faith (Luke 22:32). Called to be the messenger of the gospel, Peter's successor could never do too much. With addresses to all groups, liturgies in all churches, journeys to every country, John Paul II is accepted everywhere. He has developed a new style accepted and admired by Catholics, other Christians, and non-Christians.

This task is today more necessary than ever before, for faith is no longer to be taken for granted and the faithful no longer form the majority in many a community; a task more delicate than ever, for an opponent is no longer to be worsted in apologetic contests but persuaded by the power of the gospel as lived; more sanctifying than ever, for it is no longer merely a question of salvation of the soul, supernatural grace, eternal life, but also of integral, immanent, historical salvation that preaches a better, more just, more human life, and struggles for it for all humanity here and now.[164] John Paul II without a doubt represents the highest moral authority in the world. He should be the first and chief evangelizer in the world. This office may and should continue.

The Task of Approval/Disapproval. 'Feed my sheep, feed my lambs' (John 21:15); 'I give to you the keys of the kingdom of Heaven' (Matt. 16:18). These words have often in the course of history been misapplied, by ideologically basing an absolutist monarchical power on them. It was forgotten that Jesus himself relativized these power-giving words when he indeed conceded that Peter had spoken out of divine inspiration, not merely 'from flesh and blood', but at once gave him a sharp reproof, as not having divine insight but playing the part of 'Satan' (Matt. 16:23).

The successor of Peter cannot, therefore, be denied — biblically, historically, or dogmatically — an ultimate power of leadership, or better a service of leadership, but its limits are also biblically, historically, and dogmatically well founded.[165]

Rome remains therefore the last court of appeal and should give approval to important decisions in the church. Rome can also when necessary exercise a veto power, but this should be the exception. Rome may act in reaching final decisions, but will do so credibly, and in a way that will be accepted by all, only when such decisions result not from mere authority but also from competence, when those behind them not only speak down from their isolation at the top of the pyramid, but from lived, experienced, warm contact and dialogue with local churches.

The Dutch Synod in Rome of 1980 must today be considered rather a fearful example of this appeal function. When it was announced, it was expected that the pope would with his charism bring the two groups of bishops together, with exchange and compromise. Instead the stronger group was simply confronted with the Roman line, put into the minority through the presence of the curial cardinals entitled to vote, and had no choice but to bow to their dictates.

171

The Task of Animation. 'Your old men will dream dreams'. The events of Pentecost had the onlookers thinking of these words of the prophet Joel (Acts 2:16). Just as from the church at Pentecost, so also from Rome there should come dreams, inspirations, utopias, models, hopes. In addition an exchange of such values ought to be furthered among local churches. Once local churches have the necessary freedom, dead bones will spring to new life (Ezek. 37:1–10), fresh blood will flow through the whole church from base level, local churches will take new theological and pastoral initiatives, develop new aspects, gather new experiences; and if these prove their worth, they will be taken up by other churches.

John Naisbitt, in his book on megatrends, notes that all the tendencies, new ideas, and initiatives in the U.S.A. have come from only five of the fifty states, but they then spread out nationwide. Similarly, the local churches do not all need to be equally active. They do not all have the same charisms. God so arranges that there are giving and receiving churches, and so all grow together into a *horizontal koinonia*. From the point of view of *vertical koinonia*, Rome would have the task of directing and fueling this exchange, acting as a clearing house for the best ideas from churches. There was an example of this in January 1983 in Rome at the meeting between a delegation from the U.S.A. Bishops' Conference and representatives of various European episcopal conferences on the question of nuclear arms and disarmament, at which the Vatican took the lead in the discussion. This then set in motion a whole chain reaction of similar statements from European episcopal conferences, so that today the prophetic voice of the church must be listened to on the matter of world peace.

Chapter Eleven

New Church Activity

A Widened Mission

I almost have to excuse myself for having spoken thus far of mainly internal church structures and questions. That sprang from the subject of this book and has its importance. But now it must be very plainly said that the church must take great care not to fall into narcissism, over concern for itself. That would be a very unfortunate divergence from the right path. Church questions become almost indifferent in view of world problems. It should never be said, 'The world can perish so long as the church survives', but rather — although it will never occur — 'the church can perish so long as the world survives'. God's love from the beginning was for humanity as a whole; and the church was willed and founded as a prophetic guardian for humanity on its way through history.

The mission of the church can be described thus: it is to interpret the world — that is, human beings, one and all — all regions and religions, thoroughly and with no reservations; it is to set a new worldview before our eyes, shot through with God's all-embracing love as Jesus has taught us. That is what was meant by the kingdom of God of whose coming Jesus was the witness and guarantor. That is what was meant by the mandate to evangelize, to preach God's message to the ends of the earth, to 'shalomize', set shalom — peace, salvation, justice — before the eyes of all.

The church is to transform the world. Jesus did not send his disciples out into the world empty-handed. They were to have no care for their personal needs, take no money or change of clothes with them, but they were to show great care for others, be signs to them, heal diseases and drive out devils — that is, free them from physical and psychological evil. Jesus did just that as he was daily pressed in upon by the crowds; his disciples must do it in an outflowing of love reaching as far as the ends of the earth. What the church undertook in the course of the centuries in works of civilization and charity was in keeping with this. In the context of the present day that would certainly mean no longer merely giving alms, no longer merely helping out on individual occasions, but tearing out evil by the roots, changing unjust systems, transforming the world.

The church is to christianize the world. If Jesus' disciples preach the word of God effectively, there will always be sympathizers who will watch and wonder at Christians, who will want to know more about them and their Jesus, will then perhaps enlist in the army of catechumens and in the end be baptized, not to 'save their souls', as though before they were damned, but to become full members of this church and themselves take their full part in its mission.

The church had therefore to be 'salt of the earth, light of the world' (Matt. 5:13), the means to an end, entirely directed toward humanity. But then all too soon its institutional aspect developed in such a way that it became an end in itself. Christians wanted to build up a great and powerful church. They went on the missions to baptize 'heathens' as quickly as possible and snatch them from perdition, because in the meantime God's all-embracing love had been narrowed down to the small circle of Christendom, and beyond this was seen only barbarism and the worship of idols. The trumpet of salvation was allowed to sound only within the church, not to the open marketplace of the world. The festival of fraternity was celebrated only within the 'clan', and with everyone else there was only quarrelling and even war. We were for so long a 'church against' — against the Jews, against the Muslims, against the heathen, against the heretics. We can truly take no pleasure in this story and can only rejoice that it is past history and that today we are accustomed to join in dialogue and common prayer with all these groups.[166]

Even the ecumenical councils were fundamentally directed toward the church as church. Outsiders had *anathema sit* fired at them. There was often talk of 'renewal of the church in head and members', but never, until Vatican II, was anything said of a positive possibility of salvation for all peoples, of a positive saving function in the non-Christian religions also, of the all-embracing love of God for all peoples, yet this is what would correspond to the teaching of Jesus.

174

The Opening Introduced by Vatican II

All the more for such reasons did Catholics breathe a sigh of relief at the opening of Vatican II. Taking the lead, the charismatic John XXIII, with his new style, changed the world climate in a matter of weeks. In his first audience the ice had been broken when he declared simply: 'Do not be afraid of me; I am Joseph your brother!' In a short time a new atmosphere was created in relation to other Christians, non-Christians, even Marxists. In accordance with this the council then produced in its pastoral deliberations *Unitatis Redintegratio*, on ecumenism; *Orientalium Ecclesiarum*, on dialogue with non-Christian religions; *Dignitatis Humanae*, on religious freedom.

The question remains, how far the new directioning from the top has worked its way through the whole fabric of the church.

It was said above that today the church everywhere lives in a 'mission situation', that therefore the challenge of evangelization is greater than ever before. For the years to come this accentuates the task of increasingly building into the Christian proclamation of the gospel the ideas and insights of postconciliar agencies and encouraging convinced Christians in their basic communities in every way to pioneer on the local level dialogue with other Christians, with non-Christians, with unbelievers, and campaign for justice and peace.

One need not blind oneself to the fact that such activity has to reckon with a certain mistrust on the part of traditional Christians, perhaps even the hierarchy, just as also in Rome there is a certain tension between the new secretariats and the old congregations. Traditionalists are sometimes afraid that if they let something new 'go too far', their own position will be threatened. But that exposes a false premise, as if 'their own position' were an end in itself to be guarded like hidden treasure. The only 'position' worthy of the church as institution is one that fosters openings for dialogue with the world and the proclamation of God's salvation to all the world.

Not only on the local level but also on the world level should ecumenism today be practised in its widest sense and in the most generous fashion. The time for polarization, exclusivism, divisions, belongs to the past, not to the future. The great rifts within Christianity — at the start of the second millennium for the

Eastern churches (1045), in the middle of that millennium for the Reformation churches — should not survive beyond the end of the present millennium. Now that the years 1960–1968 have seen the unfolding of ecumenical discussion, the years 1980–2000 should experience concrete ecumenical events so that we can hand over to the third millennium not an inheritance of bitterness and Christian divisiveness, but the charge of promoting osmosis between one church and another, and between church and world.

Chapter Twelve

New Church Unity

Assuming that the churches in the six continents will one day go about their tasks with greater decentralization, and that 'pluriformity' will become synonymous with 'catholicity', the worrisome question arises, Who or what will then hold all the churches together? One who has ecumenical unity at heart cannot at the same time easily speak of centrifugal forces. Or can one? Christian dialectic consists in striving for unity in diversity. Enough has already been said on legitimate pluriformity. Vertical *koinonia* too has been discussed as a force for unity. It remains to pursue horizontal *koininia* as a means whereby the various churches can grow among themselves into a living organism.

In the past great emphasis was put on unilateral 'aid to the missions', a one-way system, the flow of money, personnel, and ideas from the North to the South. This system did not favour unity but dependence, and with dependence humiliation, and with humiliation revolt. Today we must promote 'interchurch service'. All the churches have something to offer and something to receive. Mutual giving and receiving creates unity.

In interchurch service, this mutual giving and receiving can be detailed on five ascending levels of exchange.

Exchange of Money

Even though charity was thought by many Christians to be largely a matter of money — when the missionary had finished preaching, the faithful got out their purses and gave their mite — and even though money in fact always represents an important contribution by the rich to the poor and was recommended by the Apostle Paul in behalf of the Jerusalem community (2 Cor. 8), still this kind of help remains on the lowest level of *koinonia*. This does not imply that it is undesirable but rather that the other levels are much more meaningful.

First World Christians are still very generous toward the under-privileged in the Third World. In Germany, for example, Missio in 1982 collected 163 million marks in freewill offerings; the missionary orders and institutes collected an additional 161 million marks. Of course no return flow of money can be expected from the South, but the poor churches help one another, and more and more.

The task falls to missionary officials to see to it that monies are distributed aright, to use them carefully, sometimes for ecumenical projects, sometimes as contributions to encourage development schemes in the Third World. They have also to raise their voices in behalf of church groups with regard to governments and multi-national companies, so that greater justice be done in that direction. At the start of the first development decade, in 1960, the rich countries pledged themselves to contribute 1 percent of their gross national product for the development of the poor nations. At the UNCTAD conference of 1981 in Paris and Cancún, Mexico, however, it had to be acknowledged that on an average only .062 percent had been given — not even a tenth of what had been promised. The thirty-one poorest countries still have a per capita income of $70 to $150 a year.

Europe must rethink its position in the world. With the Constantinian era, and with the later colonial period, there was a return to the Old Testament mentality. Europeans believed themselves alone to be the chosen people and to enjoy a divinely guaranteed position above all other peoples. The Spanish and Portuguese made for South America, the French and British for North America, conscious of crossing the 'Red Sea' and conquering the 'promised land'. They had no reservations about subduing the inhabitants or even simply rooting them out. The same thing occurred with the colonial powers in Africa and Asia, especially with the Boers in South Africa.

Meanwhile colonialism came to an end with the wave of independence, but it was replaced by neocolonialism. When up to 1982 the developing countries were in debt to the tune of $548 milliard (billion), it was due in no small part to the fact that the industrial products they had to import rose around 500 percent in price within a 20-year period, whereas the raw materials they were able to sell fell by around 50 percent in price. If Europe wants to find itself a place in the new world constellation, it must see its function as being for the good of all peoples, and pass from the earlier mentality of overlordship and pillage to the New Testament spirit of service, sharing, and peaceful approaches. 'Who will be greatest among you must be your servant.... Anyone who has two coats should give to the person who has none. ... When someone strikes you on the right cheek, offer also the left'. World development makes us realize that such concepts, which hitherto were taken for the utopias of some dreamer, must soon become hard realities of practical politics if the world is to regain sanity.

At the moment a lamentable crisis reigns over the whole world, but especially in the Third World. In the first two development decades a system was allowed to grow up by which corruption, bureaucracy, individual and collective selfishness, ruled on a wide scale, and cheated the poor of their hopes. We have to start again at the very beginning and pass through the third development decade with emphasis on self-reliance, living standards, and economic independence in the Third World, through development carried on from within, according to the principles of subsidiarity and participation. And so we would follow along the way to a better future, one that does not mean giving help from our superfluity but creating better conditions for a common future.[167] Hope for the world today is indivisible. H. Dietz warns Europe not to think only of its own hopes and have no concern for the hopes of those in need. To do that would be unfaithful to the humanism of the West:

> It is now a question above all of fulfilling the hopes that are weakening on the borders of Europe. ... The struggle over Europe will be decided by the quality of its hope, above all in the world of the hopeless. The Third World will decide our fate.[168]

Exchange of Personnel

Interchange of personnel stands on a considerably higher plane than that of money. The persons in question here, moreover, are not the workforce of a business concern; they are mediators between the churches. On them depend also the other stages of *koinonia*.

179

We have already seen that Western missionaries are greatly declining in numbers. According to J. Schoemakers:

The Dutch missionaries are writing the last chapter of the history of their massive presence and their influence on the young churches. The majority are handing over their entire enterprise to local church authorities.[169]

The same has to be said of the missionaries of other countries.

Although the young churches have difficulty in filling gaps, they are not thinking only of themselves but are ready to take on a missionary effort in their turn. No church can be merely a local church. It must take part in the missionary task of the whole church. Pope Paul VI called on Africans on his first visit to Africa, in Uganda in 1969, to be their own missionaries. He made a similar appeal to Asians on his first visit to Asia, in 1970 in Manila.

Already the North-South flow is being complemented by a new East-West flow. There are, for example, at present 225 Japanese and 800 Filipino Catholic missionaries in other parts of Asia or in Africa and Latin America. In India, since the closing of the frontiers to foreign missionaries, hundreds of priests and thousands of sisters have moved from the south to the north where they have to learn a new language and insert themselves into a new culture, and to that extent are as much 'on mission' as First World missionaries were in former times. In Africa, religious institutes have been formed in Nigeria, Zaire, Uganda, and Tanzania to train missionaries for poorer churches. Latin America too, where the proportion of laity to clergy is at its highest, is becoming conscious that every church must be missionary. Individual bishops first of all initiated centre/periphery action by having urban Catholics establish community centres and act as animators for the rural poor who were migrating there, then there began a movement for the benefit of poorer areas of the country — for example, from southern to northern Brazil. A conference in Lima in 1981 aroused interest in reaching out to other continents, especially exchanges between the most Catholic continent, Latin America, and the least Christian continent, Asia, to build a kind of bridge.[170]

Even if Western missionaries are declining in numbers they will never quite die out. God will always give the missionary vocation to generous souls. So there will always be missionaries. The world of tomorrow will be more and more mixed — ethnically, racially, religiously. In earlier centuries Western colonial officials, soldiers, traders, and missionaries went to other continents; today diplomats, students, those seeking work, and refugees from those continents are heading to the West. It is a time of reverse migration! So many are looking for fresh pastures! London schools have counted pupils of fifty-five mother tongues; in the case of twelve languages the number of pupils amounted to easily over a thousand. The Committee for Racial Equality came to the conclusion in a memorandum to the government that the languages of ethnic minorities should not be referred to as 'foreign languages' but as languages of the various communities in the United Kingdom. Their presence in Great Britain is a result of its imperial past. Now it is a question of building a greater and fuller community of all people.[171]

In such a multiracial world missionaries will always be needed and they will be there, God's messengers to the peoples, messengers between churches and cultures, to exchange values, give hope, and build a unified human family.

Exchange of Theology

Third World theology not only brings the young churches to self-realization; it is becoming also for the Western church a challenge and an enrichment. At the EATWOT conference in New Delhi in 1981 there was emphasis on the 'irruption' of the Third World, in the sense that the poor, oppressed, despised masses are arising and carrying out their 'modern exodus'; but also in the sense that Third World theology poses a challenge for Western theology.[172]

Taking account of this contextual theology can help us to break out of our narrow bounds and more easily solve our problems. An Indian Jesuit once said to me:

We shall no longer feed ourselves on the European theology taught us in the seminary. All self-reliance and creativity were taken from us then. Meanwhile we have learnt to express ourselves, create our own theology to meet our own problems. For the state of the 650 million non-Christians who are poor and starving, Christ must be the answer. Our problems are no longer intercommunion with Protestants but how we can practise with our Hindu friends *communicatio in sacris*, which is the only true communication.

Of course divine revelation does not merely answer *our* questions and needs, but opens up a wide horizon of questions we had never thought of ourselves. There cannot be *communicatio in sacris*, in the old sense of the term, with Hindus. But such statements should make us think, and make us notice things that even from the ecclesiastical standpoint were ignored until now out of a European sense of superiority.

'Comparative theology' [173] is rightly advocated today, to be able to conduct a theological interchange on the world level and know one another, inspire one another, learn from one another. We have to be grateful to those publishers who with a certain risk to themselves have made Third World theology known in the West.[174] Theological boundaries today do not run so much *between* confessions and religions as *through them*. Rightly did EATWOT from the start build on an ecumenical basis, as did many theological societies in Western countries. Today there is frequently an interchange of guest lecturers; this must be so in the future also, more and more, not merely between the churches but also between religions, for in the end we are all, as thinking human beings, philosophers, theologians, creatures in search of meaning.

Exchange of Pastoral Experience

One step higher than theology is the exchange of pastoral experiences, attitudes, practices, just as vigorous life stands higher than all theory. Therefore 'comparative pastoral care' is being advocated.[175] This does not mean simply to imitate other churches. The Holy Spirit wants no carbon copies, only originals. The Spirit has a special message to be given to each church (Rev. 2–3). But this same Spirit also gives inspiration through other peoples and churches. Just as at the beginning there were Pauline communities centred on freedom, Johannine on love, Petrine on authority, so today there could and should be Western, Latin American, African, Asian churches all with their own characteristics, and yet able to learn from one another and together form the one church. The Western churches, for example, would do well to adopt something of the mystical element in the Eastern churches; and the Eastern would have something to learn of turning outward to the world and striving for justice. Something similar could then happen also among the various continental churches.

Now that the Western churches as a result of their own crisis period have grown rather tired and weary, they are the more open to suggestions from other continents: from Latin America, basic communities and services without a priest; from Africa, creative liturgy; from Asia, far-reaching dialogue. Once again, such an exchange does not take place merely between Catholic churches, but across confessional lines. Protestant churches in Africa, for example, admire the liturgical renewal in the Catholic Church, encourage more frequent celebration of the Eucharist, and recommend for it the Roman Missal and Lectionary.[176] Conversely, the African independent churches, with their radical loyalty to the gospel and to African cultures, exercise a great fascination over Catholic observers who suffer under the rigid structures of their church.[177]

The aim of pastoral exchange is also served by visits that priests, bishops, and bishops' conferences make to one another these days. The Lutheran bishops of the Scandinavian countries held their 1982 synod in São Paolo, Brazil, so as to make contact with that church and learn from experiences there. A group of Indian bishops made a pastoral visit to Germany in 1978, and a group of German bishops went to India in 1982. The intention was to become better partners in the one church, quite apart from any question of finance.[178]

Exchange of Lifestyles

We come now to the topmost step in ecclesial exchange. All the churches today are faced with the same threat and the same challenge: to live the faith in a secularized and unjust world. The sole credible response is orthopraxis, the self-evident actions of persons who have encountered Christ and now go through the world as his disciples, bearing witness to his lifestyle: performing good works everywhere and freeing persons from every ill (Acts 10:38).

All the churches are on view today in the world. None lives in a cave. After the Catholic Western Church had for too long a monopoly on saints and exported their veneration throughout the world, we are now beginning to learn also of saints from Latin America, Africa, and Asia,[179] even discovering with surprise 'saintly Protestants' and 'good heathen'.[180] With the worldwide emulation in spirituality of today, it is no longer being in the right that counts, but rather having more to offer of the experience of

God and credibility in lifestyle. This is a healthy development, a healing needed by all churches and religions. We have the good fortune to be living in an ecclesial period of exceptional vitality.

I have tried to mark out to some extent the way the church can perhaps go in the next decade on the basis of present tendencies and the signs of the times. But who knows? Reality is always presenting us with fresh surprises. History, especially church history, does not follow absolute laws. Humanly and theologically it is an unfathomable mystery.

It would be wrong not to care about the future. Conleth Overman has studied three possible scenarios for the future of the U.S.A.[181] First there is the *ideal* future, a utopia where creative imagination finds alternatives, where all are in the service of others, where the Charter of Human Rights has become a reality. Specialists give this vision 30 percent probability. Secondly follows the *plausible* future, constructed and manipulated by experts. They have a solution to every problem and are convinced that even the narrow straits of world economic crisis, ecology, and the arms race can be bridged. This vision is given a 50–50 chance of success. In the third place follows the *likely* future, in which everything goes on as before, holding fast to consumerism, looking more to quantity than to quality, living from day to day, and inspired more by a backward-looking than by a forward-looking attitude. This future is given 70 percent probability. Fundamentally, a sorry outlook. Is it perhaps to be applied to the church also?

If we want to leave this path in history and really enter on a new future, we must first change so that we see anew, feel anew, think anew, will anew. That was the aim of this book. It lies within us to change the probability figures so that perhaps even a utopian future could become a reality. It would already be much if by the year 2000 the rearguard of the church could arrive at the point where the vanguard is today.

Epilogue

Perspectives on Pastoral Ministry in the Future

by Karl Rahner

Inasmuch as I have always attempted to give a pastoral orientation to my theology, I should like in this contribution also to point out a bridge between dogmatic and pastoral theology and treat a theme that is not as yet to be found, in all clarity and detail, in the general consciousness of the church and its pastoral theology, but certainly should be. What I mean is hard to convey in ordinary terms; I hope it will become clear in the course of these considerations.

What I have in mind is the need to develop a strategic pastoral plan for the world church as such. I do not mean to suggest that I have myself discovered and developed such a plan, and I will present it to you in the following pages. What I mean is that no such plan exists as yet. But I think that such a plan — a global strategy for the world church as such — will gradually be seen as a postulate for the era of a world church.

With that said, the question can remain open here as to *who* could be the one to develop such a plan, whether it ought to be the world episcopate with and under the pope, or the whole body of pastoral theologians in the world, or a special commission set up in Rome — or perhaps that such a plan must spring from the working together of all these parties.

When I say that consciousness of this task is as yet hardly a fact, I am not of course passing judgement on what is actually going on in the pastoral theological consciousness of those who have a direct responsibility for the church as a whole, nor do I deny that there are attempts of a tangible kind at planning a pastoral and theological strategy such as proposed here for a world church. Work along this line has been presented by Walbert

Bühlmann in earlier books and is further developed here. I only mean that this theme has not been given the attention — neither in the church at large nor in Rome — that would make it an institutional commonplace. My modest intention is to effect some small opening of consciousness to the fact that the church, in its pastoral theology and pastoral planning, should elaborate an express and full conceptualization of such a strategy for its work as a world church.

It could be said that with the establishment of the Synod of Bishops by Paul VI such a task had been foreseen and taken up. If so, then I certainly would not want to underestimate or play down the importance of that episcopal body in its aim and in its conclusions. But I do not think that any synod gathering up to now has considered, even in general, what the *individual* local churches and their bishops have to do as individuals, and indeed in fulfilling their task in the immediate *present*. I do not think that the synod has given explicit consideration to the church as world church and as a *whole*, in its pastoral strategy as that of the one and entire church, and for the *future*.

No one who thinks it possible to answer this question with an unqualified affirmative can have anything against my intention here of presenting the need and the possibility of such a worldwide pastoral strategy.

A preliminary remark on what follows will not be out of place. In 1981 the Vienna Institute of Pastoral Theology celebrated its fiftieth anniversary. I was allowed to give a lecture to mark the occasion, though on a subject not directly related to the tasks and aims of that institute. The address was published in the Vienna periodical of pastoral theology *Diakonia*. I think it could also serve as a kind of resumé for this book by my friend Walbert Bühlmann. Therefore I have gladly agreed to his request to be allowed to put it at the end of his book. I have at the same time slightly reworked the earlier text. Of course in such a concluding essay, things will be said that have been dealt with more exactly and at greater length by Bühlmann himself.

Perhaps another observation should be added to what has been said. Someone might think that a strategy for a world church would already have been sought out and implemented by the various dicasteries of the central government of the church in

186

Rome. There is a Roman congregation for the evangelization of the peoples, a congregation for the Eastern churches, one for bishops, for the clergy, for sacramental discipline and the liturgy, for religious and secular institutes, for Catholic teaching, and so on; and there is a secretariat of state. It could be conjectured that Roman authorities are far-sighted, given to thinking over not only the immediate here-and-now requirements within their area of competence but questioning and weighing up requirements for the more distant future, and so they have already thought about and are developing a joint strategy for the pastoral task of the church. If and insofar as such is the case, it should not be undervalued. But it can be asked, with a certain scepticism, whether such a plan is being worked on in Rome. It would be a well-kept secret. But such a plan should be made known to the church as a whole, for ultimately it can be well thought out only if the whole church brings its experience to it.

I do not think that any member of the Synod of Bishops has so far heard of any such fundamental idea for a pastoral strategy for a world church as such. It can further be wondered whether the historically very haphazard development and divisioning of the Roman dicasteries still in existence today, in spite of the curial reform initiated by Paul VI, would have the punch and far-sightedness necessary for conceiving and developing such a plan. It may be wondered whether the individual dicasteries in their traditional isolation from one another are suited to such a joint plan and to the collaboration required for its realization. The difficulties over jurisdiction that arise between the Secretariat of State and the individual congregations and secretariats show that the ideal association and collaboration fundamental to a single well-considered strategic plan is still something to be desired. And finally, even if all that should in relatively ideal fashion be found in Rome, no decree has as yet gone out forbidding anyone to think along with such a project.

The World in the Future

If there is to be an examination of the nature and necessity of a strategic pastoral plan for the task pertaining to a world church as such, an all-embracing and systematic plan, then it must follow upon a consideration of two facts that have not been present before, but which are very important for the church today. They make understandable, by their conjunction, the possibility, nature, and necessity of such a strategic pastoral plan for a world church, and of an agent to carry out such a plan. First, there is a *world church* today, and secondly there are at least the beginnings of a secular *world strategy* for the future. The two together make the nature and necessity of a strategic pastoral plan for a world church intelligible.

There is a world church today. Christianity of course, with its message of salvation, was always intended for the whole of humanity, was potentially always a world church. But in fact the church, whether the Jewish-Christian or the church of Roman-Hellenistic civilization and of the West, was not actually a world church. And when, in the sixteenth century, following in the train of European imperialism and colonialism, it started out on its way to the whole world and to all peoples, the result of the missionary work of the church in modern times, however unavoidable it may have been, was that the church was primarily a Western Christianity exported throughout the world. The church really remained a Western church with mission stations in other parts of the world. Today, as became evident during the Second Vatican Council, the church is beginning to become a world church in fact. There is everywhere an indigenous episcopacy and clergy. The autonomy and independence of the large regional churches were basically recognized by the council. Everywhere, even if varying in intensity, there are the beginnings of a theology linked with diverse cultural ambiences. The inculturation of Christianity in various cultures is recognized, at least in principle, as being a duty of the church. This inculturation in diverse cultures, which remain diverse notwithstanding a certain one-world internationalization, means that these Christianities will remain distinct; they will form component parts of the one church. The former mission churches are already beginning, even though hesitantly, to come forward with positive, effective contributions to the life of the whole church. Everywhere there are questions about, and probings for a solution to the problem of, how church unity can be harmonized with legitimate pluriformity, so that the church will truly be a world church.

The new identity of the church as world church is in fact, even if not by its very nature, conditioned by a newly developed unity in human interrelatedness worldwide and the worldwide unity given to trading and planning. In the past the fate and history of individual peoples were separated from those of other peoples by a kind of 'no-man's-land': the reality and history of Prussia at the time of the Fredericks was unconnected with the reality and history of Thailand at the same time. Today everything is interdependent. The life and fate of every region of the earth is tangibly affected by everything that is happening elsewhere in the world. That is why there have been world wars, which were scarcely possible earlier; that is why there is a UNO and superpowers whose spheres of influence are coterminous with our earth. The unity of human history today is simply a fact; humankind is one not only in its origin and as an *a posteriori* idea conceived in our hands, but as an immediately graspable reality.

At the same time, by reason of mutually conditioning relationships, this humankind is *reflectively planning* its future, *compelled* to do so. Earlier the future was the more or less unplanned, unreflected, discontinuous outcome of chance that was thrust upon human beings by nature as a passively suffered fate, and a result of what they themselves were able to do in their present without wanting or being able to plan further. But now the future has entered the sphere of consciousness of the whole of humanity or at least is on the way to it. The future will be an unfolding of a *plan for the future*, and so the world and nature are not simply the foreordained and necessarily accepted sphere of a resigned humanity, but the material for a theatre of operations that humanity has itself built according to plan. For this there are artificial materials not at all available to nature itself, energy resources contrived and channelled by human ingenuity, and so on.

Of course this global planning of the human future is still in its first beginnings because a peace-seeking world government has yet to be installed. And of course such planning has its limits, if only because there is as yet no way to sift all the information from a totally universal computer for rational world-planning, quite apart from other limitations. And reflective world-planning is conditioned by the fact that humankind now has the means of destroying itself in various ways. We are aware of some of them today: nuclear annihilation; overpopulation with all its consequences; destruction of the environmental conditions necessary for human life; psychological dangers to the human collective consciousness that we can only begin to conjecture.

But all this does not do away with the fact that humanity is about to become a united subject actively planning and *compelled* to plan its future. The thought that we could go back to a naive, unreflecting stage of consciousness and functioning is a nostalgic dream whose realization would have to be paid for by wiping out a large part of humanity. Humanity is at the stage of reflective self-planning, or at least the beginnings of this kind of planning are within our grasp. Even though Marxist socialism in the long run shows itself in need of revamping, that does not mean that the individualism possible in the West with its small population of earlier times is not an obsolete way of life. Humanity everywhere will have to find a plan for new and better forms of socialization. There lies before us a task of worldwide political planning for which the UNO is only a modest beginning: it points in the direction of a type of world government (along with, it is to be hoped, an enduring pluralism of peoples and cultures) that already a hundred years ago neoscholastic philosophers advocated on the grounds of natural law. Biogenetic mutation and manipulation is not the answer. But that the biological aspects of human life will and must be planned and directed in some way, and not only by braking population expansion, has not been ruled out. That in the future the management, improvement, and care of the ecological conditions necessary for human life will have to be rationally planned worldwide is also self-evident. All these separate efforts and plannings are signs that corporate human consciousness is slowly entering the stage of worldwide reflective planning.

The Church in the Future

The church has in fact become a world church (at least incipiently) and at a time when humanity is becoming the planning, active subject of its own development. In the new theological and practical consciousness of humanity, the church must plan itself and its future in a new, hitherto unrealizable way. There must be global, active, strategic pastoral planning of the world church.

Before I set about concretizing this thesis further, there is a caution to be set alongside my basic theory, a caution that derives from the nature of creaturely freedom, not from that of absolute freedom. It is evident that human planning, as such, carries with it no absolute guarantee of realization. Those who set limits are

190

themselves limited; the future is always a source of surprises. Even at our freest, we always work with a given material, a material never entirely transparent; there spring from it again and again, in spite of all our planning, unforeseen surprises. Human freedom, though sovereign with respect to its own determinations, is always subject to determinations beyond its reach.

It follows that planning done by the church, ecclesiastical futurology, carries with it no guarantee of realization and the church has no choice but to go on its way to an unknown future. It must even be said that the church is the community of precisely those who, in reflective understanding, await the unplannable as their salvation, accept the incomprehensibility of God in the coming of the kingdom as their blessedness, and believe that watching and waiting for this unaccountable future of humanity is a fundamental duty of the church. The church is the sacrament of the unplanned future, because the future is no other than the eternal incomprehensibility of God.

But neither human freedom nor the church are thereby dispensed from planning. Human beings can still see the blessedness of heaven open to them when everything they have built up falls in ruins about them; but even so they must use foresight, plan the house of life anew each time, and always seek to build better. And the church, looking forward in hope to the coming of the incomprehensibility of God, must always be also a church of adaptability as a community, a church of order, of justice, of missionary zeal, and therefore a church of human planning. This it always was, fundamentally, but today it must be so as a world church under the conditions of a world become one, of a global planning by humanity, of reflexive futurology. Insofar as here more tasks arise than we can envisage, as a solution for which perhaps quite new, newly-structured agents must be found in the church, a few further suggestions should therefore now be made even if they promise to be neither systematic nor complete.

I think that, to instance a first example of a strategy for a world church as such, a searching reflection and thorough planning in reference to the church's consciousness of itself, the actual believing consciousness of the church, will have to be undertaken. The variance between what is officially taught as the faith of the church and what in fact is believed by the majority of its members has for various reasons, which it will not be possible to examine here, grown enormously greater than was earlier the case. Granted that in the church there ought to be and can be no manipulation of the collective consciousness, as in totalitarian states, yet the connection between official church teaching and the facts at base level is no longer effectively accomplished by those means alone that sufficed earlier. Today the Congregation for the Doctrine of the Faith, encyclicals, papal addresses with their traditional formulations, pastoral letters with their traditional tone and content, sermons with a narrowly Catholic content and aimed far too little or too timidly at the ear of the unbeliever or the marginal Catholic, the catechisms that are still just as narrowly Catholic 'as before, are just not enough any longer to carry the wonderful message of Christianity to human beings as they in fact are today, and so also to lessen the gap between the official faith of the church and the faith that, by Christian conviction, really exists in the minds of Christians and is known to non-Christians. How a new formation and direction of de facto faith-consciousness could be planned and organized, how exactly the agent of such planning is to be thought of, how the instruction of the people can today pass from becoming merely an ever increasingly ineffective reliance on ecclesiastical authority to an instruction called forth by the inner grandeur of the matter itself — all these are questions that I do not know how to answer, but they are urgent, and in the framework of a world pastoral strategy will have to be answered.

This task raises many theological questions. The teaching office of the church cannot simply wait passively for theologians' answers, but must take part in helping and organizing, so that such problems will be made known and, so far as possible, be dealt with. I have just recently asked why there is no papal encyclical forthcoming on atheism today; I am still left wondering why papal encyclicals deal with the incarnation of the eternal Word without making the slightest attempt to smooth the way toward this basic Christian teaching for the unbeliever of today, to whom it appears sheer nonsense.

A few years ago a member of the Congregation for the Doctrine of the Faith said to me that the magisterium had only to watch that Christian teaching not be falsified or watered down, its interpretation and apologetic being the concern of theologians. That is not how things are today. The apologetic and interpretation of the corpus of Christian teaching by theologians today should at

192

least be encouraged and furthered by the magisterium. The magisterium should at the least make theologians aware of problems
waiting to be dealt with. There are very many of them but, it
seems to me, the magisterium becomes aware of them even later
than do theologians. Are there not, for example, lurking behind
the alarming falling off in frequent confession, complicated theological problems left almost untouched by both the magisterium
and the theologians?

On the Feast of Christ the King, what am I to think of Christ's
rule over the whole cosmos when at the same time I have to think
of it as a universe of 20 milliard light-years? Does not moral
theology often appeal to 'natural law' when in fact there is question
of the thought patterns of Western civilization? These are only
random examples. But should there not be in the church a reflective and informed strategy to educate public opinion on these
questions — and a thousand others?

At a given point, or so I think, general statements will become
clear. I suspect that persons in the early church knew what they
were supposed to believe when they heard the Apostles' Creed (at
least if combined with a brief instruction). I also suspect that, in
spite of all the normative significance this creed has and also will
have in the future, most persons would understand nothing or almost
nothing if I recite this creed to them today, and even if I try to
explain it briefly. They will ask me straightaway how God is to
be thought of if not enthroned in the 'heaven of heavens' but still
at work millions of light-years away — if God there be. Where are
the new contemporary elements of the creed (I am not thinking
of the words but of the subject matter) by the help of which even
an unbeliever of today could at least rightly understand what
Christians really believe?

A methodological policy for systematic and practical theology
will have to work, untrammelled and courageously, toward a
globalization in theology and in evangelization. Certainly Christianity cannot in theory or in practice deny its own historical origins.
In the future, everywhere in the world and in all the cultures of the
world, it will still have to be taught that it came from Palestine and
penetrated Western culture. But if and because Christianity is now
at last to become a world religion — that is, a religion also of those
peoples for whom the Mediterranean and the West are not the
places from which their being and their history originated —

nothing remains for Christianity except to become global — to become less historically coloured in theory and practice: to let historical events, insofar as they do not condition its actual nature, fall back quietly into a (merely) historical background (only). We have to ask ourselves what Christian theory and practice would look like when, to the world outside the West, elements of its historical conditioning fade away — just as perhaps for us Jewish theology at the time of Jesus has become unknown and a matter of indifference. Such changes will inevitably come, but we should already be learning to see them today as an exercise in a reflective methodological policy for systematic and practical theology.

A quite other but important group of questions on a truly world-wide strategy for the church has been raised on the connection, which still remains unclear, between the church as a whole and the regional churches taken individually. The Second Vatican Council did indeed solemnly declare that local churches are not just administrative subdivisions of one homogeneously structured universal church distinguishable merely by a few entirely secondary subsidiary characteristics. But by and large (if we abstract from the small uniate churches of the Middle East) this general principle remains suspended in midair. In Rome as homogeneous a canon law as possible is desired for the whole church, even if the new code is only for the 'Latin church'. The liturgies in other parts of the world are translations of the Roman liturgy. Appeal can of course be made to the principle that the unity of the church necessitates some unified detail in the universal church — but not so that the principle of independence and differentiation is sabotaged or merely paid lip-service. What independence and initiative of a concrete, tangible kind has Rome made room for in the churches in Latin America or Indonesia? I admit, the consequences of a dialetical relationship between universal church and individual churches are in practice not easily discernible. But where is there an example of such questions being boldly thought through in principle and with the cooperation of the universal church, and care taken that conclusions be put into effect?

The church acknowledged in the Second Vatican Council loud and clear its responsibility for the world, its responsibility for peace and justice in the world. It has also in this respect done not a little in past decades, even if not a little that was done and explained in this connection at the highest level was sabotaged lower down by inertia or silent opposition. But could not more still be thought of in this connection? Has the church today the courage to initiate more concrete demands for social change, for peace and disarmament, even if afterward such movements founder on refusal within the church itself, especially among politicians? Is there in Rome a centre for studying all these questions radically, systematically, with exactitude, and not just out of praiseworthy benevolence on the part of this or that official, but boldly pursued all the way to concrete solutions? Of course there are those in Rome who busy themselves with such problems, who represent the Holy See at all possible congresses and meetings, but a unified, courageous, active representation in the church of a shared responsibility for the world is not plainly visible in Rome. Yes, it seems that in spite of papal journeys throughout the world, the will in Rome is to withdraw from this task rather than contribute to it, and that Rome is anxious and nervous, and tends to take refuge in the sacristy when Christians in the world actively seek to assume their responsibility of serious social criticism.

There is a further task (of course alongside many others not mentioned) that seems to me to belong to the still largely misunderstood worldwide pastoral strategy of the world church as such. I should like to call this the question of the worldwide diaspora situation of the church. In practice the church still works mostly on the assumption that there are, as perhaps in Poland, more or less intact homogeneous Catholic blocs forming social groupings, as was the case until well into the twentieth century. At that time, for example, marriage between two Catholics was taken for granted and a mixed marriage could be treated as the rare exception, only allowed with caution; Catholic professional associations could be formed easily; Catholic schools could be advocated; cultural life in art, literature, and society could still widely found under Catholic auspices within the church. Today this is seldom the case. Christians everywhere live so much in a diaspora that, even in groups faithful to the magisterium of the church, those living as dedicated, thoroughgoing Catholics are often only a small minority. This state of things, which is to be found not only in the so-called missions but also among traditionally Christian peoples, has, or so I think, not yet been given really systematic and courageous theological and pastoral reflection in the church.

Diaspora Catholics everywhere speak the language of their milieu,

195

which is a pagan one. What, then, must the language of the church be, so that it can really be understood? In a glossary of the words a child in a primary school must learn and understand according to the norms of one state in the Federal Republic of Germany, perhaps one percent have a religious connotation. What today are the self-evident principles of an existential kind from which to start out in order to make Christianity understandable and credible? If, in the early church, a moral code that accepted slavery could be tolerated (perhaps unreflectively), what objectively immoral or false, but common, practices could the church overlook in silence today (though with reflective consciousness), to save exhausting its powers on ineffectual protests? Can the church today without more ado presume, as it did earlier, that outside and even inside the church the necessary commitment to marriage exists from the outset? In the interests of concrete ecclesiastical concern over morality, must not the socio-political presuppositions of diverse cultures be studied and calculated more painstakingly than before, when Christian morality was simply exported to mission countries unquestioned and unadapted? What use is it, a South American bishop has lately asked, if the church in a particular country considers harmless the extreme value set in getting married when the majority of children are born out of wedlock? On what front of the moral struggle (certainly not on all of them at once) should the church clearly and decidedly fight in order to witness in a pagan world to the greatness and worth of Christian morality? If, as in all ages of the church, Christian morality also today singles out certain points at issue without thereby abandoning or denying others, then it could well be, for example, that to condemn the arms race would for the moral consciousness of a secularized world be a more important index of Christian morality than to mount a campaign against 'the pill'. There have always been shifts of accent in moral matters (the popes at the time of Louis XIV suffered no grey hairs over his immoral war policies, and no one took it ill of them). But today such shifts of accent could and should be planned as part of a worldwide pastoral strategy. If this diaspora situation is not to be seen only as something to be lamented, then why should so much effort be expended to make pastoral ministry everywhere the same? Should not the church strive rather to cultivate fruitful oases in a secularized world as in a desert, even if this low-profile, soft-pedalled presence of the church cannot be everywhere? In any

196

case the worldwide pastoral strategy necessitated by the diaspora situation found everywhere sets tasks that for far too long have not been clearly seen or fulfilled.

There has been considerable talk about a retreat from middle-class Christianity, the 'service-station church'. It is of course not possible to decide here what is right in such a challenging situation, what can be done today in this regard, how to programme for a more distant future, what would be an appropriate or inappropriate transfer of models from other countries and cultures to European circumstances, what is merely utopian, what exactly will be the development of the secular world community of the future. But certainly there lies in this an important and correct perspective on the future, which has to be seen, reflected on, and planned. If, for example, the church in the future still insists on celibacy, very far-reaching changes will be called for, not all of which have been thought out by Rome, much less acted on, but which will inevitably come, if the church is not to shrivel into a small sect. With a small body of celibate clergymen, the laity will necessarily achieve greater self-reliance, influence, and importance than it has now. Lay persons will become, from below, in basic communities, the agents of the self-realization of the church.

The average Christian takes it for granted, of course, that the church of the future will go on being the church of today and yesterday, with the same social structures, 'indestructible by divine right', as is commonly assumed. But nevertheless in the year 2200 the church must and will look very different in its outward appearance from what we are accustomed to today. Is this future image to come upon the church unquestioned in advance? Is it something that will 'happen' by small degrees without much foresight, or even be wrested at times piecemeal from the contemporary situation, like the church of mediaeval feudalism following on the church of the fathers? Or must it not also, keeping in mind the present-day state of collective human consciousness, be a task of the church, even if not as a top priority, to *look ahead* and *plan ahead* as much as possible? Can and must there not be in the church a more far-seeing worldwide strategy of pastoral care than hitherto? This seems to me a genuine question for the church, one that is not perceived clearly enough. Simply to pose this question, even though haltingly and gropingly, seems to me also a way in which pastoral theology can and must be pursued. That is what is done — germinally, but effectively — in this book by Walbert Bühlmann.

Notes

1   These points are covered and further developed in other of my writings: *Wo der Glaube lebt: Einblicke in die Lage der Weltkirche*, Freiburg, 7th ed., 1978; *Missionsprozess in Addis Abeba*, Frankfurt, 1977 (Engl. translation, *The Missions on Trial*, Slough, 1978; Maryknoll, N.Y., 1979); *Alle haben denselben Gott*, Frankfurt, 1978 (Engl. translation, *All Have the Same God*, Slough, 1978; *The Search for God*, Maryknoll, 1980); *Ein Missionsorden fragt nach seiner Zukunft*, Münsterschwarzach, 1979; *Wenn Gott zu allen Menschen geht: Für eine neue Erfahrung der Auserwählung*, Freiburg, 1981.

2   *Lumen Gentium*, 13, 23; *Sacrosanctum Concilium*, 37–40; *Ad Gentes*, passim; *Evangelii Nuntiandi*, 63.

3   E.g., L. Bertsch and F. Schlösser, eds., *Kirchliche und nichtkirchliche Religiosität*, Freiburg, 1978; *Kirchlich distanzierte Christen*, Vienna, Österreichisches Pastoralinstitut, 1978; J. Höffner, *Pastoral der Kirchenfremden*, Bonn, 1980.

4   For what has been done in this regard in the U.S.A., see my 'Evangelizierung der kirchlich Distanzierten: Modelle aus den Vereinigten Staaten', *Diakonia*, Vienna, 1980, pp. 210–12.

5   See Hans-Jürgen Prien, *Die Geschichte des Christentums in Lateinamerika*, Göttingen, 1978, pp. 33–57; 'America', in *Enciclopedia Italiana*, Rome, I (1968), 515–35.

6   See Prien, *Geschichte*, pp. 58–326; R. Ricard, *La "conquête spirituelle" du Mexique*, Paris, 1933.

7   See M. J. MacLod, *Spanish Central America: A Socio-economic History, 1520–1720*, University of California Press, 1973, pp. 47–54.

8   Cited in Prien, *Geschichte*, p. 167. See also J. Höffner, *Christentum und Menschenwürde*, Trier, 1947, p. 90. See also my 'Die Rechte der Person und der Nation und ihre Bedeutung für die Mission', *Neue Zeitschrift für Missionswissenschaft*, 1957, p. 192–207, 241–55.

9   R. Konetzky, *Süd- und Mittelamerika*, Frankfurt, I (1965), 334–42; his judgements are well balanced.

10 See W. Henkel, 'Proposte del Terzo Sinodo Provinciale Messicano (1585) per una più efficace evangelizzazione', *Euntes Docete*, Rome, 1979, pp. 455–64.

11 Prien, *Geschichte*, p. 33.

12 In G. T. Taynal, *Histoire philosophique et politique des établissements et du commerce des Européens dans les deux Indes*, Paris, 1962; see also U. Bitterli, *Die "Wilden" and die "Zivilizierten": Grundzüge einer Geistes- und Kulturgeschichte der europäischübeerseeischen Begegnung*, Munich, 1976.

13 See José Comblin, *The Church and the National Security State*, Maryknoll, N.Y., 1979.

14 See V. Bennholdt et al., eds., *Lateinamerika: Analysen und Berichte*, Berlin, I (1977), 7–8.
15 See *Herder Korrespondenz*, 1983, pp. 6–8.
16 See Prien, *Geschichte*, pp. 1026–41; Gustavo Gutiérrez, *A Theology of Liberation*, Maryknoll, N.Y., 1973.
17 See J. Holland and P. Henriot, *Social Analysis: Linking Faith and Justice*, Washington, 1980.
18 See the various reports on these conferences. On the New Delhi conference, see *SEDOS Bulletin*, Rome, 1982, the issues from July to November; L. Wiedemann, ed., *Herausgefordert durch die Armen: Dokumente der Vereinigung von Dritte-Welt-Theologen, 1967–1983*, Freiburg, 1983.
19 The papers of these conferences have all been published by Orbis Books, Maryknoll, N.Y.: Sergio Torres and Virginia Fabella, eds. (Dar es Salaam, 1976), *The Emergent Gospel: Theology from the Underside of History*, 1978 (co-published by G. Chapman, London); Kofi Appiah-Kubi and Sergio Torres, eds. (Accra, 1977), *African Theology en Route*, 1979; Virginia Fabella, ed. (Wennappuwa, 1979), *Asia's Struggle for Full Humanity: Towards a Relevant Theology*, 1980; Sergio Torres and John Eagleson, eds. (Sao Paulo, 1980), *The Challenge of Basic Christian Communities*, 1981; Virginia Fabella and Sergio Torres, eds. (Geneva, 1983), *Doing Theology in a Divided World*, 1985.
20 Maryknoll, N.Y., 1980.
21 See B. Joinet, *Tanzanie: Manger d'abord*, Paris, 1981.
22 See V. Matthies, *Das "Horn von Afrika" in den internationalen Beziehungen*, Munich, 1976; I. Grey, *The Communist Challenge to Africa: An Analysis of Contemporary Soviet, Chinese, and Cuban Policies*, Surrey, 1977; A. Mbuyinga, *Panafricanisme et néo-colonialisme: La faillite de l'O.U.A.*, Paris, 1979.
23 See my *Wenn Gott* (n. 1, above), pp. 93–95, with the references there cited; see also A. Imfeld, ed., *Verlernen, was mich stumm macht: Lesebuch zur afrikanischen Kultur*, Zurich, 1980, pp. 26–60.
24 See V. Mulago, 'L'Africanité et Evangélisation', *Evangelizzazione e Culture*, Rome, Università Urbaniana, 3 (1976), 7–20. See also M. Ntetem, *Die negro-afrikanische Stammesinitiation: Religionsgeschichtliche Darstellung, theologische Verwertung, Möglichkeit der Christianisierung*, Münsterschwarzach, 1983; A. T. Sanon and R. Luneau, *Enraciner l'Evangile: Initiations africaines et pédagogie de la foi*, Paris, 1983.
25 See, e.g., the series *Classiques africains* published by Edition Armand Colin, Paris, in more than twenty volumes.
26 See my *Sie folgten dem Ruf: Afrikanische Zeugen des Glaubens*, Mainz, 1982, pp. 95, 99. See also T. Sundermeier, *Christus, der schwarze Befreier*, Erlangen, 1973.
27 See my 'L'autre face de l'histoire des missions', *Neue Zeitschrift für Missionswissenschaft*, 1982, pp. 127ff.
28 In my 'L'autre face', pp. 129–32. See also M. P. Hebga, *Emancipation d'Eglises sous tutelle: Essai sur l'ère post-missionnaire*, Paris, 1976; R. Luneau and J. M. Ela, *Voici le temps des héritiers: Eglises d'Afrique et voies nouvelles*, Paris, 1981.
29 See *Herder Korrespondenz*, Jan. 1983, pp. 23–30.

30 See K. Julian, 'Christian Sacraments and African Religious Rites', *Evangelizzazione e Culture*, 3 (1976) 51–68.

31 See W. Brandmüller, *Konzilsgeschichte*, Paderborn, 1979. See also *Pour un Concile Africain*, Paris, 1978.

32 See H. Nakamura, *Ways of Thinking of Eastern Peoples*, Honolulu, 1974.

33 *The Vedic Experience: An Anthology of the Vedas for Modern Man and Contemporary Celebration*, London, 1977.

34 See D. S. Amalorpavadass, *Research Seminar on Non-biblical Scriptures*, Bangalore, 1975.

35 See P. Rossano, 'Sulla presenza e attività dello Spirito Santo nelle religioni e nelle culture non cristiane', *Prospettive della Missiologia oggi*, Rome, Università Gregoriana, 1982, pp. 59–71; T. Michel, 'Criteria for Discerning the Movement of the Holy Spirit in Islam', in *Credo in Spiritum Sanctum*, Atti del Congresso Teologico Internazionale di Pneumatologia, Rome, Università Urbaniana, II (1983) 1411–26.

36 See my *All Have the Same God (The Search for God)* (n. 1, above).

37 See P. Gerlitz, *Kommt die Welteinheitsreligion?*, Hamburg, 1968; see also the prophetic utterances of Nicholas of Cusa (1401–1446) in his *De pace et de unitate fidei*.

38 'Censorship and the Future of Asian Theology', *Anawim*, New Delhi, 29 (1981) 1–10.

39 See P. Schwarzenau, *Der grössere Gott: Christentum und die Weltreligionen*, Stuttgart, 1977, p. 13.

40 See D. Acharuparambil, 'The Problem of Presenting Christianity to Hinduism', *Evangelizzazione e Culture*, 3 (1976) 163–82.

41 See my *Wenn Gott*, pp. 71–119.

42 *Saints for Sinners: The Failure of St. Francis Xavier*, London, 1936. See also G. Schürhammer, *Franz Xaver: Sein Leben und seine Zeit*, Freiburg, 2 vols., 1955, 1973.

43 See W. Henkel, 'Christentum und Kultur bei Chateaubriand und sein Einfluss auf das 19. Jahrhundert', *Evangelizzazione e Culture*, 2 (1975) 364–73.

44 *Katholische Missionsgeschichte*, Steyl, 1924, pp. 1ff.; idem, 'Konfessionelle Missionspolemik', *Zeitschrift für Missionswissenschaft*, 1920, pp. 93–101.

45 See M. D. Chenu, *Dieu est noir*, Paris, 1977.

46 See J. Schütte, *Die katholische Chinamission im Spiegel der rotchinesischen Presse*, Münster, 1957.

47 *The Role of the Missionaries in the Conquest*, Johannesburg, 1952.

48 *Des prêtres noirs s'interrogent*, Paris, 1956.

49 *Missions on Trial* (n. 1, above); 'L'autre face' (n. 27, above), pp. 124–35.

50 See J. Meier, 'Zehn Jahre "Studienkommission für Lateinamerikanische Kirchengeschichte" ', *Neue Zeitschrift für Missionswissenschaft*, 1983, pp. 61–66.

51 See also Bitterli, *Die "Wilden"* (n. 12, above).

52 *Histoire Générale de l'Afrique Noire*, Paris, 2 vols., 1970, 1971.

53 *Histoire de l'Afrique Noire*, Paris, 1972.

54 J. D. Frage and R. Oliver, eds., Cambridge, 8 vols., 1976–83.

55 *Histoire Générale de l'Afrique Noire*, Paris, UNESCO, 1980.

56 Geschichte des Christentums in Lateinamerika, Göttingen, 1978.
57 See J. Splett, 'Die theologische Dimension der Geschichte', Zeitschrift für katholische Theologie, 1978, pp. 302–17.
58 See E. Biser, 'Friede', in Lexikon für Theologie und Kirche, 4, 366–69; R. Friedli, Frieden wagen: Ein Beitrag der Religionen zur Gewaltanalyse und zur Friedensarbeit, Fribourg, 1981; M. van Lay, Kirche im Entkolonisieurungskonflikt, Mainz, 1981; B. Häring, 'Peace on earth', in Free and Faithful in Christ, III, Slough/New York, (1981), pp. 391–422.
59 Häring, ibid.
60 Although Pope Paul VI on several occasions acknowledged fault, Pope John Paul II seems to have the tendency to extenuate everything. Compare Redemptor Hominis, 12, with Familiaris Consortio, 10.
61 See my Wenn Gott, pp. 71–119, and The Missions on Trial.
62 J. B. Metz, Zur Theologie der Welt, Mainz, 1969, p. 93.
63 See Torres and Fabella, Emergent Gospel (n. 19, above).
64 See A. Pecci (president of the Club of Rome), Die Zukunft in unserer Hand, Vienna, 1981, p. 108.
65 La S. Sede e il disarmo, Vatican City, 1977.
66 See H. Rzepkowski, 'Deutsche Missionare', in Missio pastoral, Aachen, I (1980) 33–39.
67 Herder Korrespondenz, Dec. 1981, pp. 624–30.
68 See Friedli, Frieden wagen (n. 58, above), p. 181.
69 Ibid., pp. 201–18.
70 See the entire vol. 3 of Häring, Free and Faithful in Christ (n. 58, above); see also C. Grannis, The Risk of the Cross: Christian Discipleship in the Nuclear Age, New York, 1981.
71 Worthy of mention here is the American initiative that led to the legislation signed by President Reagan in October 1984 'to establish an independent, non-profit, national institute [the U.S. Peace Institute] to serve the people and the government through the widest possible range of education and training, basic and applied research opportunities, and peace information services as the means to promote international peace, and the resolution of conflicts among the nations and peoples of the world without resort to violence'.
72 These five levels of exchange will be developed in greater detail in chap. 12, below.
73 See K. Esser, 'Franz von Assisi und die Katherer seiner Zeit', Archivium Franciscanum-Historicum, 51 (1985) 225–64; idem, 'Die religiösen Bewegungen des Hochmittelalters von Franz von Assisi', in Festschrift J. Lortz: Glaube und Geschichte, II (1958) 287–315.
74 See my 'Missionsverständnis des heiligen Franziskus nach der Regula non bullata', in A. Camps and G. Hunold, eds., Erschaffe mir ein neues Volk, Mettingen, 1982, pp. 13–29.
75 See Grand Larousse Encyclopédique, Paris, IV (1961) 867.
76 Heinrich Fries, in R. Bärenz, ed., Die Kirche und die Zukunft des Christentums, Munich, 1982, p. 46.
77 For statistics on the Catholic Church I have used the Annuarium Statisticum Ecclesiae 1970, Vatican City, 1973 (and subsequent editions), and the Annuario Pontificio, 1960. For statistics on all the Christian churches I have used Donald B. Barrett, ed., World Christian Encyclopedia: A Comparative Study of Churches and Religions in the Modern World A.D. 1900–2000, Oxford, 1982.
78 See my Wo der Glaube lebt (n. 1, above), p. 29.

79 Ibid., pp. 158–60.
80 Rzepkowski, 'Deutsche Missionare' (n. 66, above), pp. 33–39.
81 Barrett, *Encyclopedia*, p. 17.
82 For literature, sometimes polemical, on this subject, see J. Power, *Le Missioni non sono finite*, Bologna, 1970; J. Masson, *La Missione continua*, Bologna, 1975; G. Butturini, *La "fine delle Missioni"*, Bologna, 1979; E. Kendall, *The End of an Era: Africa and the Missionary*, London, 1979.
83 See my *Wenn Gott* (n. 1, above), pp. 186–249.
84 Among other biographies, see *Gandhi ci parla di Gesù*, Bologna, EMI, 1980.
85 See *The Image of Christianity in Japan*, Tokyo, 1980.
86 See Barrett, *Encyclopedia*, esp. pp. 18ff., 117–122, 796–98, and the simplified table on p. 798.
87 See T. Rendtdorff, *Christentum ausserhalb der Kirche*, Hamburg, 1969; J. Amstutz, 'Über die Allgegenwart der Gnade', *Neue Zeitschrift fur Missionswissenschaft*, 1982, pp. 81–109, esp. 107ff.
88 See the 60-page document by the German bishops' conference, *Muslime in Deutschland*, Bonn, 1982.
89 Dietrich Bonhoeffer, *Widerstand und Ergebung: Briefe und Aufzeichnungen aus der Haft* (E. Bethge, ed.), Munich, 1964.
90 *Gottesvergiftung*, Suhrkamp Taschenbuch, 1980; see also J. Türk, ed., *Glaube und Unglaube*, Mainz, 1971.
91 P. M. Zulehner, *"Leutereligion": Eine neue Gestalt des Christentums auf dem Weg durch die achtziger Jahre*, Freiburg, 1982, p. 57; idem, *Religion im Leben der Österreicher*, Freiburg, 1981, p. 35.
92 'Entkirchlichung in der Grossstadt: München Statistik', *Herder Korrespondenz*, Sept. 1975, pp. 428–30.
93 J. W. Varroll, ed., *Religion in America*, New York, 1979, esp. G. Gallup, 'A Coming Religious Survival?', pp. 111–15.
94 Barrett, *Encyclopedia*, p. 5.
95 See Karl Rahner, 'Theologische Bedeutung der Position des Christen in der modernen Welt', *Sendung und Gnade*, Innsbruck, 4th ed., 1966, pp. 13–47; idem, *Strukturwandel der Kirche als Aufgabe und Chance*, Freiburg, 3rd ed., 1973, pp. 21–48; N. Mette, *Kirchlich distanzierte Christenheit: Eine Herausforderung für die praktische Kirchentheorie*, Munich, 1982.
96 There is a wealth of material on the question of office in the church; see, e.g., K. Kertelge, *Gemeinde und Amt im Neuen Testament*, Munich, 1972; E. Schillebeeckx, *Das kirchliche Amt*, Düsseldorf, 1981; J. Fuellenbach, *Ecclesiastical Office and the Primacy of Rome*, Washington, 1980; H. J. Venetz, *So fing es mit der Kirche an: Ein Blick in das Neue Testament*, Zurich, 1981.
97 A. Acerbi, *Due ecclesiologie: Ecclesiologia giuridica ed ecclesiologia di comunione nella "Lumen gentium"*, Bologna, 1975; H. Wieh, *Konzil und Gemeinde*, Frankfurt, 1978.
98 E. Sauser, *Woher kommt die Kirche? Ortskirche in der Frühzeit und Kirchenbewusstsein heute*, Frankfurt, 1978; H. Frankenmölle, ed., *Kirche von unten. Alternative Gemeinde: Modelle — Erfahrungen — Reflexionen*, Mainz, 1981; J. Cappellaro, J. Mira, and J. Jimenez, *Pfarrgemeinde der Zukunft: Eine Gemeinschaft von Gemeinschaften*, Thaur, Tirol, 1979; G. Hartmann, *Christliche Basisgruppen und ihre*

befreiende Praxis, Mainz, 1980.

99 *Der aufgeweckte Siebenschläfer*, Würzburg, 1962.

100 See my *Wenn Gott*, pp. 71–119.

101 Cited in D. Günter Jacob, 'Die Zukunft der Kirche in der Welt des Jahres 1985', *Junge Kirche: Protestantische Monatshefte*, Dortmund, 7 (1967) 1–16.

102 *Let My People Go: A Study of the Catholic Church in West Nigeria*, Brussels, 1974, p. 303.

103 See P. Angela, *La vasca di Archimede*, Milan, 1975, pp. 11–18; D. Meadows, *The Limits to Growth*, New York, 1972; Club of Rome, *Das menschliche Dilemma: Zukunft und Lernen — Bericht für die achtziger Jahre*, Munich, 1979.

104 See T. Mommsen, *Römische Geschichte*, Berlin, 5 vols., 1868–85; W. B. Durant, *Caesar und Christus: Eine Kulturgeschichte Roms und des Christentums*, Bern, 1956, pp. 466–68, 531–33, 748–53.

105 See W. D. Hussey, *The British Empire and Commonwealth*, Cambridge, 1968; J. Morris, *Heaven's Command: An Imperial Progress*, London, 1973; Lord Hailey, *An African Survey*, Oxford, 1957, pp. 51ff., 201ff., 414–17.

106 World Conference on Agrarian Reform and Rural Development, Rome, FAO, 1979.

107 New York, Warner Books, 6th ed.,1983.

108 See his Epilogue at the end of this book.

109 See G. Alberigo, ed., *Kirche im Wandel*, Düsseldorf, 1982; J. M. R. Tillard, *L'évêque de Rome*, Paris, 1982, p. 65; R. Minnerath, *Le Pape, évêque universel ou premier des évêques?*, Paris, 1978; P. Granfield, *The Papacy in Transition*, Dublin, 1984, pp. 17–33; G. Feliciani, *Le Conferenze Episcopali*, Bologna, 1974.

110 See, e.g., the address to the CCEE on Dec. 21, 1978; the European bishops' message, Subiaco, Sept. 28, 1980; and his addresses on the occasion of the Austrian Katholikentag, Vienna, 1983.

111 Synodus Episcoporum, *De evangelisatione mundi huius temporis*, Vatican City, 1974, pp. 18ff.

112 W. de Vries, 'The Origin of the Eastern Patriarchates and their Relationship to the Power of Rome', in T. E. Bird, ed., *Archiepiscopal and Patriarchal Autonomy*, New York, 1972, pp. 14–21; K. Mörsdorf, 'Patriarch', *Lexikon für Theologie und Kirche*, 8, 174–77; J. Spiteris, *La critica bizantina del primato romano nel secolo XII*, Rome, 1979.

113 See his address on the 400th anniversary of Matteo Ricci's arrival in China, *Osservatore Romano*, Oct. 25–26, 1982.

114 Related by A. Camps, who took part in the meeting. See also J. J. Spae, *Church and China towards Reconciliation?*, Chicago, 1980; Wei Tsing-Sing, *Le Saint Siège et la Chine*, Allais, 1971.

115 See Brandmüller, *Konzilsgeschichte* (n. 31, above), esp. vol. 1; H. J. Sieben, *Die Konzilsidee der alten Kirche*, 1979, pp. 511–16; J. Metzler, *Die Synoden in China, Japan, und Korea*, 7 (1980) 301ff.

116 See Colloque International de Kinshasa, *Religions africaines et christianisme*, pp. 289–91; the idea had surfaced a year earlier in the Colloque d'Abidjan (1977), *Civilisation noire et Eglise catholique*, Paris, 1978, p. 342. See also *Pour un Concile africain*, Paris, 1978.

117 See W. Bassett and R. Goedert, *The Choosing of Bishops*, Hartford, 1971.

118   J. Grootaers and J. A. Selling, *The 1980 Synod of Bishops on the Role of the Family: An Exposition of the Event and an Analysis of its Texts*, Louvain, 1983.

119   See J. Tomko, 'Il Sinodo dei vescovi, luogo di communione ecclesiale', *Osservatore Romano*, Oct. 20, 1982. The 1983 code of Canon Law (can. 342–44) stresses more than once the merely consultative nature of the Synod of Bishops.

120   See, e.g., *Dominicae Coenae*, the lenten letter of the pope to all the bishops in 1980 (*Acta Apostolicae Sedis*, 1980, no. 10). In the same vein there is every year a call in favour of Latin (e.g., *Osservatore Romano*, Nov. 27–28, 1978), although the Congregation for the Sacraments had to learn, from a survey of bishops, that only the elderly and some intellectuals attended Mass in Latin (*Notitiae*, Rome, 12 [1981] 509–611, esp. 604–6).

121   *Dominicae Coenae*, 11; also *Redemptor Hominis*, 21.

122   See my *Wenn Gott*, pp. 60–68.

123   See H. Jedin, *Handbuch der Kirchengeschichte*, Freiburg, I (1965) 172–80, 279–81, 307–87; A. G. Weiler, *Geschichte der Kirche*, Zurich, I (1963) 332–37; M. Testard, *Chrétiens latins des premiers siècles*, Paris, 1981.

124   Abidjan (n. 116, above), p. 207.

125   Ibid., p. 267.

126   Hebga, *Emancipation* (n. 28, above), pp. 159ff.

127   Abidjan, p. 56; see also my 'L'autre face' (n. 27, above), pp. 124–35; Luneau and Ela, *Voici* (n. 28, above); V. J. Donavan, *Christianity Rediscovered: An Epistle from the Masai*, Maryknoll, N.Y., 1982; J. G. Healey, *A Fifth Gospel: The Experience of Black Christian Values*, Maryknoll, N.Y., 1981.

128   *Lexikon für Theologie und Kirche*, 7, 222ff.

129   *Acta Apostolicae Sedis*, 1977, p. 284.

130   'Sociologische Überlegungen zur Zukunft des Christentums', in Bärenz, *Kirche* (n. 76, above), pp. 68–95, esp. 76–88.

131   B. Mondin, *Le nuove ecclesiologie*, Rome, 1980.

132   Leonardo Boff, *Iglesia: Carisma y poder — Enseyos de ecclesiología militante*, Santander, 1982, pp. 65–77.

133   So, e.g., *Familiaris Consortio*, 10, and in various addresses given in Africa.

134   See the enthusiastic recognition address by John Paul II over Matteo Ricci (*Osservatore Romano*, Oct. 27, 1982), where unfortunately no mention is made of how long his path-breaking example was forbidden by Rome. Rahner's dictum is found in *Entschluss*, Vienna, 7/8 (1983) 28.

135   See my 'Die Basisgemeinden: Ort der aktiven Kirche', *Franziskanische Studien*, Werl, 1983, pp. 9–15.

136   See B. Luykx, *Culte chrétien en Afrique*, Immensee, 1974.

137   See H. Hochegger, *Le langage des gestes rituels*, Bandundu, Zaire, CEEBA, 1983; also Julian, 'Christian Sacraments' (n. 30, above).

138   See M. Pompilio, *Il quinto Evangelio*, Milan, 4th ed., 1975; J. Müller, *Missionarische Anpassung als theologisches Prinzip*, Münster, 1973.

139   See G. Stachel, 'Dreizehntausend Laien studieren Theologie für etwa dreitausend Stellen', *Diakonia*, 1983, pp. 212–18.

140   See Nakamura, *Ways* (n. 32, above), pp. 286–94.

141 See Leonardo Boff, *Theologie hört aufs Volk*, Düsseldorf, 1982; A. Exeler and N. Mette, eds., *Theologie des Volkes*, Mainz, 1978; F. Castillo, *Theologie aus der Praxis des Volkes*, Munich, 1978; Frankenmölle, *Kirche von unten* (n. 98, above).

142 See G. Caprile, *Il Sinodo dei vescovi 1980*, Rome, 1982, pp. 415ff., 437, 511; D. A. Seeber, 'Schwierigkeiten mit der Moralverküngdigung', *Herder Korrespondenz*, 1982, pp. 105–7; Archbishop R. G. Weakland, in *America*, 1982, p. 455.

143 *Osservatore Romano*, Oct. 19, 1982.

144 See L. Bressan, *Il divorzio nelle Chiese orientali*, Bologna, 1976; H. Herrmann, *Ehe und Recht: Versuch einer kritischen Darstellung*, Freiburg, 1972.

145 Paul VI to a group of French bishops (*Osservatore Romano*, March 27, 1977); John Paul II to the bishops of Switzerland (*Osservatore Romano*, July 10, 1982), and as early as his written message to all priests (April 8, 1979, no. 10).

146 *Osservatore Romano*, April 2, 1982.

147 See G. Denzler, ed., *Priester für heute: Antworten auf das Schreiben Papst Johannes Pauls II. an die Priester*, Munich, 1980; E. Klostermann, *Gemeinde ohne Priester*, Mainz, 1981; Solidaritätsgruppe katholischer Priester der Diözese Speyer, *Gemeinde ohne Priester — Priester ohne Zukunft?*, Frankfurt, 1983; H. Mynarek, *Eros und Klerus*, Düsseldorf, 1978; R. Hickey, *Africa: The Case for an Auxiliary Priesthood*, London, 1979; W. R. Burrows, *New Ministries: The Global Context*, Maryknoll, N.Y., 1980; M. A. Santaner, *Homme et pouvoir: Eglise et ministère*, Paris, 1980.

148 See K. Piskaty, 'The Process of Contextualization and its Limits in the New Codex Juris Canonici', *Verbum SVD*, St. Augustin, 1983, pp. 163–71.

149 Some years ago a priest from the Third World, who had a diploma from the Superior Catechetical Institute in Paris, wrote a catechism from the Superior Catechetical Institute in Paris, wrote a catechism for children. Someone sent a copy of it to the apostolic nuncio, who sent it to Rome. From Rome came a written instruction ordering that, the next time the book was to be printed, some changes had to be added: creation was *ex nihilo*; heaven and hell are places; the eucharistic presence takes place by transubstantiation — all this in a book for children!

150 See Zulehner, *Religion* (n. 91, above), pp. 63f., 123.

151 *Muss die Kirche die Jugend verlieren?*, Freiburg, 1981, pp. 11f., 70f.

152 Zulehner, *"Leutereligion"* (n. 91, above).

153 J. B. Metz, *Jenseits der bürgerlichen Religion: Reden über die Zukunft des Chrisentums*, Mainz, 1980.

154 H. Hermann, *Die sieben Todsünden der Kirche*, Reinbek bei Hamburg, 1978, pp. 231–35.

155 See Avery Dulles, *The Survival of Dogma: Faith, Authority, and Dogma in a Changing World*, New York, 1973, p. 129.

156 See 'The Institutional Church in the Future', *Pro Mundi Vita Bulletin*, Brussels, July 1980; C. Falconi, *La contestazione nella Chiesa: Storia e documenti del movimento cattolico antiautoritario in Italia e nel mondo*, Milan, 1969; Peter Hebblethwaite, *The Runaway Church*, London, 1975; R. Schermann, *Woran die Kirche krankt: Kritische Betrachtungen eines engagierten Priesters*, Düsseldorf, 1981.

157 See G. Caprile, *Il Concilio Vaticano II*, Rome, 1969, V, 415.
158 Card. Massaia, *Lettere e scritti minori*, Rome, III (1978) esp. pp. 212, 259–63, 279f.
159 See W. Weber, *Macht, Dienst, und Herrschaft in Kirche und Gesellschaft*, Freiburg, 1974; H. Mynareck, *Herren und Knechte der Kirche*, Cologne, 1973; Boff, *Iglesia* (n. 132, above).
160 *Osservatore Romano*, Nov. 10, 1979.
161 See ibid., Oct. 4 and Nov. 23–26, 1982.
162 To mention only a few of the books of this type: N. Lohfink, *Kirchenträume: Reden gegen den Trend*, Freiburg, 1982; P. M. Zulehner, *Kirche, Anwalt der Menschen: Wer keiner Mut zum Träumen hat, hat keine Kraft zum Kämpfen*, Freiburg, 1980; G. Zizzola, *Quale Papa?*, Rome, 1978; Andrew Greeley, *The Making of the Popes: The Politics of Intrigue in the Vatican*, Kansas City, 1978; J. Bourdarias, *Les fumées du Vatican*, Paris, 1979; Morris West, *The Clowns of God*, New York, 1981.
163 In *Concilium* (Italian ed.), 8 (1975) 133.
164 See the excellent amplifications of this thematic in *Evangelii Nuntiandi* (1975).
165 See Minnerath, *Le Pape* (n. 109, above); H. Stirnimann, ed., *Papsttum und Petrusdienst*, Frankfurt, 1975; K. Lehmann, ed., *Das Petrusamt: Geschichtliche Stationen seines Verständnisses und gegenwärtige Standpunkte*, Freiburg, 1982.
166 See my *Wenn Gott* (n. 1, above), part 2.
167 R. Heckel, *Selbstverantwortung (Self-reliance): Der dritten Entwicklungsdekade entgegen*, Rome, Päpstl. Kommission Justitia et Pax, 1978.
168 H. Dietz, *Europas letzte Stunde*, Freiburg, 1981, pp. 148, 159.
169 Cited in *Mondo e Missione*, Milan, 1982, p. 527.
170 Segundo Galilea, *Responsabilità missionaria dell'America latina*, Bologna, 1982.
171 'Minderheitssprachen in Grossbritanien', *Neue Zürcher Zeitung*, Sept. 9, 1982.
172 See *SEDOS Bulletin*, Rome 1982, pp. 219–22, 273–78, 290–96.
173 Anton Exeler, 'Vergleichende Theologie statt Missionswissenschaft?', in H. Waldenfels, ed., *Denn ich bin bei euch: Perspektiven im christlichen Missionsbewusstsein heute*, Zurich, 1978, pp. 199–211.
174 E.g., Missionswissenschaftliche Institut Missio, Aachen; EMI, Bologna; Orbis Books, Maryknoll, N.Y.
175 Anton Exeler, 'Wege einer vergleichenden Pastoral', in *Evangelisation in der Dritten Welt: Anstösse für Europa*, Freiburg, 1981, pp. 92–121; my *Wenn Gott*, pp. 178–83.
176 See B. Bürki, *L'assemblée dominicale: Introduction à la liturgie des Eglises protestantes d'Afrique*, Immensee, 1976, pp. 33, 145.
177 See my 'L'autre face' (n. 27, above), pp. 124–35, esp. 132f.
178 See R. H., 'Deutsche Bischöfe: Mehr Kontakt zur Dritten Welt', *Die katholische Missionen*, 1982, pp. 108ff.
179 See my *Sie folgten* (n. 26, above); E. L. Stehle, *Sie verteidigten die Menschenwürde: Zeugen des Glaubens in Lateinamerika*, Mainz, 1982; Martin Lange and Reinhold Iblacker, eds., *Christenverfolgung in Südamerika: Zeugen der Hoffnung*, Freiburg, 1980 (Engl. translation, *Witnesses of Hope: The Persecution of Christians in Latin America*, Maryknoll, N.Y., 1981).

[180] J. Dournes, *Gott liebt die Heiden*, Freiburg, 1966; Jean Daniélou, *Die heiligen Heiden des Alten Testaments*, Stuttgart, 1955.

[181] Overman, *Four Alternative Futures* (n. 107, above).